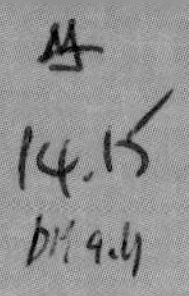

OCR H

Democracy and Dictatorship in Germany 1919–1963

Professor Mary Fulbrook and David Williamson with Nick Fellows and Mike W Series consultant: Chris Taylor

www.heinemann.co.uk

✓ Free online support
✓ Useful weblinks
✓ 24 hour online ordering

01865 888080

Official Publisher Partnership

Heinemann is an imprint of Pearson Education Limited, a company incorporated in England and Wales, having its registered office at Edinburgh Gate, Harlow, Essex, CM20 2JE. Registered company number: 872828

www.heinemann.co.uk

Heinemann is a registered trademark of Pearson Education Ltd

COLEG CYMUN... ABERGELE
AB... COLLEGE
LEARNING RESOUR...
ABERGELE 9/11
124131 943.086 FUL

Text © Mary Fulbrook and David Williamson, 2008

First published 2008

12 11 10 09 08[1]
10 9 8 7 6 5 4 3 2

British Library Cataloguing in Publication Data is available from the British Library on request.

131891

ISBN 978-0435312251

Copyright notice
All rights reserved. No part of this publication may be reproduced in any form or by any means (including photocopying or storing it in any medium by electronic means and whether or not transiently or incidentally to some other use of this publication) without the written permission of the copyright owner, except in accordance with the provisions of the Copyright, Designs and Patents Act 1988 or under the terms of a licence issued by the Copyright Licensing Agency, Saffron House, 6–10 Kirby Street, London EC1N 8TS (www.cla.co.uk). Applications for the copyright owner's written permission should be addressed to the publisher.

Edited by Alexander Gray
Designed by Pearson
Typeset by Saxon Graphics Ltd
Original illustrations © Saxon Graphics Ltd, 2008
Cover design by Bigtop Design Ltd
Picture research by Cristina Lombardo
Cover photo/illustration: Three soldiers reading a newspaper © Corbis
Printed in China (EPC/02)

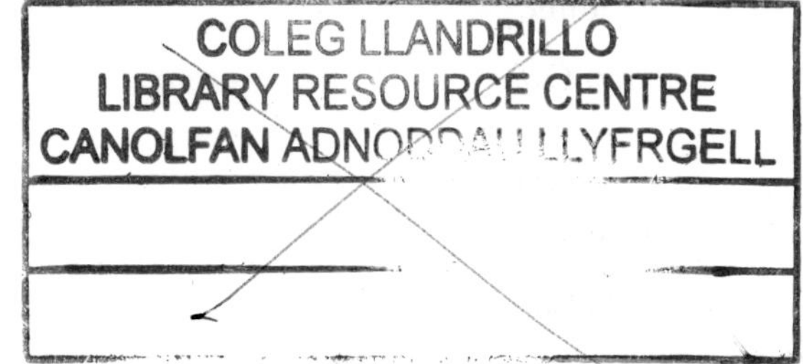

Acknowledgements
We would like to thank David Williamson and Mary Fulbrook for their invaluable help in the development and trialling of this course. The authors and publisher would also like to thank the following individuals and organisations for permission to reproduce photographs:

Photos and images
Figure 1.1: C. Henrich/Coll. Archiv f.Kunst & Geschichte/akg-images; Figures 1.2, 1.4, 1.5, 1.8, 2.3, 2.4, 2.5, 3.1, 3.2, 3.5, 3.6, 4.1, 4.2, 4.4, and 6.1: akg-images/akg-images; Figure 1.4: ullstein bild /akg-images; Figures 1.6 and 3.4: Imagno/Hulton Archive/Getty Images; Figure 4.3: PK-photo/Deskau/akg-images; Figure 4.5: Bildarchiv Pisarek/akg-images; Figure 5.1: Fred Ramage/Keystone/Hulton Archive/Getty Images; Figure 5.4: George Konig/Keystone/Hulton Archive/Getty Images; Figures 5.7, 5.9 and 6.2: Keystone/Hulton Archive/Getty Images; Figure 5.8: Binder /akg-images; Figure 6.3: Keystone/Stringer/ Hulton Archive/Getty Images.

Written sources
p. 16 Source C, First Series Vol IX, HMSO. p. 32 Source A, B; p. 64 Source A, p. 65 Source B: J. Noakes & G. Pridham (eds), Vol: 1 The Rise to Power, Exeter Uni. Press. p. 62 Source, p. 77 Source A, p. 78 Source D; p. 92 Source A; p. 108 Source A, D; p. 111 Source C; p. 112 Source D; p. 115 Source B: J. Noakes & G. Pridham (eds), Vol: 2 State Economy, Exeter Uni. Press. p. 122 Source D; p. 123 Source E: J. Noakes & G. Pridham (eds), Vol: 3 Foreign Policy, Exeter Uni. Press. p. 112 Source E: J. Noakes & G. Pridham (eds), Vol: 4 The German Home Front, Exeter Uni. Press. p. 77 Source B: I. Kershaw, Hitler Hubris Vol: 1, Allen Lane (Penguin). p. 92 Source B: Richard J. Evans, The Third Reich in Power 2006, Penguin. p. 156 Source D: Translated by Mary Fulbrook. p. 186 Source A: Unknown, News Magazine, The Times. p. 187 Source E: Unknown, Financial Times July 1952, Newspaper.

Every effort has been made to contact copyright holders of material reproduced in this book. Any omissions will be rectified in subsequent printings if notice is given to the publishers.

Websites
The websites used in this book were correct and up-to-date at the time of publication. It is essential for tutors to preview each website before using it in class so as to ensure that the URL is still accurate, relevant and appropriate. We suggest that tutors bookmark useful websites and consider enabling students to access them through the school/college intranet.

Contents

	Introduction	4
1	How strong was Weimer Germany in the 1920s?	8
	Exam Café	34
2	How and why did the Nazi Party come to power in 1933?	38
	Exam Café	58
3	How effectively did Hitler establish and consolidate Nazi authority 1933–45?	62
	Exam Café	88
4	Economy and society 1933–45: To what extent did the Nazis transform German economic policy and society?	92
	Exam Café	124
5	The division of Germany after 1945 and the establishment of Communist GDR up to1963.	128
	Exam Café	158
6	Adenauer's Chancellorship1949–63: How far did Western democratic structures (political, democratic, social) succeed in the Federal Republic?	164
	Exam Café	182
	Bibliography	188
	Glossary	189
	Index	191

How to use this book

Notes for teachers

This book, *Democracy and Dictatorship in Germany 1919-63,* is designed to support OCR's History A specification. It is divided into two units: F962 Option B, Study Topic 8 and F964, Option B, Study Topic 4. Each of the six chapters covers one of the Key issues in Unit F962 and Chapters 3, 4, 5 and 6 cover the Key issues in Unit F964. The chapters focus on two types of historical skill required: Period studies (Unit F962, Chapters 1–6) and Enquiries (Unit F964, Chapter 3-6).

Period studies

Students examine historical factors and their importance. Students should be developing skills to cross-reference, link, and compare for higher level answers. The chapters include activities:

- to encourage them to think about why one factor is more important than another.
- to give them the skills to look at the pros and cons of each factor as they go through and gauge its importance in different contexts.

These activities will encourage a cumulative approach leading to summative questions such as 'bearing all this in mind, why did this happen?'

Enquiries

Chapters 3-6 include two types of exercises:

- sophisticated comparison of two sources as evidence for something. Students should assess content and provenance and compare the two.
- five sources central to the answer.

Higher level answers will not sequentially describe source A, source B, source C, source D, source E and conclude but will link throughout the answer. Students can use their own knowledge, gained through further reading (*see* Bibliography, page 000) to evaluate the sources and are encouraged to formulate their own considered opinions.

Students should be grouping sources into those with the same view or those with a different interpretation. They should be able to establish the value of sources and decide which are more useful than others.

Please note: the sources in this book, for the most part, are longer than those used in the examination.

Exam support

Each chapter also has detailed exam preparation and support in the Exam Café with further support on the CD-ROM.

The Exam Café focuses on the type of questions assessed in the exam in either period studies or enquiries. It is divided into three areas: Relax, Refresh, Result!

- **Relax** is an area for sharing revision tips.
- **Refresh your memory** is an area for revising content.
- **Result** is the examiner's area: it includes exam questions, student answers with examiner comments, and tips on how to achieve a higher level answer.

Understanding the nature of, and the reasons for, change, divergence and continuity in political, economic and social structures in Germany during 1919-63 needs to run throughout teaching and learning for OCR History A Units F962/F964.

Democracy and Dictatorship in Germany 1919-63 has been written specifically to provide teachers and students with a taught course that exactly reflects the key issues and skills in the specification topics. Each chapter begins with key questions on a key issue which are then discussed in sequence, with supporting activities.

Additionally, each chapter includes a final review of what has been learnt, together with some review questions to help student's self-assessment of their knowledge.

Methods of assessment

The AS GCE is made up of two units: candidates can do either Unit F961 and F964 or F962 and F963. Centres choose one or two study topics from each unit. This book supports one unit in F962 and one unit in F964. They cannot be taken together.

The question paper for F962 is an essay question paper. It will be assessed by two answers, each of which might be drawn from one or more than one key issue. Candidates can answer from a choice of three essay questions from one or two study topics. Each question is worth a maximum of 50 marks.

F964 is a document study paper. Four or five unseen sources are set for each exercise. The question paper contains a two-part document study question for each study topic. Candidates answer one question from the study topic they have studied. Question (a) is worth 30 marks and question (b) worth 70 marks.

Each paper is 1.5 hours long and is 50% of the total AS GCE marks.

Notes for students

This book has been specifically written to support you through the OCR A GCE History course. *Democracy and Dictatorship in Germany 1919-63* will help you to understand the facts and concepts that underlie the topics you are studying. It can be used as a reference throughout your course.

You should refer back to this book during your revision. The Exam Café sections at the end of each chapter and on the CD-ROM will be particularly helpful as you prepare for your exam.

Each chapter in the book makes use of the following features:

Key questions

Each chapter will start by asking some Key Questions. The content of the chapter will help you to find answers to these Key Questions.

Key Questions:

In weighing up the strengths and weaknesses of the Weimar Republic the following key questions need to be answered:

- What were the consequences for Germany of defeat in the First World War?
- What was the impact of the Treaty of Versailles on post-war Germany?
- What was the structure of the newly established democratic Republic?
- Why were the years 1920–24 a period of repeated crises?
- What was the impact of the French and Belgian invasion of the Ruhr on Germany in 1923–24?
- Why was Bavaria hostile to the Weimar government?
- To what extent was the period 1924–29 a time of recovery?
- How did Chancellor Stresemann attempt to restore German influence in Europe,

Sources

We have included lots of sources throughout the book to allow you to practice your historical skills. *Note:* the sources tend to be longer than they would be in the exam.

Source

(A) At his trial Hitler made a dismissive reference to the Bavarian police and was rebuked by the president of the Court. Hitler replied as follows:

...it is not you gentlemen, who pass judgement on us. That judgement is spoken by the eternal court of history. What judgement you will hand down, I know. But that court will judge us, the Quartermaster-General of the old Army (Ludendorff), his officers and soldiers, as Germans who wanted only the good of their own people and Fatherland. You may pronounce us guilty a thousand times over, but the goddess of the eternal court of history will smile and tear to tatters the brief of the State prosecutor and the sentence of this court. For she acquits us.

A. Bullock (1990). *Hitler: A Study in Tyranny* (pp. 119–20). London: Penguin.

(B) Looking back at the trial nearly ten years later Hitler observed:

When the Kapp Putsch was at an end, and those who were responsible for it were brought before the Republican courts, then each held up his hand and swore he knew nothing, had intended nothing, wished nothing. That was what destroyed the bourgeois world – that they had not the courage to stand by their act, that they had not the courage to step before the judge and say: 'Yes that is what we wanted to do; we wanted to destroy the state....' It is not decisive whether one conquers; what is necessary is that one must with heroism and courage make oneself responsible for the consequences.

A. Bullock (1990). *Hitler: A Study in Tyranny* (p. 117). London: Penguin.

Activities

The activities have been designed to help you understand the specification content and develop your historical skills. Key activities are marked as either ***Period Studies*** or in the activity box and also in the top corner of each page with a **P** or an **E**.

ACTIVITY

To what extent was Stresemann's foreign policy a success?

Information

You should be thinking like an historian throughout your history course. These highlight content to provide extra detail to the main questions in the chapter.

Hindenburg's election to the Presidency in April 1925

President Ebert died in February 1925. The president was elected directly by the people. In the first ballot the winner needed an absolute majority, but in the second a simple majority was enough. **Hindenburg** was the candidate of the Right and won by a small majority of 900,000. Politically, Hindenburg's election was a serious blow for the Republic. Although he respected the constitution, his general aim was to exclude, if at all possible, the SPD from government, whilst including the right-wing DNVP. Ironically, between September 1930 and January 1933 he became the Republic's last defence against Hitler see p. 52).

Case studies

Case studies are used to further illustrate the main questions. Most of the examples can be applied in some way to the topic you are studying for your AS exam.

Case study: The revolution in Munich

After the King of Bavaria abdicated on 7 November 1918, a weak USPD-SPD coalition government was formed by Kurt Eisner. When he was assassinated on 12 February by a Munich university student, Graf Anton von Arco-Valley, a group of USPD members and anarchists set up a 'soviet republic'. On 13 April, this in turn was taken over by a group of left-wing extremists, who were led by the Communist Eugen Leviné. He set up a dictatorship based on the Russian model. Two weeks later, after bitter fighting, which involved atrocities on both sides, it was swept away by troops of the *Reichswehr* (the new German army) and *Freikorps*. These events had a lasting impact on the Bavarians and help to explain why Munich became such a strong centre of the radical Right, and the base from which Adolf Hitler was to build up the Nazi Party.

Definitions

Definitions of new words can be found in the margin next to where the word appears in the text to help put the word in context. All definitions can also be found in the Glossary (page 000).

Special interest parties
Parties which are formed to campaign on specific issues, in this case financial compensation from the government for losses during the inflation years.

Exam support

In our unique Exam Café you'll find lots of ideas to help prepare for your exams. Exam Café is at the end of each chapter. You can **Relax** because there's handy revision advice from fellow students, **Refresh your Memory** with summaries and checklists of the key ideas you need to revise and **Get that Result** through practising exam-style questions, accompanied by hints and tips on getting the very best grades.

Student answers are often extended into the CD-ROM. Look for the

CD-ROM

You'll find a free CD-ROM in the back of the book. This contains:

- **Exam Café** with a wealth of interactive exam preparation material: interactive multiple choice questions, revision flashcards, exam-style questions with model answers and examiner feedback and much more!
- **Chapters 1–6** – an electronic copy of the book with easy-to-navigate menus and zoom capability for all content.

How strong was Weimar Germany in the 1920s?

Source

A wounded German soldier, who was recovering in an army hospital on 9 November 1918, recalled his feelings of the time about the political turmoil in the aftermath of the war:

I shall never forget the scene when a comrade without an arm came into the room and threw himself on the bed crying. The red rabble, which had never heard a bullet whistle, had assaulted him and torn off all insignia and medals. We screamed with rage. For this kind of Germany we had sacrificed our blood and our health, and braved all the torments of hell and a world of enemies for years.

Richard Evans (2004). *The Coming of the Third Reich* (p. 70). London: Penguin.

Key Questions:

In weighing up the strengths and weaknesses of the Weimar Republic the following key questions need to be answered:

- What were the consequences for Germany of defeat in the First World War?
- What was the impact of the Treaty of Versailles on post-war Germany?
- What was the structure of the newly established democratic Republic?
- Why were the years 1920–24 a period of repeated crises?
- What was the impact of the French and Belgian invasion of the Ruhr on Germany in 1923–24?
- Why was Bavaria hostile to the Weimar government?
- To what extent was the period 1924–29 a time of recovery?
- How did Chancellor Stresemann attempt to restore German influence in Europe, 1925–29?
- How stable was the Weimar Republic, 1924–29?
- How did Hitler rebuild the Nazi Party, 1925–29?
- What was the situation in 1929?

The Weimar Republic was created in the wake of Germany's defeat in the First World War. Its first government had to sign the Treaty of Versailles and deal with the economic and political crises that beset Germany in the years that followed. It is not surprising therefore that the Weimar Republic is often seen as a brief, doomed regime that led to the Third Reich. Yet it is also possible to look at the Weimar Republic in a different way and ask why it lasted as long as it did, and whether it was 'doomed' to collapse.

What were the consequences for Germany of defeat in the First World War?

In March 1918 the Supreme Command of the Imperial German Army launched a massive attack against the British and French troops in France. At first the offensive was successful and made some significant gains, but in the end the sheer war weariness of the German army,

COLEG LLANDRILLO COLLEGE
LIBRARY RESOURCE CENTRE
CANOLFAN ADNODDAU LLYFRGELL

and the growing strength of the Allies, who could increasingly draw on American troops, once the United States declared war on Germany in 1917 as a result of submarine attacks on her shipping, ensured that the German advance ground to a halt. It was then the Allies' turn to advance, and by late September the Germans were in full retreat. On 29 September the army's Chief of Staff, Erich von Ludendorff, informed both his superiors, Field Marshal von Hindenburg and the German Chancellor Georg von Hertling, that the war was effectively lost and the only solution was to appeal to Washington for an **armistice.** The United States was more ready to negotiate a lenient peace with Berlin than Britain and France, provided Germany was ready to democratise her constitution. Consequently, in an effort to make this appeal more persuasive to the Americans, Ludendorff urged the creation of a more democratic regime which would, he hoped, convince Washington that the Germans were serious about making peace.

For most Germans defeat came as a surprise, although they had been subjected to a rigorous naval blockade by the British and food was very scarce. In March 1918 Russia had been forced to make peace with Germany, and German troops still occupied northern France and much of Belgium. Once the news of the armistice appeal became public the demand for peace gathered an unstoppable momentum. The German Admiralty however, opposed an armistice and decided on its own to pursue the war in defiance of the people's wish. It ordered the German High Seas fleet to attack the British fleet. In protest the crews of the fleet in the Wilhelmshaven and Kiel declared on 30 October that they would not sail beyond Heligoland to take the offensive. When the officers arrested the ring leaders, the sailors mutinied and together with the dockers set up **soviets** or Councils on the Soviet pattern. Over the following days soldiers' and workers' councils sprang up in all the large cities of the Reich.

Armistice

A temporary end to war hostilities so that negotiations for a peace treaty can begin.

Soviets

These were elected councils set up throughout Russia during the Bolshevik Revolution of 1917.

ACTIVITY

Compare Sources A and B as evidence for the impact of the revolution on Germany. Why did the revolution occur in November 1918?

Source

(A) The German War Ministry summed up the situation in a report to the government dated 8 November 1918. (*Note*: The references to 'Red' indicate those cities that had been taken over by the Communists.)

9 a.m.	*Serious riots in Magdeburg.*
1 p.m.	*In Seventh Army Corps Reserve District rioting threatened.*
5 p.m.	*Halle and Leipzig* Red*: Düsseldorf, Halstein, Osnabrück, Lauenburg* Red*;Magdeburg, Stuttgart, Oldenburg, Brunswick and Cologne all* Red.
7.10 p.m.	*General Officer Commanding Eighteenth Army Corps Reserve at Frankfurt deposed.*

R. M. Watt (1968). *The Kings Depart* (p. 186). London: Weidenfeld and Nicolson.

(B) Theodor Wolff, a German journalist, wrote in a newspaper on 10 November:

The greatest of all revolutions has, like a suddenly onrushing storm, overturned the Imperial regime with all that belongs to it ... Yesterday morning at least in Berlin everything was still there; yesterday afternoon nothing of all that existed any longer.

K. S. Pinson (1966). *Modern Germany* (p. 196), New York: Macmillan.

SPD
The main working-class political party in Germany.

USPD (Independent Social Democratic Party)
A political party composed of former members of the SPD who believed that Ebert was being too cautious and should introduce more radical socialist reforms.

Bolshevik Revolution
In October 1917 the Russian Bolshevik communists under Lenin had seized power in Russia. The term 'Bolshevik' means majority and was given to the majority Russian Socialist Party in 1903.

National assembly
An elected assembly that draws up a constitution.

Spartacist League
A left-wing revolutionary movement founded after the First World War by Karl Liebknecht and Rosa Luxemburg. It later changed its name to the Communist Party of Germany (KPD).

BIOGRAPHY
Friederich Ebert (1871–1925)
The co-chairman of the SPD and leader of the provisional German government, 1918–19. He was then appointed the first president of the Weimar Republic in 1920.

Was there a revolution in Germany?

The German emperor, William II, who had fled to the army headquarters in Spa, abdicated on 9 November and power passed to a Council of People's Representatives under Friederich Ebert, the leader of the majority Social Democratic Party (SDP). The Council consisted of three representatives of the **SPD** and three of the **USPD**. At this stage it seemed to many observers that Germany was on the verge of a revolution comparable in scale to the **Bolshevik Revolution** in Russia.

Over the next few days the revolution spread rapidly throughout Germany:

- Workers' and soldiers' councils sprang up in Hamburg, Bremen, Düsseldorf, Berlin, and all other large cities in Germany.
- More and more soldiers were joining the soldiers' and workers' councils.

How successful was Ebert in controlling the situation in Germany?

Frederich Ebert and many SPD colleagues, as one Socialist later remarked, hated the 'revolution like sin'. To them the revolution in Russia had brought chaos and bloody civil war. Such a revolution would disrupt demobilisation, the vital distribution of food to the starving population and the preparations for the coming peace negotiations. It would too, they felt, set German against German and lead to a bitter civil war, which would effectively destroy the German state. Ebert saw the Council of People's Representatives as a temporary government until a **national assembly** was elected**.** To maintain order and to avoid Germany slipping further into revolution he needed the support of the army, and therefore he refrained in the aftermath of defeat from reforming it or creating a new force that would be more friendly towards a republican Germany. He was also helped by the country's heavy industrialists who negotiated with the trade unions the Central Working Association Agreement. This granted the unions an eight-hour working day and allowed them to establish workers' councils in all companies with a workforce larger than fifty

Splits among the working-class

The far Left, which included the **Spartacist League** and the left-wing of the USPD, wanted to have a soviet rather than an elected parliamentary system of government in Germany. If this happened power would rest with locally elected councils rather than an elected parliament, which the moderate SPD leaders favoured. They also wanted the formation of a Red Army or workers' militia and the nationalisation of all medium to large-sized farms and the key industries. In support of their cause they organised strikes and demonstrations. However this only pushed the more moderate SPD leadership further to the right and made it more determined to control the unrest. So, instead of creating a new workers' militia, the SPD looked for support to the remnants of the Imperial army and to the ***Freikorps***.

Left and Right

Throughout this book you will meet the terms Left and Right. These are designations of basic political attitudes and beliefs.

Broadly speaking, the values of the **Left** were:

- liberty, equality and fraternity, which was the slogan of the French Revolution
- upholding human rights and holding a general belief in reform and progress
- peace and internationalism
- concern with the welfare and political representation of lower classes
- often a belief in state control of economic and social functions (with Communism seeing the strongest form of state control)
- in Germany the main left wing parties with the KPD (Communist Party), SPD (Social Democratic Party) and DDP (German Democratic Party).

The values of the **Right** stressed:

- authority, social hierarchy or class, tradition of the Kaiser's Germany and order
- duties rather than rights
- reaction or opposition to reform
- nationalism
- economically and socially, value placed on private enterprise, free trade, limited state involvement, big business, private philanthropy
- In Germany the main right wing parties were the DNVP, the DVP (see p 21) and later the Nazi Party (NSDAP).

Freikorps

The *Freikorps* (Free Corps) were made up of groups of young right-wing volunteers, students and ex-soldiers. They were formed to fight Communism within Germany and to defend the eastern frontiers against the Poles and the Russians. They hated the Jews, democracy, the new Republic and the SPD. In 1933 Hermann Göring, a leading Nazi, called them the 'first soldiers of the Third Reich'.

Figure 1.1 The defeat of the Bavarian Soviet Republic by *Freikorps*, Munich, 1st/2nd May 1919.

Parliamentary republic

A republic in which the government is responsible to an elected parliament.

The first Congress of Workers' and Soldiers' Councils' meeting in Berlin in December 1918 made it clear that the majority of German workers and soldiers did not want a communist revolution. Instead it decided there should be elections for a national assembly, which would then draw up a constitution for a new **parliamentary republic** and the election of a government. Until this government was elected, there would be no further reforms.

The Spartacist Revolt, 5–12 January 1919

This decision to hand over power to an elected parliament without first carrying out reforms, such as socialisation of industry or the creation of a workers' militia, led to the resignation of the Independent Socialists from the Council and the formation of the German Communist Party (KPD) by the leaders of the Spartacist League. On 5 January the Communists attempted to seize power in Berlin, but were ruthlessly repressed by the military and the *Freikorps*. Two of the KPD's leaders, Karl Liebknecht and Rosa Luxemburg, were murdered on January 15. Over the next four months a series of strikes and riots broke out throughout the country, and soviets were set up in Munich, Bremen, Mühlheim and Halle. The army and the *Freikorps* brutally crushed these, which in turn led to an increasing polarisation in German society. On the one hand, the unrest had confirmed the fears on the Right that the Communists were planning a revolution in Germany. They feared that this would lead to civil war and to the loss of their businesses, farms and property. On the other hand, the intervention of the army and the *Freikorps* confirmed the suspicions of the KPD, the USPD, and even some members of the SPD, that the army was essentially an undemocratic force.

BIOGRAPHY

Karl Liebknecht (1871–1919) and Rosa Luxemburg (1870–1919)

These were left-wing revolutionaries who publicly opposed the war and were jailed in 1916 for anti-war activities. They were released in October 1918 and founded the Spartacist League which became the German Communist Party.

Figure 1.2 Karl Liebknecht (centre) and Rosa Luxemberg became popular martyrs for left-wing groups after their murder.

Coalition

A government made up of members from several parties.

Case study: The revolution in Munich

After the King of Bavaria abdicated on 7 November 1918, a weak USPD-SPD coalition government was formed by Kurt Eisner. When he was assassinated on 12 February by a Munich university student, Graf Anton von Arco-Valley, a group of USPD members and anarchists set up a 'soviet republic'. On 13 April, this in turn was taken over by a group of left-wing extremists, who were led by the Communist Eugen Leviné. He set up a dictatorship based on the Russian model. Two weeks later, after bitter fighting, which involved atrocities on both sides, it was swept away by troops of the *Reichswehr* (the new German army) and *Freikorps*. These events had a lasting impact on the Bavarians and help to explain why Munich became such a strong centre of the radical Right, and the base from which Adolf Hitler was to build up the Nazi Party.

The formation of the Weimar Coalition

In the national elections on 19 January 1919 the moderate democratic parties, the SPD, the Centre (the German Catholic Party) and the German Democratic Party (DDP) formed a coalition and won a decisive majority. The National Assembly met in Weimar to avoid threats of riots in Berlin. The SPD, which had gained 38 per cent of the vote, provided both the first President of the Reich, Ebert, and the Chancellor, Philipp Scheidemann. The government was based on a **coalition** formed by the SPD, DDP and the Centre Party – the Weimar Great Coalition.

The immediate tasks of the government were to draft a new constitution and to negotiate a peace treaty with the Allied powers and include the USA.

Coalition

A government made up of members from several parties.

Conclusion

The first consequence of defeat for Germany had been an outbreak of strikes and mutinies. Throughout the country soviets were set up and a government was formed by a Council of People's Representatives. Ebert and most members of the SPD were determined that as soon as possible power should be given to a proper elected parliament to prevent the Communists taking over in Germany. Consequently, they made the key decision to hold elections in January for a National Assembly and a new government. In the meantime they worked with the army, the moderate trade unions and the industrialists to restore order and revive the economy.

The Communists and USPD responded by organising a series of demonstrations and uprisings; these were brutally put down. To stop the Communists taking over, Ebert agreed to the creation of the *Freikorps* – by Gustav Noske, the Minister of Defence – which, to many workers, seemed a betrayal of all the SPD stood for, given that the *Freikorps* hated the SPD almost as much as they hated the Communists.

ACTIVITY

To what extent was Ebert's main aim to avoid a Communist revolution in Germany?

ACTIVITY

Compare Sources A and B (see next page) as evidence for the views of Ebert's opponents on both the Right and the Left. To what extent did these views become the main reason for Ebert's decision to hold elections in January?

Sources

(A) On 19 January 1919 the commander of one of the *Freikorps* wrote in his diary:

I will set down here in my journal … that I will not forget these days of criminals, lies, barbarity. The days of the revolution will forever be a blight on the history of Germany … As the rabble hates me … I remain strong. The day will yet come when I knock the truth into these people and tear the mask from the faces of the whole miserable, pathetic lot… .

R. Waite (1970). *The Vanguard of Nazism* (p. 57). Cambridge, Mass: Harvard University Press.

(B) Ernst Däumig, a member of the USPD, told the Congress of Workers' and Soldiers' Councils on 19 December 1918:

… salvation will come not by slavish imitation of the old democratic principle but by the new democratic principle of the Soviet system. The German proletariat [workers] is too good to sink to the stage of the western democracies. The German people with its servility must be shaken out of its lethargy…This can happen only when the people are actively participating in the fashioning of its destiny.

K. S. Pinson (1966). *Modern Germany* (p. 371). New York: Macmillan.

What was the impact of the Treaty of Versailles on post-war Germany?

ACTIVITY

Assess the reasons for the survival of the Weimar Republic, 1919–23.

Initially, the German government hoped that it could negotiate a moderate peace with the European Allies and the USA. Its overriding aim was to protect the potential strength of the German economy to leave the way clear for recovery. It had no intention of paying reparations to the Allies, apart from the cost of rebuilding the devastated areas of Belgium and northern France. It was also prepared to return Alsace-Lorraine, which was annexed in 1871, to France and cede a minimal amount of territory to the new state of Poland. These concessions were to be counterbalanced by the Allies agreeing to allow Austria and the other German-speaking areas of the former **Habsburg Empire** to become part of the Reich. The Germans also assumed that the new democratic Reich would play a key role in the new League of Nations and would remain a great power.

Habsburg Empire

The Austro-Hungarian Empire, including the German-speaking areas of Sudetenland and Austria, which collapsed in November 1918.

The German delegation to the peace treaty was summoned to Paris on 7 May 1919 to be presented with the draft terms of the treaty. What confronted them was very different from the more moderate terms they had expected.

- The demand for reparations was consideraby increased by the British suggestion that family allowances and pensions for the wounded should be included in the final total.
- Upper Silesia, which contained important coal and steel works, and most of the provinces of West Prussia and Posen were to be ceded to Poland; only in Marienwerder was there to be a **plebiscite** on whether the people were prepared to become part of Poland; Danzig was to become a free city under the protection of the League of Nations.
- There was also to be a plebiscite in Schleswig to give the Danish population there a chance to vote for its return to Denmark.
- In the west, besides the return of Alsace-Lorraine to France, Eupen and Malmedy were to be given to Belgium and the Saar was to be looked after by the League of Nations for 15 years, after which there would be a plebiscite; the Rhineland was to be occupied for a period of 15 years by Allied troops.

Plebiscite

A plebiscite is a referendum or a vote by the people of a country on a particular issue.

- Germany would lose all her colonies and foreign investments, as well as most of her merchant navy.

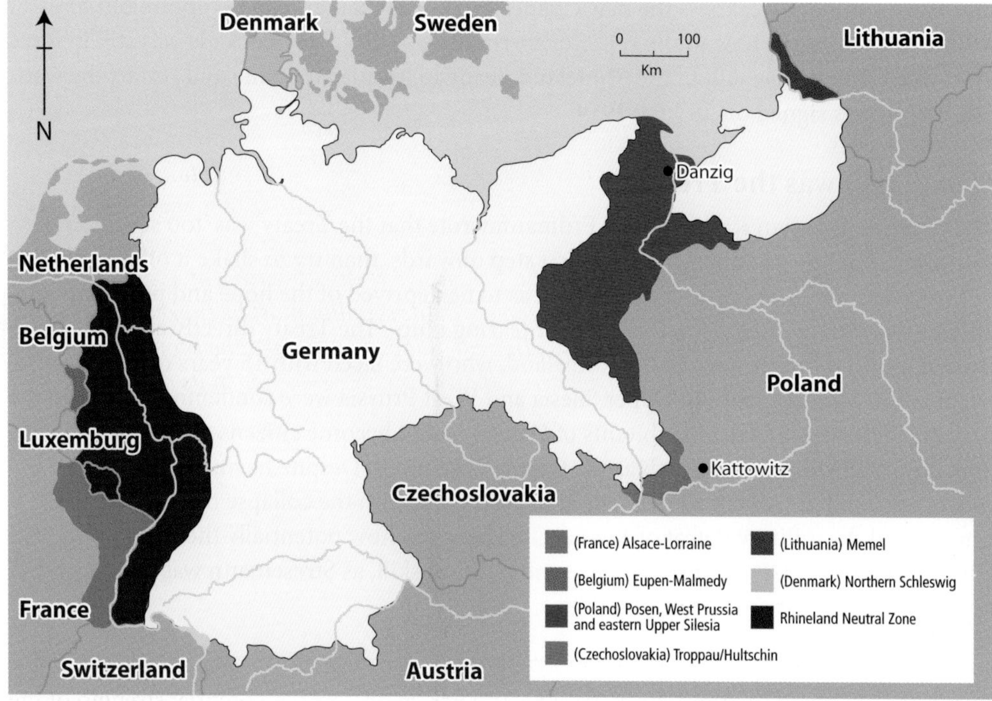

Figure 1.3 Germany became a smaller country after Versailles, losing much of its territory to the newly formed countries around it

- The German army was to be cut down to 100,000 men, its navy to 15,000, and the general staff was to be disbanded. Germany was forbidden to have tanks, aircraft, submarines and poison gas.
- Article 231 of the Treaty declared that Germany and her allies were responsible for starting the war.

The German government had 14 days to consider these terms. It found them unacceptable and argued that the Treaty was a dictated peace, or *Diktat*, and that Germany was not alone in starting the war. This had little effect on the Allies and America. On 16 June the German delegation was handed the final version of the Treaty, in which the only major concession made by the Allies was that of holding a plebiscite in Upper Silesia to determine whether the area should be Polish or German.

Figure 1.4 The German delegates receive the terms of the Versailles Treaty from the Allies, Versailles, 7 May 1919

The Treaty aroused a storm of protest in Germany and triggered a political crisis splitting the government, which led to the resignation of Chancellor Scheidemann. However, given Germany's military weakness the new Chancellor, Gustav Bauer, had no option but to accept it. They had to bow to the superior forces of the Allies. The blockade was still in force and Allied troops were still in the Rhineland, ready to invade Germany and restart the war. The Treaty was signed on 28 June 1919.

How harsh was the Treaty?

The German historian Karl Dietrich-Erdmann wrote that the Treaty was 'too severe, since Germany could do no other, from the first step onwards, than try to shake it off; too lenient, because Germany was not so far weakened as to be deprived of the hope and possibility of either extricating herself from the treaty or tearing it up'. The Treaty directly affected the lives of millions of Germans in the Rhineland, who were faced with 15 years of Allied occupation. Millions more in Upper Silesia and West Prussia were condemned to live in the new Polish state, while the inhabitants of Danzig had to become citizens of an independent 'free city'. But it was not as harsh as the Germans believed. Despite having to pay reparations and the loss of 13 per cent of her territory, with the collapse of the Austrian Empire and the military defeat of Russia, Germany was now potentially the strongest power in Central Europe. Given time, patience and political skill, as Stresemann was later to show, revision of the Treaty would be possible.

Sources

(A) The German government accompanied the signature of the Treaty with the following statement:

...Surrendering to superior force but without retracting its opinion regarding the unheard of injustice of the peace conditions, the government of the German Republic declares its readiness to accept and sign the peace conditions imposed by the Allied and Associated governments.

D. Williamson (1994). *War and Peace* (p. 38). London: Hodder.

(B) The Pan-German newspaper *Deutsche Zeitung* published this on its front page on 28 June:

Vengeance! German nation! Today in the Hall of Mirrors of Versailles the disgraceful treaty is being signed. Do not forget it! In the place where, in the glorious year of 1871, the German empire in all its glory had its origin, today German honour is being carried to its grave. Do not forget it! The German people will, with unceasing labour, press forward to reconquer the place among the nations to which it is entitled. Then will come vengeance for the shame of 1919.

K. S. Pinson (1966). *Modern Germany* (p. 398). New York: Macmillan.

(C) A German government proclamation issued on the date of the coming into force of the Treaty on 10 January 1920:

The unfavourable result of the war has surrendered us defenceless to the mercy of our adversaries, and imposes upon us great sacrifices under the name of peace. The hardest, however, which is forced upon us is the surrender of German districts in the east, west and north. Thousands of our fellow Germans must submit to the rule of foreign states without the possibility of asserting their right of self-determination.

... In this dark hour, let us appreciate the treasure which remains our common property, and which no outside power can take away from us.

Together we keep the language, which our mother taught us, together with the realm of thought, of speech, of ideas, in which the greatest minds of our people have striven to express the highest and noblest ideas of German civilisation. By all the fibres of our being, by our love and by our whole life we remain united.

Documents on British Foreign Policy (1960). First Series, Vol. IX (pp. 17–18). London: HMSO.

ACTIVITY **Period Studies**

1 Look at the map on p. 15 and read Source C carefully. How important was the loss of 'German' territory by the Treaty of Versailles?

2 Read all three sources and use your own knowledge. To what extent was the settlement of the East more resented by the Germans than that in the West?

3 The Versailles Treaty was 'too severe, since Germany could do no other, from the first step onwards, than try to shake it off; too lenient, because Germany was not so far weakened as to be deprived of the hope and possibility of either extricating herself from the treaty or tearing it up'. How far do you agree with this view of the Treaty of Versailles?

What was the structure of the newly established democratic Republic?

The newly elected National Assembly (Weimar Coalition) set up a committee to draw up a new constitution. Under it Germany remained a **federation**, but the power of the central government was strengthened over the individual **states**, whose ruling families had been forced to abdicate in November 1918. The Upper House, or the ***Reichsrat***, lost its power to veto bills passed up from the ***Reichstag***. The government of Germany was made responsible to the *Reichstag*, which was elected according to **proportional representation** by universal suffrage. The head of state was the Reich President, who was directly elected by the people for an initial period of seven years, although he could stand for re-election. He had the power to choose the Chancellor, order a referendum, and Article 48 (see page 18) empowered him to proclaim a state of emergency to safeguard public security provided he had the backing of the *Reichstag*. The constitution also contained sections on individual rights and the duty of the state to provide welfare for its citizens. The SPD also managed to secure articles guaranteeing the socialisation of 'suitable' industries which were privately owned.

Federation

A system of government whereby several states form a unity but run their own internal affairs independently.

Reichsrat

This was the German Upper House of parliament or senate. The equivalent in Britain is the House of Lords.

Reichstag

This was the Lower House or elected chamber of parliament. The equivalent in Britain is the House of Commons.

Proportional representation

The principle whereby parties are represented in parliament in direct proportion to the number of votes they poll.

Key elements of the Weimar Constitution

The President: elected directly by universal franchise, had powers to choose the Chancellor and declare an emergency.

The Reichsrat: the upper house or senate where the individual German states were represented.

The Reichstag: the lower house elected by universal franchise.

ACTIVITY
Period Studies

1. Assess how democratic the Weimar constitution was.

2. Given the situation in 1919, to what extent was it necessary to include Article 48 in the Reich constitution?

It was argued after 1945 that the Weimar constitution helped the rise to power of the Nazi Party. There is some truth in this. Proportional representation did indeed increase the influence of the small parties and make the formation of a strong government more difficult. There were, for instance, between 13 February 1919 and 30 January 1933 twenty different cabinets. Article 48 gave wide-ranging powers to the President, which were abused in the period 1930–33 (see chapter 2). Similarly, the demand for a referendum was exploited by the nationalist Right during the debate over the Young Plan in 1929 (see pages 30–31).

On the other hand, it is possible to exaggerate this argument. It is likely, for instance, that proportional representation ensured that the Nazis won less seats than they would

ACTIVITY
Period Studies

1. Assess how democratic the Weimar constitution was.

2. Given the situation in 1919, to what extent was it necessary to include Article 48 in the Reich constitution?

otherwise have done in the years 1930–33. The historian Richard Evans has also pointed out that despite the frequent change in cabinets there was considerable continuity is some ministries. Gustav Stresemann, for instance, was Foreign Minister from 1924 to 1929, Heinrich Braun was Minister of Labour from June 1920 to June 1928, and Otto Gessler was Army Minister from March 1920 to January 1928. 'All in all', Evans argues, 'the Weimar Germany's constitution was no worse than the constitutions of most other countries in the 1920s and a good deal more democratic than many'.

German states

The unified Germany in 1871 was a federation of states, which were represented in the *Reichsrat*, and which had considerable powers of self-government. In 1919, the states lost some but by no means all their powers and were called *Länder*.

The use of Article 48 played a key role in weakening the Weimar Republic in 1930–32 and in appointing Hitler in 1933. It was therefore heavily criticised after 1945, however all constitutions have provisions for giving emergency powers to governments in times of crisis. What is often forgotten is that the *Reichstag* had the power to order the government to 'rescind' it.

Source

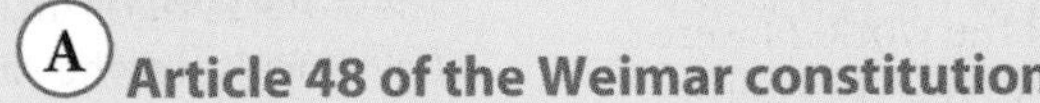

A Article 48 of the Weimar constitution

The key emergency powers which enabled the issue of legislation by Presidential decree were contained in paragraph 2 of the Weimar constitution

II. *If a state does not fulfill the responsibilities assigned to it under the constitution or laws of the Reich, the Reich President can take the appropriate measures to restore law and order with the assistance of the armed forces.*

In the event of a serious disturbance or threat to law and order, the Reich President may take the necessary measures for restoring law and order, intervening if necessary with armed forces. To achieve this he may temporarily suspend either completely or partially the basic rights in Articles 114, 115, 117, 118, 123, 124 and 153.

W. Michalka and G Niedhart (1980). *Die Ungeliebte Republik. Dokumente zur Innen-und Aussenpolitik Weimars 1918–1933* (p. 62). Munich: dtv. (Translated by the author.)

B National election results 1919–30 in the Weimar Republic

Date	KPD	USPD	SPD	DDP	Centre/ BVP	DVP	DNVP	NSDAP	Others
19.1.19	-	7.6	37.9	18.6	19.7	4.4	10.3	-	1.5
6.6.20	2.1	17.9	21.6	8.3	17.6	13.9	14.9	-	3.7
4.5.24	12.6	1.1*	20.5	5.7	16.6	9.2	19.5	6.5	8.3
7.12.24	9.0	-	26.0	6.3	17.3	10.1	20.5	3.0	7.8
20.5.28	10.6	-	29.8	4.9	15.2	8.7	14.2	2.6	14.0
14.9.30	13.1	-	24.5	3.8	14.8	4.9	7.0	18.3	13.6

* In 1924 the USPD rejoined the SPD.

T. Childers (1982) *Inflation, stabilisation and political realignment in Germany, 1924–28*, in G. D. Feldman *et al*. (eds). The German Inflation Reconsidered (p. 430). Berlin: de Gruyter.

Why were the years 1920–23 a period of repeated crises?

The economic and social legacy of the war

The German historian Wolfgang Mommsen argued that 'the seedbed of extremist nationalism and the eventual rise to power of the National Socialists was a set of social and economic factors that had their origins in the Great World War'. The legacy of the war certainly created a heavy burden for the new republic:

- The British naval blockade had ruined the German export trade.
- The government was burdened with a debt of 250.7 billion marks by November 1918, which was made worse by welfare payments to war invalids and widows and reparations.
- On the assumption that Germany would win the war and reparations from the defeated powers would pay for it, war expenditure was financed by loans, bonds and the printing of money rather than by taxation, and consequently inflation gathered pace. Prices rose by 250 per cent during the war.
- The war divided society into winners and losers: apart from the owners of the war industries who made large fortunes, those who gained most were the skilled workers in these industries, while the middle classes who lived on fixed incomes and interest from their savings were the greatest losers.

ACTIVITY

Period Studies

Assess the reasons why the legacy of the Great War for the German people and the Weimar Republic was so negative.

Threats to the Weimar Republic, 1919–20?

By early 1920 the authority and prestige of the Weimar coalition was already badly damaged and it faced threats from both the Left and Right. On the one hand, many of the workers were disappointed that their demands for the **nationalisation** of key industries and the formation of **workers' factory councils** with real power to decide issues in their factories had come to nothing. They were looking to the USPD, or even to the KPD. On the other hand, the old nationalist Right, which had been shell-shocked by the events of November 1918, was re-emerging. The attitude of the army was ambiguous. While it hated the Weimar Republic, some officers were ready to overthrow it; others urged the army to remain aloof from politics and concentrate on creating a tightly-knit professional force, which could one day be expanded again. The professional classes, that is university and school teachers, judges and civil servants, etc., were also for the most part hostile to the new regime.

Nationalisation
The taking over of factories by the state in the name of the people.

Workers' factory councils

These were bodies made up of members who were elected by the workers to represent their interests in the workplace.

Völkisch

The *völkisch* ideology preached the preservation of a traditional German, national and racial community. It was anti-Semitic and formed an important component of Nazi ideology.

How serious was the threat from the Right?

In Bavaria, a mass of ***Völkisch*** and extreme right-wing groups sprang into existence; among them was the German Worker's Party. It was at a meeting of this Party in the autumn of 1919 that Hitler made his first political appearance, when he addressed the Party on the Treaty of Versailles and the Jews.

At the Commission of Enquiry, which was set up by the government to establish the reasons for Germany's defeat in the Great War, Hindenburg used the term 'stab in back' to explain how the German army had apparently been 'sabotaged' by the strikes and unrest at home. The term was immediately seized upon by the Nationalistic Right as further evidence of the role of Jews and Bolsheviks in undermining Germany. Leading Weimar politicians, such as **Matthias Erzberger** and Friedrich Ebert, who had signed the peace treaty, became the target of constant abuse and threats and were called the 'November Criminals' because they had supported the armistace of November 1918.

BIOGRAPHY

Matthias Erzberger (1875–1921)

A Centre Party deputy and Finance Minister in 1919–21. He was assassinated by right-wing paramilitaries.

The Kapp Putsch

This was the atmosphere in which Ludendorff, Wolfgang Kapp, a founder member of the patriotic Fatherland Party, which had been set up to back the war effort in 1916, and General Lüttwitz, the commander of the *Reichswehr* in central and eastern Germany, created the National Association. Its object was to replace the Republic with a right-wing authoritarian regime. Their chance came when the government, obeying orders from the Allied Disarmament Commission, began to disband the *Freikorps*. Exploiting the anger and resentment of the *Freikorps*, Luttwitz on 10 March called for Ebert's resignation and for the reprieve of the *Freikorps*. When the government refused, one of the *Freikorps*, the Ehrhardt Marine Brigade, marched into Berlin and proclaimed Kapp as Chancellor. General Reinhardt, the *Reichswehr* Commander-in-Chief, was ready to crush the putsch, but, when his generals refused, the government fled, first to Dresden and then to Stuttgart.

ACTIVITY

Period Studies

Assess the reasons for the failure of the Kapp Putsch.

Figure 1.5 The Kapp Putsch: Lüttwitz troops in Unter den Linden, March 1920.

The trade unions retaliated by organising a general strike which paralysed all the public services such as water, electricity and gas. Kapp was defeated and on 18 March both he and Lüttwitz fled to Sweden to avoid arrest. The Putsch did, however, succeed in Bavaria where the *Reichswehr* commanders in Munich managed to replace the existing Bavarian government with a right-wing regime, which called itself a 'focus of order' in a nation threatened by Communism. From that point on Bavaria rapidly became, to quote the German historian Eberhard Kolb, 'an **Eldorado** for extreme right-wing organisations and the leading personalities of militant right-wing radicalism'.

How serious was the threat from the left?

The Ruhr uprising, April 1920

The trade unions hoped, now that the putsch had been defeated, that the government would purge hostile right-wing elements in the army and administration, and press on more quickly with setting up workers' councils and nationalisation of **heavy industry**. However, the outbreak of a workers' uprising in the Ruhr in April again made the government turn to its nationalist enemies for help.

The Communists, assisted by many members of the USPD, had drawn up plans for creating a **Red Army** and seizing key public buildings, such as banks, railway stations and post

Eldorado

An imaginary country or city where the streets are literally paved with gold. In other words, in this context a place which was sympathetic to the *Völkisch* and nationalistic Right.

Heavy industry

These are industries in which large and heavy equipment is used to manufacture products or extract minerals, for example shipbuilding and coalmining.

Red Army

A German Communist workers' army. It took its name from the Revolutionary Red Army in Russia.

offices. When the Kapp Putsch broke out, the Communists immediately called out their followers in the Ruhr and formed an army of about 80,000 men. By 20 March they controlled most of the Ruhr. In early April the *Freikorps* and the army launched a full-scale offensive against the 'Red Army' and ruthlessly crushed it; some 5000 of the insurgents sought refuge in the British Rhineland Zone.

ACTIVITY

Compare Sources A and B as evidence for the attitude of workers to the Weimar Government.

Source

(A) Brigadier-General Morgan, who was a member of the Inter-Allied Military Control Commission, 1920–24, describes in his memoirs the impact of the general strike, which defeated the Kapp Putsch:

At seven o'clock on the Sunday morning I returned ... to my quarters at the [Hotel] Adlon. I went into the bathroom to wash my hands and turned on the tap. There was a gurgling sound ... but no water appeared ... The next moment the electric light went out ... I was vaguely conscious of something peculiar about my room. Normally a faint light, like early dawn, suffused it even in the watches of the night. Its two big windows, leading to the balcony, looked out onto Unter den Linden, and the great arc lamps of that thoroughfare, and the sky signs opposite, diffused so much light, that my windows were, even in the dead of night, faintly visible in silhouette from within ... A wall of blackness seemed to shut in the hotel like a fog.

I recalled the confident prophecy of my chauffeur that the 'Arbeiterschaft'[the workers] would have something to say to the Kappists. The trade unions had now struck and struck heavily. They had proclaimed a general strike with the gloves off. No 'essential services' had been exempted. Water, light, power, communications, the very arteries of life were completely cut off.

J. H. Morgan (1945). *Assize of Arms* (pp. 67–68). London: Methuen.

(B) A member of the von Epp *Freikorps* told his family in a letter about his experiences in the Ruhr when crushing the workers' revolt there.

If I were to tell you everything, you would say I was lying to you. No pardon is given. We shoot even the wounded. The enthusiasm is terrific – unbelievable. Our battalion has had two deaths; the Reds 2–300. Anyone who falls into our hands first gets the rifle butt and then is finished off with a bullet. ...

R. G. L. Waite (1970). *The Vanguard of Nazism* (p. 182). Cambridge, Mass: Harvard University Press.

Why were the elections of 6 June 1920 a disaster for the Weimar coalition?

After both the Kapp Putsch and the Ruhr uprising had been defeated the government brought forward the date of the first election to be held under the new constitution to early June. The results were a disaster for the Weimar coalition. The SPD and DDP lost many seats, while the USPD and the right-wing **DVP** and **DNVP** clocked up impressive gains. A new **minority coalition government** was formed under the Centre politician, Konstantin Fehrenbach. It was composed of the Centre, the Democratic Party and the DVP. It contained no SPD members, and was determined to drop the previous government's plans for introducing further economic and social reforms.

DVP
The German People's Party (before 1918 it was known as the National Liberal Party).

DNVP (The *German National People's Party*)
This political party was formed in 1919 as an amalgamation of the pre-war conservative parties.

Minority coalition government
A coalition government that does not have a majority in the *Reichstag*.

Why did the Republic remain under pressure in 1920–22?

ACTIVITY

Why did the Weimar coalition parties do so badly in the election of June 1920?

Gold standard

A monetary system by which the value of a currency is defined in terms of gold.

Separatists

Those who wanted a separate Rhineland looking to Paris as the centre of power rather than to Berlin.

Entente

The Anglo-French wartime alliance against Germany.

The bitter arguments with the Allies over reparation payments (see below) gave successive German governments every excuse to delay stabilising the currency and allowing inflation to escalate. To end inflation government expenditure on welfare would have to be cut and the *Reichsmark* would have to be tied to the **gold standard**. This, however, risked creating unemployment and causing unrest in the industrial areas. Consequently the government continued, as in the war years, to print money, which inevitably fuelled inflation.

The growing strength of the Communist Party, with which the left-wing of the USPD had amalgamated in October 1920, showed that, despite the defeat of the Ruhr uprising, the threat from the Left was far from over. In the spring of 1921, for example, uprisings broke out in Merseburg, Halle and Mansfeld, although order was quickly restored by the police.

The struggle with the Allies over the execution of the peace terms encouraged the growth of the radical Right. Patriotic leagues and secret societies replaced the *Freikorps*, which were dissolved in 1921. Some of these became terrorist groups, which assassinated **separatists** and informers who had helped the French in the Rhineland. They also murdered leading socialists and democratic politicians. In the summer of 1921 both Karl Gareis, the USPD leader, and Matthias Erzberger were murdered, and a year later, **Walther Rathenau**, the Foreign Minister, was shot because he was attempting to pursue a policy of cooperation with the ***Entente*** as a means of persuading Britain and France to revise the Treaty of Versailles.

BIOGRAPHY

Walther Rathenau (1867–1922)

Rathenau was a prominent Jewish businessman, writer and philosopher, the son of Emil, the founder of the AEG. Early in the war he had headed the Raw Materials Department which played a key role in countering the British blockade. In 1921 he became Minister for Reconstruction and then a year later Foreign Minister. His policy was to seek agreement with France so that Germany could solve the reparation crisis. The Right saw him as a dangerous traitor.

Rathenau's murder temporarily rallied support to the Republic. A Law for the Protection of the Republic was passed, despite opposition from both the Nationalists and the Communists, which enabled the government to prohibit extremist organisations, but its effectiveness was limited by both the judiciary's and the Bavarian government's reluctance to act on it.

What was the reparation problem, 1921–22?

Reparation Commission

An inter-Allied committee that sat in Berlin to work out how much Germany should pay in reparations.

'Fulfilment'

The policy of showing good will and attempting to fulfil the Treaty of Versailles in an effort to gain concessions from the Allies.

At the end of April 1921 the **Reparation Commission** fixed the German debt at 132 billion gold marks or £6,600,000,000. The amount was accepted by the Allied leaders, who on 5 May 1921 dispatched an ultimatum to Berlin giving the Germans a week to accept the new payment schedule, after which the Ruhr would be occupied.

In Berlin the government resigned, and a new Centre-SPD-DP coalition, led by Joseph Wirth, was formed on 10 May. It was based on the Weimar coalition of the Centre, Democratic and SPD parties, and was determined to pursue a policy of '**fulfilment**' rather than confrontation and to cooperate closely with the British in the hope that they would be able to persuade the French to make concessions over both reparations and Upper Silesia.

By the autumn of 1921 Wirth's reparation policy was also running into considerable difficulties. On 31 August the first installment of reparations had been paid punctually, but, as the government, like its predecessors, still refused to stabilise the currency, cut expenditure and impose new taxes, it was becoming ever clearer that Germany would not be able to pay the second installment punctually.

Case Study: The Upper Silesian plebiscite 1921

For the next six months the Upper Silesian issue dominated German politics. A majority in the industrial area and 60 per cent of the total vote had opted to be part of Germany in the plebiscite in April 1921. However, to stop any attempt to restore the industrial region to Germany, a Polish force led by Wojciech Korfanty attempted to occupy the region. His forces, unofficially supported by the French, quickly established themselves along the so-called Korfanty line some 80 kilometres to the west of Kattowitz (see map, page 15). German self-defence forces backed by volunteers, many of whom were former members of the *Freikorps*, then moved into Silesia and attacked the insurgents. The British bitterly condemned the Korfanty uprising, but were unable to secure any major concessions from the French, and in August they agreed to submit the whole Upper Silesian question for a decision to the League of Nations. Here the French secured a decision which gave the key industrial triangle to the Poles. The German policy of closer cooperation with Britain had failed to save Upper Silesia, and Wirth resigned in protest, although he returned to power four days later.

Conclusion

Although the Weimar Republic survived both the Kapp Putsch and the Ruhr uprising, it continued to be attacked by the extreme Right and the extreme Left. The Right was strengthened in the elections of June 1920 and former members of the *Freikorps* carried out a wave of assassinations of politicians who were associated with accepting or carrying out the terms of the Treaty of Versailles. The relentless pressure put on Germany by France to pay reparations also strengthened the nationalist Right.

ACTIVITY

Why did the Weimar Republic managed to survive the years of crisis, 1920–23?

How serious a threat was the French and Belgian invasion of the Ruhr to Germany in 1923?

The Ruhr occupation and hyperinflation, 1923

The crisis over reparations came to a head in January 1923, when the Reparation Commission declared Germany to be in default on deliveries of timber and coal. The French and Belgians immediately occupied the Ruhr, despite British opposition.

The Ruhr occupation temporarily united the German nation behind the government. Reparation payments were suspended, and the Ruhr workers went on strike. In the short term these tactics were successful, and deliveries of coal and steel to the French were drastically reduced, but at the cost of putting enormous pressure on the German economy. Inflation had been a growing problem since the war – the cost of the war itself and then the reparations that followed put enormous pressures on the government to find more money to balance the books. To pay the strikers and compensate for the lost tax revenues from the Ruhr, the government had to print more money, which caused inflation to accelerate into out-of-control 'hyperinflation', and by August 1923 the German mark was virtually valueless. The trade unions could do nothing to help and the democratic process just seemed to be making everything far worse than it ever had been before.

ACTIVITY

Period Studies

'Wirth's policy of fulfillment merely strengthened the nationalist Right and the opponents of the Weimar Republic.' How far do you agree with this view of the policy of fulfillment?

ACTIVITY

Compare Sources A and B as evidence for the lasting harm the hyperinflation crisis did to the Weimar Republic in the eyes of its citizens.

Source

(A) The following table shows the rise in hyperinflation from the beginning of the war up to 1923. (Note: The figures are US dollar quotations for the Reichsmark, 1914–23)

Month	Year	($US)
July	*1914*	*4.2*
January	*1919*	*8.9*
January	*1920*	*64.8*
July	*1920*	*39.5*
January	*1921*	*64.9*
January	*1922*	*493.2*
January	*1923*	*17, 972.0*
July	*1923*	*353, 412.0*
August	*1923*	*4, 620, 455.0*
September	*1923*	*98,860,000.0*
October	*1923*	*4,200,000,000,000.0*

G. Craig (1978). *Germany, 1866–1945* (p. 450). Oxford: Oxford University Press.

(B) The historian Richard Evans sums up the impact of inflation on the German people:

At its height, the hyperinflation seemed terrifying. Money lost its meaning almost completely. Printing presses were unable to keep up with the need to produce banknotes of ever more astronomical denominations, and municipalities began to print their own emergency money, using one side of the paper only. Employees collected their wages in shopping baskets or wheelbarrows, so numerous were the banknotes needed to make up their pay packets; and immediately rushed to the shops to buy supplies before the continuing plunge in the value of money put them out of reach.

Richard Evans (2004). *The Coming of the Third Reich* (p. 106). London: Penguin.

War bonds

These were certificates issued and sold by the German government during the war promising to repay people who bought them their money, plus interest added, by a specific date.

This completed the ruin of those people such as civil servants, pensioners and widows who were dependent on fixed incomes and interest income from **war bonds** and insurance annuities. Of course there were others who benefited from the inflation. Industrialists, for instance, could secure loans from banks to expand their factories or buy up other plants, and then they could pay off the loan which inflation had made almost worthless. Speculators, too, were able to buy up antiques or the treasured possessions of the German middle classes who had to sell all they could on the black market to survive.

Why did passive resistance fail?

By midsummer 1923 it was clear that Germany could no longer maintain the passive resistance campaign. In July public order was threatened by strikes and rioting in the cities in unoccupied Germany. Large gangs of heavily-armed young men regularly attacked farms and carried off any surplus food. When the Cuno government resigned in September, the political situation was almost as bad as October 1918 except that, to quote the historian Charles Maier, 'the measure of defeat was no longer the progress of the Allied armies, but the rout of the mark from 200,000 to 2 million per dollar within a fortnight'. **Gustav Stresemann** formed a 'Great Coalition' of the Centre Party, the SPD, DDP and DVP and had no alternative but to end the passive resistance campaign on 26 September.

Why was the autumn of 1923 a period of acute crisis for the Weimar Republic?

The Great Coalition now faced a period of acute crisis, which could easily have ended in the creation of a dictatorship:

- Some DNVP politicians, generals and industrialists were planning to replace parliamentary government with a dictatorship.
- The KPD, encouraged by the Russian Bolsheviks, were planning uprisings in Saxony.
- In Bavaria patriotic, nationalist and paramilitary organisations were also planning a coup against the central government.

To deal with these threats Stresemann had little option but to declare an emergency under Article 48 and hand over to the army the responsibility for keeping order. On 10 October the Communists in Saxony began to organise for the 'revolution' by forming an armed militia. Stresemann acted decisively and demanded the dissolution of the Red Militia and the sacking of Communist members of the Saxony Government. When these requests were ignored the army moved in and arrested both the Communist and the Socialist members of the Saxony Cabinet.

What were the causes of the Munich Putsch?

The situation in Bavaria was more complex than elsewhere in Germany. Since the Kapp Putsch, Bavaria had been governed by a conservative Catholic regime under **Gustav von Kahr**. He wanted to bring the nationalist Right together to form a powerful bloc, so that he could turn Bavaria into what he called a 'cell' or oasis of order and restore the traditional values of pre-war Germany. One of the strongest forces on the right was the new Nazi Party, which was led by Adolf Hitler.

What was Adolf Hitler's career up to 1923?

Hitler was born in Braunau am Inn, Upper Austria, in 1889. In *Mein Kampf* he described his childhood as impoverished and hard, but actually his father, Alois, an Austrian customs official, earned enough money to keep his family quite comfortably. In 1905 Hitler left school without any academic qualifications and was rejected for a place at the Academy of Fine Arts in Vienna. When his mother died in 1907, he inherited a small sum of money. However, up to August 1914 he had no work, and as his inheritance ran out he lived an increasingly impoverished life, first in Vienna and then in Munich. He gained a smattering of knowledge about contemporary **Social Darwinism**, *Völkisch* and racist thinking.

In August 1914 Hitler volunteered to join a Bavarian regiment and fought for the next four years on the western front with considerable courage and was awarded the Iron Cross (First Class). In 1918 he was wounded in a British gas attack, but was able to return to his regiment in Munich in late November. Here he witnessed the rise and fall of the Munich

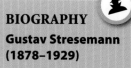

BIOGRAPHY

Gustav Stresemann (1878–1929)

He was the most well-known liberal politician in the Weimar Republic. In the Great War he was an extreme nationalist. He became leader of the DVP in 1919 and was at first critical of the Weimar Republic, but he began to support it after Rathenau's assassination. He was Chancellor from August to November 1923, and Foreign Minister from August 1923 until his death in October 1929. He successfully began the process of revising the Treaty of Versailles (see pp. 30–31).

BIOGRAPHY

Gustav Ritter von Kahr (1862–1934)

A right-wing politician who was murdered on Hitler's orders during the 1934 purge (see page 000).

Social Darwinism

This applied Charles Darwin's theories of evolution and natural selection to human society and taught the doctrine that different countries and races were in a struggle in which only the 'fittest' would survive.

SA *Sturmabeilung* (Stormtroopers)

Literally this is the Assault Section of the Nazi Party. It was founded in 1921 to protect party meetings from being disrupted by the Communists. It was dissolved after the Munich Putsch.

'soviet republic' in April 1919 (see page 13). After its collapse on 3 May, Hitler was appointed a *V-Mann,* or informer, in his regiment, to help stop the spread of Communist propaganda amongst the troops. This brought him into touch with the German Workers' Party, which was one of the many small *Völkisch*-radical groups which had been formed in Germany in 1919–20. In April 1920 he began to work full-time for the Party, which changed its name in February to the German National Socialist Workers' Party (NSDAP). By 1922 he had established complete control over the Party, which, strengthened by the creation of the paramilitary **SA *Sturmabeilung*** in August 1921, had become the most dynamic force on the Right in Bavaria.

Hitler's potential as a political leader lay in the way he was able to exploit the fear, anger and resentment of the impoverished middle classes in the post-war period. National Socialism would have existed without Hitler, but he managed to turn it into a major force in Bavaria.

Kampfbund

This literally means a Fighting League or Association.

Putsch

An attempt to seize power by force.

Why did the Munich Putsch fail?

In early September 1923 the Nazi Party joined the ***Kampfbund*,** an association of right-wing militant groups in Bavaria, to plan their tactics against the Republic. The SA became part of the military wing of the *Kampfbund*, while Hitler was given its political leadership. Hitler's task was to win over public opinion to support a ***Putsch*** in Munich as a preliminary to establishing a dictatorship in Berlin, which would most likely be headed by Ludendorff, although Hitler would be a member.

For the Putsch to be successful it was vital to win the backing of:

- von Kahr, the Bavarian State Commissioner
- von Seisser, the head of the Bavarian police
- General von Lossow, the commander of the Bavarian *Reichswehr*.

On 3 November, however, Seisser was told by General von Seeckt, the head of the German army, that he was not willing to oppose the elected and legal government in Berlin. This was unwelcome news to Seisser and his colleagues, who began to have serious doubts about the possible success of a *putsch*. This left Hitler in a difficult position. His followers were clamouring for action, and were convinced that if he delayed for too long the favourable moment would pass. Hitler therefore adopted the high-risk strategy of trying to force von Kahr into supporting his plans by seizing him and his colleagues while at a public meeting at the *Bürgerbräukeller* beer hall on the evening of 8 November. Initially this appeared to work. Bowing to force they agreed to support him, but then Hitler was suddenly called away and left them in the charge of Ludendorff. The latter allowed them to go home once they had given him their word of honour that they would support Hitler. This promise was not kept and the following morning they ordered the police to break up the *Kampfbund's* planned march into the city centre. Sixteen Nazis and three policemen were killed.

ACTIVITY

Period Studies

'The Munich Putsch was a disastrous failure for the Nazi Party.'

How far do you agree with this assessment?

A few days later Hitler was arrested by the police. In February 1924 he was given the minimum sentence of five years' imprisonment with the understanding that he would be released early on probation. The publicity the putsch received and his subsequent trial gave Hitler nationwide publicity in the media. He was imprisoned in Landsberg fortress where he dictated his book *Mein Kampf*, or *My Struggle*, to his secretary, Rudolf Hess. He was released from prison in December 1924.

Figure 1.6 Hitler's imprisonment in Landsberg prison was not a harsh sentence – his fame guaranteed him comfortable quarters and a considerable amount of personal freedom.

ACTIVITY

Compare Sources A and B. How far would you say Hitler's actions actually reflected his 'heroic' descriptions?

Source

(A) At his trial Hitler made a dismissive reference to the Bavarian police and was rebuked by the president of the Court. Hitler replied as follows:

...it is not you gentlemen, who pass judgement on us. That judgement is spoken by the eternal court of history. What judgement you will hand down, I know. But that court will judge us, the Quartermaster-General of the old Army (Ludendorff), his officers and soldiers, as Germans who wanted only the good of their own people and Fatherland. You may pronounce us guilty a thousand times over, but the goddess of the eternal court of history will smile and tear to tatters the brief of the State prosecutor and the sentence of this court. For she acquits us.

A. Bullock (1990). *Hitler: A Study in Tyranny* (pp. 119–20). London: Penguin.

(B) Looking back at the trial nearly ten years later Hitler observed:

When the Kapp Putsch was at an end, and those who were responsible for it were brought before the Republican courts, then each held up his hand and swore he knew nothing, had intended nothing, wished nothing. That was what destroyed the bourgeois world – that they had not the courage to stand by their act, that they had not the courage to step before the judge and say: 'Yes that is what we wanted to do; we wanted to destroy the state....' It is not decisive whether one conquers; what is necessary is that one must with heroism and courage make oneself responsible for the consequences.

A. Bullock (1990). *Hitler: A Study in Tyranny* (p. 117). London: Penguin.

Conclusion

The crisis triggered by the French occupation of the Ruhr nearly destroyed the Weimar Republic. Hyperinflation impoverished large numbers of Germans, and provided extremists on both the Left and Right with the chance to bring down the Republic. By

September the government could no longer maintain passive resistance and had to cooperate with the French. Internally it faced trouble from both the Communists and the Nationalist Right in Bavaria

ACTIVITY

'The Weimar Republic survived the multiple crises of 1923 more by luck than political skill'.

How far do you agree with this view?

To what extent can the period 1924–29 be called the 'Golden Years' of the Weimar Republic?

The economy

In November 1923 the government began to stabilise the currency, when the devalued *Reichsmark* was replaced with a temporary currency, the *Rentenmark*, whose value was guaranteed by bonds based on the assets of German industry and agriculture. Nine months later the process of stabilising the currency was completed when the new *Reichsmark* was introduced.

By 1924 it was clear that the Republic had survived. The cost of the Ruhr occupation had caused a sharp decline in the value of the franc, and so the British and Americans were able to force the French to agree to setting up an experts' committee chaired by the American banker Charles Dawes, to look into the whole question of reparations. This produced the Dawes Plan in April 1924, which:

- did not reduce the final total of reparations, but
- did agree that reparations payments would start gradually and rise to their maximum total in five years, and
- proposed that a loan of 800 million marks should be raised for Germany.

Between 1924 and 1928 the German economy did stage a modest recovery, and by 1927 industrial production had returned to the level of 1913. Compared to the years 1919–23 and 1930–33 this was a period of relative prosperity.

ACTIVITY

How did the Dawes Plan help stabilise the German economy?

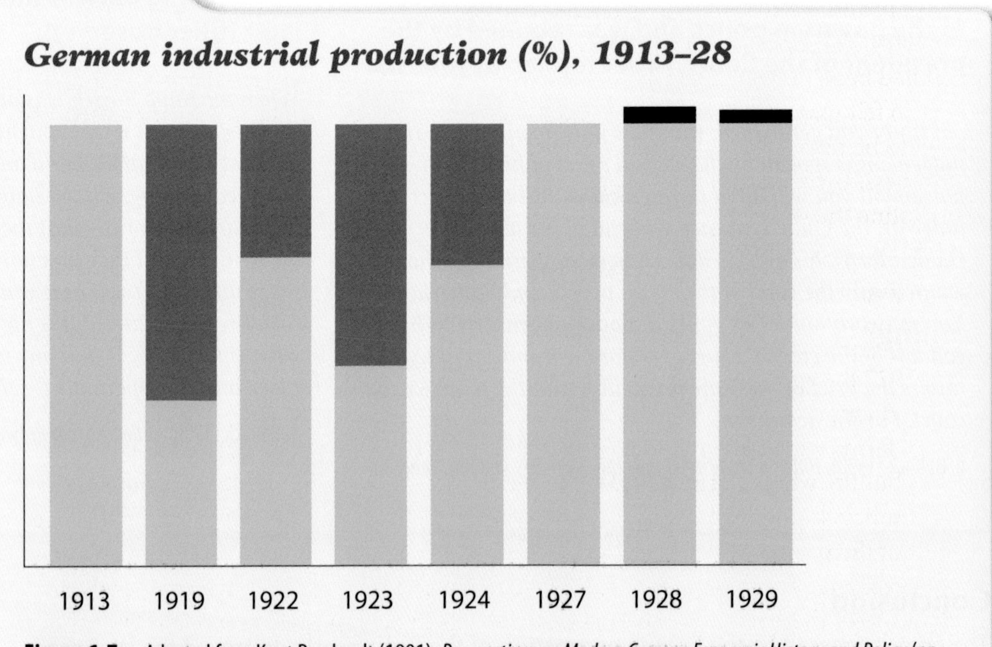

Figure 1.7 Adapted from Knut Borchardt (1991). *Perspectives on Modern German Economic History and Policy* (pp. 171–72). Cambridge: Cambridge University Press.

However, there were still severe economic problems. Above all there was the need to compensate the millions of people who had seen their savings destroyed by inflation. Financially, the government could not afford to do much to help them, but reluctantly it did in the end agree to compensate those who had lost all their investments in war bonds, at a mere 12.5 per cent of the original value to be spread over 30 years. The creditors most of whom came from the professional classess and the *Mittelstand* (see p. 95), bitterly resented this and saw it as a deliberate betrayal of them by the Weimar Republic. They were the true losers of the 'Golden Years'.

What problems did stabilisation of the currency create for industry?

The stabilisation of the currency also created problems for German industry. As prices for German exports were now much higher, industrialists did everything to simplify production techniques and reduce the number of people working for them. In the mines, for instance, by 1929 one miner in four had lost his job. Just at the time when the number of jobs available were decreasing, the workforce was being increased by young people who were born in the baby boom of the pre-1914 years. In 1925 there were five million more people in the workforce than there had been in 1907. Inevitably this led to a serious unemployment problem, which did not disappear even in the brief spells of economic expansion that occurred in 1927–29. In January 1928, for example, there were nearly two million workers unemployed. The stabilisation of the currency also made Germany an attractive market for foreign loans, particularly from the USA. This money did help revive the economy, but at the same time German industry became dangerously dependent on foreign loans. If they were withdrawn suddenly, the German economy would be in great trouble.

Why did labour relations deteriorate during the 'Golden Years'

Wage disputes and strikes became much more bitter as employers and workers fought over whether profits should be distributed mainly in the form of higher wages or else reinvested in industry. The employers felt that the system of **compulsory state arbitration of strikes**, which had been introduced in 1919, favoured the workers, and argued for its abolition. They also felt that the welfare state, which the Weimar Republic had greatly increased, also needed to be dismantled as it cost so much to run and greatly increased the burden of tax on business. Increasingly the employers felt that only an authoritarian regime would be able to discipline the workers and help business and industry thrive again.

Compulsory state arbitration of strikes

When a strike occurred the state intervened and forced the employers and workers to come to an agreement.

What was the impact of the agricultural depression on German farming?

In late 1927 the agricultural depression hit German farming with a devastating blow. Global over-production of food led to a steep fall in prices. By 1929 between a third and half of all German farms were failing to make a profit. The agricultural slump affected not only the farmers but the whole of rural society. Anger in the countryside was directed both at the welfare policy of the state, which was perceived to be favouring the urban working classes at the cost of the peasantry, and at its trade policies, which encouraged the import of foreign food in exchange for the opening up of export markets for German industrial goods. In 1928 and 1929 there were massive peasant protests in Schleswig-Holstein and Oldenburg where public officials and buildings were attacked. This hostility was to be effectively exploited by the Nazis.

ACTIVITY

Period Studies

To what extent did the German economy recover between 1925 and 1929?

How did Foreign Minister Stresemann attempt to restore German influence in Europe, 1925–29?

Source

Stresemann wrote of his aims in foreign policy to the German ex-Crown Prince William on 7 September 1925:

... there are three great tasks that confront German foreign policy in the more immediate future.

In the first place the solution of the reparation question in a sense tolerable for Germany, and the assurance of peace, which is essential for the recovery of our strength. Secondly the protection of the Germans abroad, those 10 to 12 millions of our kindred who now live under a foreign yoke in foreign lands. The third great task is the readjustment of our eastern frontiers; the recovery of Danzig, the Polish frontier, and a correction of the frontier of Upper Silesia.

D. Williamson (1994). *War and Peace* (p. 61). London: Hodder.

Demilitarisation

The banning of all military bases from an area.

Council of the League of Nations

This was one of the principal organs of the League of Nations and its function was to settle international disputes. Originally its permanent members were Britain, France, Italy and Japan and it had four non-permanent members, which were elected every three years.

ACTIVITY

Using the source, explain the aims of Stresemann's foreign policy.

Like Joseph Wirth (see p 23), Stresemann used every chance from 1924 to 1929 to revise the Treaty of Versailles. He was motivated by the desire to free Germany from the reparation payments imposed on it by France and Britain and this led him to seek alliances with western powers and, particularly, the USA. He first made sure that there would be no repetition of the Ruhr occupation by France when he proposed with British support a guarantee by the European Great Powers of the Franco-Belgian-German frontier and the permanent **demilitarisation** of the Rhineland, which led to the Locarno Treaty of 1925. In this way he managed to a certain extent to overcome French fears of a German revival and create what was called the Locarno Honeymon. A year later Germany joined the **Council of the League of Nations**. Stresemann skillfully used the goodwill that Germany gained through this more cooperative policy to extract concessions from Britain and France. In January 1927 the Allied Disarmament Commission was withdrawn from Germany, and in August Britain, France and Belgium withdrew 10,000 troops from their garrisons in the Rhineland.

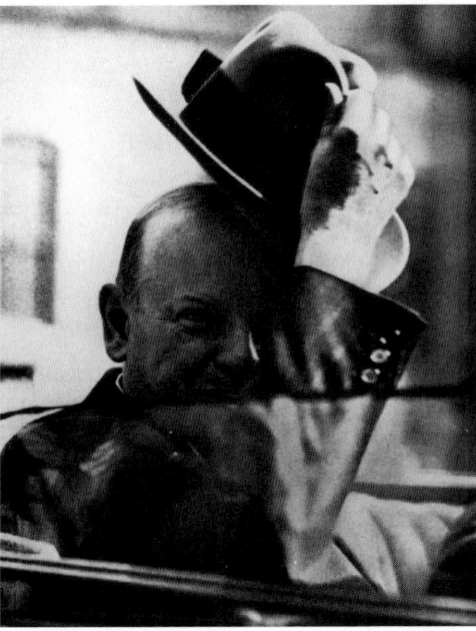

Figure 1.8 Gustav Stressemann is often described as the one great statesman of the Weimar Republic.

In 1928 the German government launched a major initiative to persuade Britain and France to evacuate the Rhineland altogether, and to agree to a revision of the Dawes Plan. During the winter of 1928–29 a committee of financial experts, which was chaired by the American banker Owen Young, considered the reparation problem. In June 1929 it recommended:

- the reduction of the overall reparation total from 132 billion (gold) marks to 40 billion (gold) marks, and
- the dismantling of the international controls over the German economy, which had been set up under the Dawes Plan.

At the Hague Conference in August 1929 Stresemann managed to achieve his aims. The Young Plan was accepted and Britain and France agreed to evacuate the Rhineland by 30 June 1930.

In December a referendum was forced on the government by the Nazi Party and the DNVP, which argued that the signature of the Hague Treaty was an act of high treason, but the government won with an overwhelming majority, and the Young Plan was officially implemented on 20 January 1930.

BIOGRAPHY

President Hindenburg (1847–1934)

Field Marshal von Hindenburg retired in 1911 but was recalled in 1914. He defeated the Russians at the battle of Tannenberg and became Commander-in-Chief of the Western Front in 1916. He became a symbol of German courage and determination. It was as a consequence of this fame that he was elected president in 1925.

How stable was the Weimar Republic, 1924–29?

Even in the relatively calm years between 1924 and 1929, the Weimar Republic continued to be governed by unstable coalitions. A strong government, which could command a majority in the *Reichstag*, needed to be based either on a coalition composed of the SPD, Centre and liberal parties (DDP and the DVP) or a Centre, DVP and DNVP grouping (see p.17). The problem however was that disagreements on economic and social questions between the SPD and the liberal parties made cooperation between them difficult to maintain, while foreign policy differences complicated relations between the DNVP, the Centre and the DVP. The DNVP was for most of the time deeply suspicious of Stresemann's attempts to improve relations with Britain and France.

ACTIVITY

To what extent was Stresemann's foreign policy a success?

Hindenburg's election to the Presidency in April 1925

President Ebert died in February 1925. The president was elected directly by the people. In the first ballot the winner needed an absolute majority, but in the second a simple majority was enough. **Hindenburg** was the candidate of the Right and won by a small majority of 900,000. Politically, Hindenburg's election was a serious blow for the Republic. Although he respected the constitution, his general aim was to exclude, if at all possible, the SPD from government, whilst including the right-wing DNVP. Ironically, between September 1930 and January 1933 he became the Republic's last defence against Hitler (see p. 51).

Towards the end of the 1920s the Centre Party began to move to the right. This made cooperation with the SPD much more difficult. The liberal parties lost many of their voters, who transferred their support to the **special interest parties**, which campaigned on behalf of those who had lost their money in the inflation period. In the 1928 election the special interest parties won 14 per cent of the vote, which was more than the total of the two Liberal parties combined. In 1930 many of these voters were to move over to the Nazis. For details of all election results see the table in Source B on page 18.

Special interest parties

Parties which are formed to campaign on specific issues, in this case financial compensation from the government for losses during the inflation years.

The Golden Age of culture?

Although German modern art and architecture had developed before 1914, in the more tolerant atmosphere of the Weimar Republic it flourished on a far greater scale. New modernistic designs for both buildings and furniture were produced on a large scale by the *Bauhaus* group. In the mid-1920s the *Neue Sachlichkeit* or New Objectivity Movement was formed by a group of painters and writers such as Erich Kastner, **Otto Dix** and Georg Grosz with the aim of coming to terms through literature and painting with the huge changes that had taken place in Germany since 1914.

This inevitably attracted a backlash of criticism from both cultural and political conservatives from all parties and classes. The film version of Erich Maria Remarque's *All Quiet on the Western Front* stirred up a bitter campaign by the nationalists, while the new forms of poetry as practised by the Berlin **Dada** group and such experimental operas as Paul Hindemith's *News of the Day* in which a naked women sang an aria in a bath, were also highly offensive to many Germans. Jazz, which one prominent critic called 'the most disgusting treason against all occidental civilized music' was also popular, particularly in night clubs, bars and dance halls in the large cities.

Dadaism

Originating in Zurich in 1916, this movement involved the visual arts, poetry and graphic design. It rejected all conventional art or literary forms.

Otto Dix (1891–1969)

Expressionist painter.

What was the situation in 1929?

The Weimar Republic never really won the loyalty of the German people, and was attacked by both the Right and the Left. On the Right it was still seen in 1929 as the regime that had betrayed Germany in November 1918, while the Left could never forget how it had crushed the workers uprising in the Ruhr in 1920. Many Germans of all political persuasions were also scandalised by the literature, art and music of the 1920s. There was also, especially amongst many of the older generation, a fear that the growth of feminism was producing a 'new' woman who was working by day in the office and, as the historian Detlev Peukert said, 'frittering away the night dancing the Charleston or watching **Ufa** and Hollywood films'. Many believed that the decline in the population was a consequence of feminine liberation

Economically, the Weimar Republic was burdened by the legacy of a lost war and by the heavy costs of running a welfare state, which was even more expensive that reparations. To maintain these welfare payments to widows, wounded ex-soldiers and the unemployed, the economy would have to enjoy a long period of sustained growth. The alternative was to make cuts in welfare, but this would anger the working classes and provoke a major political crisis. It seemed to many Germans that the Weimar Republic was incapable of producing a strong government that could take difficult decisions about welfare, industry and the unions.

On the other hand, as a contrast to this depressing picture of what the German historian Michael Stürmer called the 'history of failure', the situation in Prussia and the large cities was more optimistic. City mayors with the backing of both left-wing and right-wing parties had embarked on impressive recovery programmes, although they had had to borrow money from abroad to finance these, which in the economic crisis of 1930–33 was to cause severe problems. Prussia, which after all comprised three-fifths of the Reich, was ruled by a stable SPD, Centre and DDP coalition, which Otto Braun, its Minister-President, called the 'guarantor of the continued existence of the German Republic'. The Weimar Republic was not liked but in 1929 there was no real reason why it should collapse.

ACTIVITY

Period Studies

'By 1929 the Nazi Party was in a position to expand into a mass party if the economic situation in the Weimar Republic changed.'

How far do you agree with this assessment?

Ufa

This stands for Universal Film AG, the main film studio in Germany at the time.

Review questions

1. Assess how serious were the threats from the Left and Right to the Weimar Republic, 1919–23.
2. To what extent was there a revolution in Germany in the winter of 1918–19?
3. Assess the reasons for the survival of the Weimar Republic during the years 1919–23.
4. How stable was the Weimar Republic by 1928–29?
5. 'The Nazi Party can be dismissed as only of marginal importance during the period 1920–29'. How far do you agree with this assessment?
6. How successfully did the Weimar government tackle the issues raised by the Treaty of Versailles?

Exam**Café**

Relax, refresh, result!

Relax and prepare

Hot tips

Hattie

I wish I had written down the title of the book or article from which I was taking notes and the actual pages so that I could have gone back to it to check points I was unsure about when it came to revision.

Alex

It would have been a help to have had a copy of the Specification I was following at the very start so that I could use it as a checklist – so that I knew I had notes on all the key points. And if I had a list of past questions I could have seen the types of question set and also used them to practise planning essays.

Arman

At first I found it hard to distinguish between the armistice and the Treaty of Versailles. Which came first and which later – but especially how they were linked. But then my friend told me how she just remembered that 'A' comes before 'V' in the alphabet – so armistice before the Treaty of Versailles. This helped trigger me into remembering how many of the terms of the armistice fed into the Treaty.

Stephen

Some of the political stuff from the early years of the Weimar is difficult to get my head around – who was left wing, who was right. So I ended up making a table with headers of left wing/Communist and right wing/ Fascist and put the Spartacists in the left-wing column, the Kapp in the right-wing column. Dates or era went down the left-hand side in a different colour!

Rebecca

There's so much detail in the 1920s and 30s and so many concepts I get them confused. For instance, hyperinflation and Depression got muddled up in my mind. In the end I found it useful to train my brain to see things visually – so hyperinflation is a balloon and all the events for 1923 are in that inflated balloon. Then the Depression is a deflated balloon, with all the events and people hanging off the limp string underneath it. Linking them of course is how these economic climates helped Hitler's rise to power.

Refresh your memory

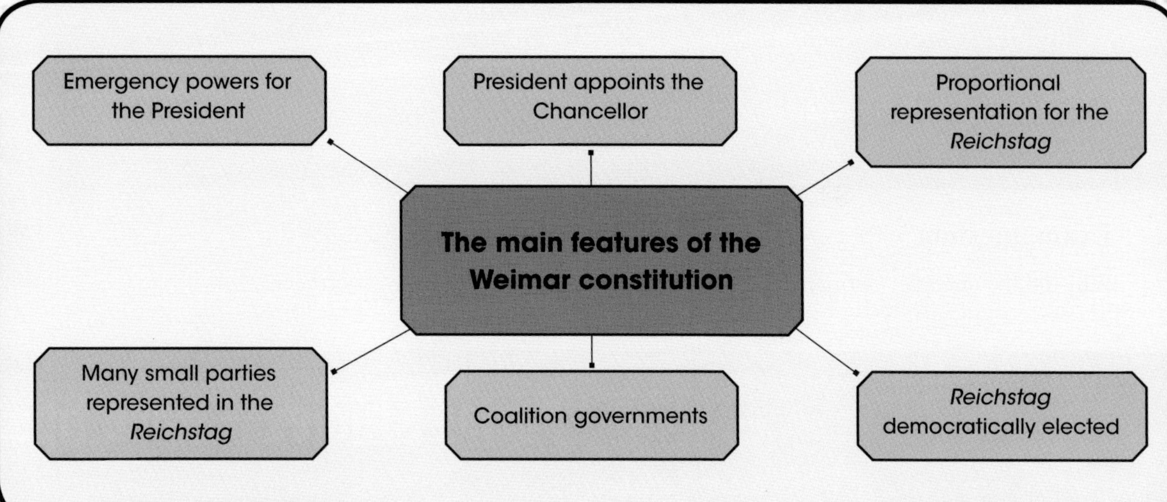

How strong was Weimar Germany in the 1920s?

- Understand the strengths and weaknesses of the Weimar constitution.
- Be able to explain and analyse the seriousness of the problems Weimar faced, 1919–23.
- Ensure you can explain why Weimar was able to survive the crises of 1923 and compare with what happened in 1929–33.
- Be able to explain how successful the foreign policy of the Golden Years was. Remember, nationalists did not support the developments.
- How much political support was there for Weimar throughout the period? What was the electoral performance of the anti-democratic parties in the elections to the *Reichstag*?
- How strong was the economy during the Weimar period? How great was the recovery during the Golden Years?

Get the result!

Writing a good AS essay

To do well in your AS exams it is important to understand the difference between a *descriptive* and *analytical* paragraph and how to write a good analytical paragraph.

Here we will focus on one paragraph from an answer to this question that considers the threat from the Communists or Spartacists.

You can find the rest of the answer on the CD ROM

Exam question

Why did the unrest in Germany in 1918–23 fail to destroy the Weimar government?

Period Studies – some tips

- Remember that in your AS exam (period studies) you will need to be able to explain the relative importance of the factors and explain how they link together if you want to reach the top mark bands. The answers must also be supported by precise factual knowledge.
- Remember, there is no right answer to an essay question. The examiner wants to know what your view is, but she or he will expect you to be able to support your view with precise factual information.

Sample answers

Tom's answer:

In January 1919 the dismissal of an official resulted in mass protests which the Communists, or Spartacists, tried to take over. They hoped that this would lead to a revolution similar to Russia. It was led by Rosa Luxemburg and Karl Liebknecht. The Communists tried to take control of Berlin and issued a proclamation deposing Ebert's government. However, the President of the Republic had the support of the Army who, supported by the Freikorps, suppressed the revolt in a week of bitter fighting. During the fighting both Spartacist leaders were shot and killed whilst they were under arrest. Within a week Berlin was back under government control.

Examiner says:

Although the factual knowledge is excellent, the reasons for the failure of the rising are only implied. Tom hints at the government's ability to gain the support of the army and the *Freikorps* and their willingness to be brutal in the suppression of the uprising. However, most of the answer simply describes what happened. You should focus on the opening sentence: Tom does not give a reason but sets the scene; the opening sentence should give a reason that you then go on and explain in the rest of the paragraph.

Tom's improved answer:

The Spartacist Uprising in Berlin failed because the government had the support of the Army and the Freikorps. President Ebert's actions in calling on the Army to crush the left-wing rising ensured that it would be short-lived as the government's forces were much stronger than those of the protestors. Although the brutal suppression did not prevent other left-wing risings, as in Bavaria in 1920, it made many potential opponents of the Republic see the futility of armed resistance and attempted revolution; instead they turned to the ballot box, reflected in the growing support for the Communist Party in elections to the Reichstag.

Examiner says:

Look at the opening sentence: it gives a clear reason for the failure of the rising and directly answers the question. There is sufficient factual knowledge, with reference to the President and the forces he used. The answer is more focused on the question.

How to tackle this type of question

- Spend time writing opening sentences to possible questions.
- The sentence should introduce an idea that is directly relevant to the question being answered. Look at the example above. Why is the second opening sentence better than the first?

For more student answers with examiner comments go the CD-ROM

How and why did the Nazi Party come to power in 1933?

Source

The British historian Ian Kershaw commented that:

Between the refoundation of the NSDAP [Nazi Party] in February 1925 and the beginning of the new political and economic turmoil that was to usher in the shattering impact of the world economic crisis, the Nazi Movement was no more than a fringe irritant in German politics. Its leader, Hitler, faced with the rebuilding of the Party from scratch after it had fractured into warring factions during his imprisonment in 1924, and banned from speaking in public in most of Germany until 1927 (in the biggest state of all, Prussia, until 1928), was confined in the political wilderness. A coincidental report by the Reich Minister of the Interior in 1927, pointing out that the NSDAP 'was not advancing', realistically described the party as 'a numerically insignificant... radical-revolutionary splinter group incapable of exerting any noticeable influence on the great mass of the population and the course of political events'.

Ian Kershaw, *Hitler, (Hubris) Vol. 1: 1889–1936*, p. 257 London: Allen Jane..

Key Questions:

In deciding why the Nazis were able to seize power in 1933, the key questions that need to be considered are:

- What was the legacy of the Weimar Republic and the Treaty of Versailles?
- What was the impact of the Great Depression?
- Did the new Brüning administration mark the death of the Weimar Republic or was it the last chance of survival?
- Why did the Brüning government fall in May 1932?
- How did the Nazi and Communist parties exploit the Depression, 1930–32?
- Why could neither von Papen nor Schleicher stabilise the situation in Germany in 1932?
- How inevitable was Hitler's appointment as Chancellor?

Within six years of the Reich Minister of the Interior's report, as quoted by Ian Kershaw above, Hitler not only led the largest party in Germany but was appointed Reich Chancellor on 30 January 1933. Why this seemingly miraculous reversal in the fortunes of Hitler and the Nazi Party occurred will be analysed and explained in this chapter.

How did Hitler rebuild the Nazi Party, 1925–29?

When Hitler came out of prison in December 1924, he had to rebuild his Party and re-establish his power. Not only was the Nazi Party outlawed, but thanks to the stabilisation of the currency, the Weimar Republic appeared to be on the road to recovery. In prison he had come to the conclusion that after the failure of the Munich Putsch the NSDAP would have to campaign through the ballot box and gain power by what he was later to call a 'legal revolution'.

He started to rebuild the Party when the ban on it was lifted in Bavaria in January 1925. As *Führer* he made sure that he had a position of absolute power as a **charismatic leader**, who was above the minor quarrels and disagreements within the Party. This *Führer* cult was the main way of uniting the Party in total obedience of the Führer. Party bureaucrats in Munich, like **Rudolph Hess** relieved Hitler of the routine administration, and were able to protect his charismatic image without posing any threat to his power. Hitler would only intervene and make a decision in an issue that involved his supreme authority.

Nationally the Nazi Party was divided into thirty-five *Gaue,* or regions, each controlled by a *Gauleiter*. Below these were the local branches, which were run by a **cadre** of activists. Each level of the Party received its orders from the one immediately above it. The organisations affiliated to the Party – the SA, the Hitler Youth, the Nazi Teachers' Association, etc. – were, however, directly responsible to *him* alone rather than being firmly integrated into the Party hierarchy.

Until 1927 the Nazi Party, following the example of Italian fascism, attempted to dominate the cities by appealing to the workers, but these tactics did not work because the Party's core supporters were the *Mittelstand* – the peasantry, the artisans and the small shopkeepers (see page.17), who had been impoverished by the war and the inflation of 1918–23. In the winter of 1927–28, with the start of the agricultural depression, Hitler gave up the Urban Plan and played down the Party's emphasis on land confiscation, which had alarmed many small farmers. Although the Nazi Party did not do well nationally in the 1928 elections, in some rural areas in North-West Germany, such as Schleswig-Holstein, the Nazis won over ten per cent of the vote.

Charismatic leader

A leader able to inspire others with devotion and enthusiasm.

Cadre

A core unit which can serve as a basis for mass expansion.

ACTIVITY

Why the Weimar Republic could only be governed by coalitions.

BIOGRAPHY

Rudolph Hess (1894–1987)

Hess was Hitler's deputy and in 1941 flew to Scotland in a doomed attempt to negotiate peace with Britain. Later he was tried at Nuremburg and imprisoned for life in Spandau jail.

What was Hitler's ideology?

Hitler never revised the Party's 1920 programme, but in practice he modified its more socialistic economic ideas to attract new supporters. *Mein Kampf,* which he wrote in prison, is a better guide to Nazi ideology. Of key importance for the future was his identification of the Jews with Russian Bolshevism, which had, to quote the historian Ernst Nolte, an 'explosive political effect'. This made Nazi propaganda more accessible to a wider middle-class public, which was terrified by the prospect of the Communists taking power in Germany. As he made clear in *Mein Kampf,* his whole programme for the future regeneration of Germany depended on creating a racially pure state, which would be strengthened by the German colonisation of *Lebensraum*, or 'living space', in western Russia. This would entail the expulsion of non-Germans from the Reich, especially Jews, extensive efforts to increase the birth rate and rebuild the military power of the German Reich.

ACTIVITY

Using Sources A and B and your own knowledge explain how the Nazi Party changed from 1919 to 1929.

Sources

(A) In 1929 Hitler wrote in an article in a newspaper recalling the early days of the German Worker's Party (the predecessor to the Nazi Party) in 1919:

Our little committee, which with its seven members in reality represented the whole Party, was nothing but the managing committee of a small whist club… To start with we met in a pathetic little room in a small pub…The committee's proceedings consisted in reading out letters received, discussing replies to them, and registering the letters that were sent off following the discussion. …

J. Noakes and G. Pridham (eds) (1998). *Nazism, 1919–45, Vol. 1: The Rise to Power, 1919–34* (2nd edn) (p. 16). Exeter: University of Exeter Press.

(B) After the election of May 1928 the Nazi newspaper, the *Racist Observer*, drew the following conclusions:

... The election results from the rural areas in particular proved that with a smaller expenditure of energy, money and time, better results can be achieved there than in the big cities. In small towns and villages mass meetings with good speakers are events and are often talked about for weeks, while in the big cities the effects of meetings with even three or four thousand people soon disappear. Local successes in which the National Socialists are running first or second are, surprisingly, almost invariably the result of the activity of the branch leader or of a few energetic members … .

J. Noakes and G. Pridham (eds) (1998). *Nazism, 1919–45, Vol.1: The Rise to Power, 1919–34* (2nd edn) (pp. 63–64). Exeter: Exeter University Press.

Weimar Republic

This was a democratic state founded in 1919 after the abdication of the Kaiser and the failure of the German revolution.

ACTIVITY

Period Studies

1. To what extent was the collapse of the Weimar Republic inevitable by 1929?

2. What was the most important weakness in 1932–33?

What was the legacy of the Weimar Republic and the Treaty of Versailles?

What were the weaknesses of the Weimar Republic?

In the last chapter we looked at why the Weimar Republic would be potentially vulnerable in a time of great economic and political crisis:

- The Weimar constitution was democratic, but deep disagreements between the parties, as well as the large number of small parties, ensured that it was very difficult to form a strong government that could make difficult decisions. The Reich President had considerable powers and, once Hindenburg was elected, these were in the hands of a man who disliked the German Social Democratic Party (SPD) and democracy in general.
- The Weimar Republic was hindered by the hostility of its elites (i.e. the judges, professors, industrialists, etc.) to parliamentary democracy and the Republic.
- The German economy was unable to deliver prosperity. This in turn prevented the Republic from creating an effective welfare state that could, at least, have reconciled large sections of its population to the new regime by compensating them generously for what they had lost in the war and experienced in the subsequent inflation. The post-1949 West German state was able to do this successfully thanks to economic growth (see Chapter 6).

- Most of the population hated the Republic. The industrialists believed it spent far too much on welfare, while many workers were unable to forget how it employed the army and the *Freikorps* to crush Communist uprisings in the early 1920s. There was also bitterness towards the Weimar politicians among the middle classes whose savings had been wiped out by inflation.
- Many Germans were also disturbed by the increasing freedom that women appeared to be gaining. Similarly they were shocked by the modern art and literature that flourished during the 1920s. Again they blamed the **permissive attitude** of the Republic for all these changes, and longed for a tougher government to 'clean up' Germany.

The legacy of Versailles

Although Stresemann had begun the long process of revising the **Treaty of Versailles** peacefully (see pages 29–31), the Treaty was still in force. Danzig had been placed under the control of the League of Nations, while Germans in German Upper Silesia and the **Danzig Corridor** were living under Polish rule. Reparations, had been cut by the Young Plan (see page 31), but had still to be paid. Secret agreements with the Soviet government enabled the army to develop new weapons in the USSR, but the army, at 100,000 men, was only a fraction of its pre-war size. Southern areas of the Rhineland were still occupied by Allied troops, and even after they were withdrawn in June 1930, the whole Rhineland was **demilitarised** and German troops were forbidden to enter it.

The German Nationalist Party (DNVP) was particularly hostile to the Treaty and never lost an opportunity to attack it. In a speech in 1927, after unveiling a memorial marking the 1914 German victory at Tannenberg over the Russians, President Hindenburg went out of his way to stress that Germany was completely free from all war guilt. Every Allied concession was viewed as not going far enough by nationalist Germans. Stresemann's acceptance of the Young Plan in 1929, which substantially cut reparation payments and led to the evacuation of the Rhineland by French troops, was also greeted with deep hostility on the Right. The Nationalist Party (DNVP), the Pan German League, the ***Stahlhelm*** and the Nazi Party managed to gain sufficient support to force the government to hold a referendum on the Young Plan in early 1930. The German people were asked to vote on a law repudiating the war guilt clause of the Treaty of Versailles and forbidding the government to accept any new agreements, such as the Young Plan, which could imply the acceptance of the Treaty. The government easily won the referendum, permitting the Young Plan, but there were still 5,825,000 Germans who voted for the proposal. The final withdrawal of French troops from the Rhineland again led to a barrage of criticism from the Nationalists because the Rhineland remained demilitarized.

ACTIVITY

Using your own knowledge, and Sources A and B, explain the hatred of the Treaty of Versailles in Germany.

Permissive attitude

An attitude which tolerates behaviour and practices that go beyond normal conventions.

Treaty of Versailles

A treaty signed in 1919 between Germany, the USA and the victorious Allied powers (see pages 14–16).

Danzig or Polish Corridor

A small corridor of land placed under Polish control so that Poland had access through German territory to the port of Danzig.

Demilitarised

A demilitarised area or zone is one in which military personnel and weapons are banned.

Stahlhelm

Literally, the League of Steel Helmets. It was a military veterans' society which was founded on 13 November 1918 by Franz Seldte.

Source

(A) The Nationalist newspaper *Kreuz-Zeitung (Paper of the Cross)* wrote in June 1930, when the last French troops had left the Rhineland:

The period of French occupation on the Rhine, that era of shame and tribulation, must be commemorated for the sake of coming generations... We know that the Rhine is not yet free. Owing to the demilitarisation of the Rhineland and the one sided disarmament of Germany, this country and above all the Rhineland itself, continues to be exposed to the caprice of our worst enemy. Evacuation which had to take place at the latest by the year 1935, was purchased at immense cost by the Young Plan... If, however, the premature evacuation of the Rhine was in actual fact a success, then we have to thank those who in tireless day to day resistance to brute force, often at the risk of their lives, finally made the French understand that their hope of detaching the Rhine and the Ruhr from the rest of Germany was vain.

National Archives, letter from Sir Horace Rumbold to the British Foreign Minister, 3 July, 1930.

(B) Dr Kaas, one of the leaders of the Centre Party, observed on the same date:

The occupation of the Rhineland... did little good and certainly no honour to France. Psychologically the most favourable hour for evacuation struck in September 1926 when Briand [French Foreign Minister] and Stresemann signed the Locarno Agreement [see page 30] and Germany entered the League of Nations. Locarno lost much of its popularity and suggestive effect in Germany in consequence. In fact it has never quite recovered. Many of the currents and cross currents of 'revenge', which are regarded with suspicion in France today, arise from the disappointment felt above all by the youth of Germany at the poverty of the results of the Locarno Treaty. There is nothing generous in the French gesture. It is merely the inevitable result of an agreement purchased at heavy cost on the German side...

National Archives, letter from Sir Horace Rumbold to the British Foreign Minister, 3 July, 1930.

ACTIVITY
Period Studies

Assess the legacy of the Versailles Treaty for the Weimar Republic.

Investment

This is money invested for profit in banks or businesses.

Interest rates

The amount or rate of interest paid at regular intervals for the loan of money.

What was the impact of the Great Depression?

The Great Depression, which the historian Robert Boyce has called 'the third global catastrophe of the century' (along with the two world wars), had an immense impact on German history. Between 1929 and 1932 the volume of world trade fell by 70 per cent. Unemployment rose to 13 million in the United States, to at least 6 million in Germany and to 3 million in Britain.

In its impact on the lives of ordinary Germans the Depression was devastating. By 1932 almost one worker in three was officially registered as unemployed. Many more were forced to accept wage cuts or part-time work merely to survive. Many were reduced to instant poverty and families were made homeless as rent and mortgages could not be paid. People tramped from city to city desperately looking for work and some were reduced to begging on the streets. By January 1933 it was calculated that the unemployed and their dependents made up a fifth of the whole population of Germany.

It was not, of course, just the workers who suffered. Desperate to save money, the government made as many of its employees redundant as possible and cut the salaries of those who remained. Many other white-collar workers saw their jobs axed, and those who managed to cling on to their jobs lived in constant fear of losing them.

By January 1932 the unemployed, together with their dependent families, made up 20 per cent of the total German population – almost thirteen million people. The unemployed were entitled to benefits, but in practice the longer the Depression lasted, the less they received. The unemployment benefit system was originally designed for only 800,000 people and could not cope with the huge numbers who needed benefits by 1932.

How did the Great Depression in Germany happen?

The German economic recovery of 1925–28 had been made possible by American **investment**. High German **interest rates** attracted American money, and by the late 1920s major German firms, such as Krupps and the United Steel Works, were depending heavily on American investments. Even the banks took out American loans to help them lend money to German businessmen. Potentially this was a dangerous position for the German economy to be in. It was made worse by the fact that most American loans were short term, often renewed on a monthly basis, and so could be cancelled at short notice.

In the autumn of 1928 there were the first signs of a global recession. Not surprisingly, American investment in the German economy began to fall, and by the spring of 1929 unemployment had increased to 2.5 million in Germany. On 'Black Tuesday'(29 October 1929) there was a dramatic collapse in the value of American shares on the New York stock market that caused billions of dollars to be wiped off the value of major American companies. American companies went bankrupt, the demand for German imports dried up and the banks began to call in the short-term loans upon which most of German industry was dependent. With no hope of further investment, German factories had to cut back on production or even close down completely. Industrial production fell rapidly and by 1932 it had dropped to just 40 per cent of its 1929 value.

Figure 2.1 Queues of the unemployed, in front of an employment office, Berlin, 1930.

Table 2.1 Unemployment in Germany (millions), January and July, 1929–33

Year	January	July
1928	1,862	1,012
1929	2,850	1,251
1930	3,218	2,765
1931	4,887	3,990
1932	6,042	5,392
1933	6,014	4,464

Source

The historian Alan Bullock wrote about the social/psychological impact and consequences of the Depression on the German people as follows:

Like men and women in a town stricken by an earthquake millions of Germans saw the apparently solid framework of their existence cracking and crumbling. In such circumstances men are no longer amenable to the arrangements of reason. In such circumstances men entertain fantastic fears, extravagant hatreds and extravagant hopes. In such circumstances the extravagant demagogy of Hitler began to attract a mass following as it had never done before.

Alan Bullock (1990). *Hitler: A Study in Tyranny* (p. 153). London: Penguin.

It was not surprising that many of the younger unemployed tried to escape from the tedium and frustration of unemployment by joining the paramilitary organisations of either the Nazis or the Communists – the Nazis' ***Sturmabteilung*** (SA), or the Communists' ***Rotfront*** (paramilitary force).

Sturmabteilung **(Stormtroopers)**

These were the Nazis' assault troops.

The Depression and the fall of the Müller government

The Depression plunged the Weimar Republic into a crisis that finally led to its dissolution. Already by the end of 1929 the **Great Coalition** was beginning to come apart. SPD **backbenchers** had rebelled against their own Chancellor, Hermann Müller, and voted in protest against the Cabinet's decision to build a **battle cruiser**. Increasingly, only support for the Young Plan held the Cabinet together. Once the referendum (see page 31) on the Plan had been won in March 1930, the differences in the Cabinet over financing the unemployment insurance system came to a head. The SPD argued that despite the steep rise in unemployment, there should be no cut in benefits, while the German People's Party (DVP) called for reductions. German industrialists were beginning to push for the abolition of the German welfare state on the grounds that it was too expensive to maintain. A compromise was put forward by the Centre Party, which proposed that any financial increase in unemployment benefit should, until the autumn, be paid for by a mixture of government subsidy and increased contributions.

This compromise proposal was rejected on 27 March 1930 by the trade unions and SPD backbenchers and the Cabinet resigned. Later, the left-wing Social Democrat, Rudolf Hilferding, bitterly criticised his party for being 'ready to let German democracy and the German Republic go to the devil... over the question of thirty *pfennigs* [pennies] for the unemployed'. He did indeed have a point, as the fall of the Grand Coalition after only two years in power fatally weakened German democracy and was to open the door to the rise of the Nazi Party. However, what was at stake for the SPD and the trade unions was the major issue of whether or not unemployment benefits should be cut. They feared that the compromise was in fact only a prelude to major reforms aimed at dismantling the welfare state.

When Chancellor Müller resigned in March 1930, President Hindenburg seized the chance to appoint **Heinrich Brüning**, the leader of the Centre Party, as Chancellor in the *Reichstag*. Hindenburg and his advisers (particularly General Schleicher, the army's political advisor within in the Defence Ministry) had been waiting to replace Müller with a more right-wing Chancellor. The army was aiming to rearm Germany and make her once again a great power and believed this required a more authoritarian government, independent of the *Reichstag*.

Figure 2.2 Hindenburg's chief advisor was Kurt von Schleicher (far right), who would later become Chancellor, with from left to right, von Pappen, Wilhelm von Gayl and von Hindenburg.

ACTIVITY

Period Studies

Assess the evidence for the impact of the Great Depression on the German people.

Great Coalition

This consisted of the German Social Democratic Party (SPD), the Democratic Party (DDP), the Centre Party (ZTR) and the German People's Party (DVP).

Backbenchers

Members of parliament who are not members of the Cabinet and sit on 'the back benches' in the *Reichstag*.

Battle cruiser

A 'pocket' or small battleship.

BIOGRAPHY

Heinrich Brüning (1885–1970)

After serving in the First World War, Brüning became an official in the Christian Trade Union Movement and, in 1924, a Centre Party deputy in the *Reichstag*. In 1929 he became the parliamentary leader of the Party. He rapidly gained a reputation for his expertise in economic and financial matters, and moved the Centre Party back to a more right-wing position.

Did the new Brüning administration mark the death of the Weimar Republic or was it the last chance of survival?

Historians argue about Brüning's role in the destruction of the Weimar Republic. In the 1930s the historianArthur Rosenberg wrote that Brüning brought about the 'death of the Weimar Republic', while Friedrich Meinecke observed in 1946 that 'the path to the abyss' only began with Brüning's fall.

Brüning's first government, which was formed on 28 March 1930, was supported by the Centre, the German People's Party (DNVP) and the Democratic Party (DP) but as it was opposed by the Social Democratic Party (SPD) it did not have a majority in the *Reichstag*. From the start, Brüning made it clear that if his government was defeated he would request the dissolution of the *Reichstag* and govern with emergency decrees. His first finance bill just managed to scrape through parliament, but the second one, involving increased taxes, **deflationary** cuts in welfare expenditure, as well as 'an emergency contribution' from those on fixed incomes, was defeated in July. When the *Reichstag* rejected as unconstitutional the government's attempts to use Article 48 (see page 18) to pass the legislation, it was promptly dissolved.

The general election of 14th September 1930 and the Nazi breakthrough

Germany went to the polls on 14 September. With hindsight one can see that this, as the historian Ian Kershaw observes, was a decision of 'breathtaking irresponsibility' since it allowed the Nazi Party to become a major political force. Legally, a new election was not due for another two years.

By 1928 Hitler together with **Gregor Strasser** managed to rebuild the Nazi Party so that it had become, to quote the historian Richard J. Evans, 'an elaborate well-organised political body whose appeal was directed virtually to every sector of the population'. They constructed a party which gave Hitler unconditional loyalty. Its propaganda was modern and sophisticated, while in the SA it had a paramilitary force that that could challenge the Communist *Rotfront* (Red Front Fighters League) and Social Democratic ***Reichsbanner*** (Reich flag).

In the subsequent electoral campaign the Nazi Party exploited the growing insecurity of the voters with great skill. Their main theme was that parliamentary democracy had demoralised the people, split society into competing, mutually-exclusive interest groups, and that only Hitler could unite the people into a new national community (*volksgemeinschaft*). In major speeches in the large cities, Hitler constantly attacked the divisions and failures of the Weimar Republic and its responsibility for the humiliation of Germany in the Versailles Treaty.

Nazi propaganda cleverly targeted different groups amongst the German electorate and was brilliantly masterminded by **Joseph Goebbels**. Different posters and leaflets were designed so as to appeal to local audiences. Campaigners were given practical training in how to appeal to different types of audience and organise their local propaganda with the maximum effect. The Nazi Party was able to do this so effectively because it had developed a series of specially designed organisations targeting different sectors of the population. There were, for instance, groups for young people, school and university students, civil servants, the war wounded, farmers and workers. Whole regions were saturated with Nazi canvassers and electoral meetings.

ACTIVITY
Period Studies

Assess the importance of the Depression in bringing about the fall of the Müller government.

Deflation

A policy aimed at reducing the amount of money in circulation so as to stop prices rising.

Reichsbanner

The Social Democratic Party's paramilitary force.

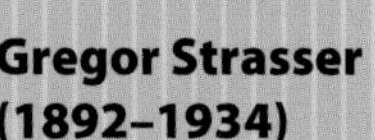

BIOGRAPHY
Gregor Strasser (1892–1934)

Gregor Strasser was the leader of the North German Nazis during the 1920s and the main representative of the 'socialist' anti-capitalist wing of the Nazi Party. Strasser believed passionately in a 'German or National Socialism'. In 1928 he played a key role in improving the Nazi Party's organisation.

BIOGRAPHY

Joseph Goebbels (1897–1945)

Goebbels was one of the few leading Nazis who had studied at university (he gained a PhD). He became the *Gauleiter* of the North Rhine district and secretary to Gregor Strasser and, in November 1926, *Gauleiter* of Berlin. Two years later he was put in charge of Party propaganda and played a major role in projecting the Nazi Party throughout the Reich in 1930–32. In March 1933 he became Minister for Popular Enlightenment and Propaganda. In July 1944 he was appointed Reich Trustee for Total War and in April 1945, shortly after Hitler's suicide, he killed his children and then himself and his wife.

According to their 25 Point Programme of 1920 the Nazis were committed to the nationalisation of big business and industry, the leasing out of department stores to small traders and the 'expropriation of land for communal purposes', which seemed to imply that the farms would be broken up. In 1930 however, Hitler was determined not to alarm the big businessmen and industrialists and reassured them that the Nazis wanted to save Germany from Communism and rebuild the economy and Germany's strength. Unlike Stresemann who wanted to see Germany as a part of the global economy, Hitler believed that Germany would only survive if she eventually established a huge area of *Lebensraum* (living space) and became as self sufficient as possible in industry and food production.

Figure 2.3 Weimar Republic/*Reichstag* Elections, 14 Sept. 1930. Passers-by care for a woman knocked over by National Socialists.

The results of the election on 14 September were 'a political earthquake': the NSDAP increased its seats from 12 to 107, and became the second largest party in the *Reichstag*.

Table 2.2 Results of the election of 14 September 1930 (number of seats)

NSDAP (Nazis)	107
DNVP (Nationalists)	41
DVP (People's Party)	30
Centre Party	68
DDP (Democratic Party, renamed in 1930 the State Party)	20
SPD (Social Democratic Party)	143
KPD (Communist Party)	77
The Economy Party	23

Where did the Nazi votes come from?

In 1930, 18.3 per cent of the electorate voted for the Nazis (6.5 million people). This went up to 37.3 per cent in July 1932. The Nazis benefited from the sharp increase in the electoral turnout in 1930 and 1932 and the large number of first-time voters who came onto the electoral roll between May 1928 and July 1932. Mass unemployment, Hitler's promises to create work and the glamour of the SA attracted many young male voters. The Nazis also gained from voters moving over from the smaller middle-class interest parties (see page 32).

By 1930 the NSDAP (Nazi Party) had set up specific organisations which were each targeted at attracting a particular section of society such as the peasants, self-employed businessmen, clerical workers, students, women, as well as many members of the professions. Although the NSDAP did best in the Protestant and rural districts of northern Germany, and did not win as many votes in the Catholic areas and cities, it did nevertheless attract votes from all sections of society. Some 27 per cent of the Nazi voters in September 1930 were manual workers.

Conclusion

Brüning's disastrous decision to hold an election in September 1930 played into the hands of the Nazis. At a time when there were already over three million unemployed, the Nazis were able to increase their number of seats in the *Reichstag* from 12 to 107. Their propaganda brilliantly appealed to different groups in German society and exploited the feeling of insecurity which the Great Depression had caused.

Land parliaments

The parliaments of the individual states (*Länder*) of Germany.

ACTIVITY ***Period Studies***

1 Assess the reasons for the Nazis' success in the election of 14 September 1930.

2 To what extent did the Great Depression increase support for the Nazi and Communist parties?

Why did the Brüning government fall in May 1932?

Brüning at first hoped to gain the backing of the NSDAP for his government in the *Reichstag*, and suggested to Hitler that 'in all ***Länd*** **parliaments** where it was arithmetically possible, the NSDAP and the Centre might combine to form a government'. But Hitler was unwilling to prop up the Brüning government. Brüning also failed to gain the support of

the DNVP, but in the end was saved by the SPD, which agreed to support his Cabinet, partly to keep Hitler from the Chancellorship, but also to keep intact its coalition with the Centre Party in the Prussian parliament.

As long as he enjoyed both the passive support of the SPD and the support of Hindenburg, Brüning could survive, but democracy in Germany was progressively weakened. The Communist and Nazi delegates made the *Reichstag* so unmanageable that it was adjourned for six months in 1931. The number of emergency decrees rose from 5 in 1930 to 66 in 1932. At the same time the freedom of the press to criticise Brüning's policies was increasingly controlled. By July 1931 it was estimated that about a hundred newspaper editions were banned every month throughout Germany. By early 1932 the Communist paper *The Red Flag* was being banned almost one day in three.

What was Brüning's economic policy?

Brüning's priority was to use the misery of the Depression to persuade the western powers to scrap reparations. He also hoped to bring about an economic recovery by cutting back on welfare costs, which would make production costs in German factories much cheaper.

He attempted to negotiate a **customs union** with Austria, which he argued would give Germany 'an adequate natural area of living space'. Inevitably this provoked sharp protests from France. The French feared that this was just a preliminary step to political union between the two countries, which had been banned by the Treaty of Versailles.

When Germany was plunged into a major banking crisis in July 1931, the French vetoed every proposal for an emergency loan until Germany gave up the idea of the customs union. Brüning retaliated by threatening to suspend reparation payments until further notice. His gamble worked because the severity of the banking crisis in Germany persuaded US President Hoover to force the French into agreeing to declare a year's **moratorium** on reparation payments.

Brüning was now near to achieving one of his aims (ending of reparations). He convinced a committee of international financial experts that Germany could no longer pay reparations even after the expiry of the moratorium. The committee agreed and proposed that both reparations and **inter-Allied debts** should be cancelled. This was adopted at the Lausanne Conference in June 1932.

Customs union

An economic union between two countries which ensures that both can trade freely with each other without paying any customs' duties.

Moratorium

A suspension of debt repayments.

Inter-Allied debts

These were debts owed by France and Britain to the USA.

The banking crisis of July 1931

This crisis was caused by the collapse of an Austrian bank, the *Kreditanstalt* in Vienna, in July 1931. Since the inflation of 1923 the German banks had only a small amount of capital in reserve, and they were immediately put under pressure by their customers, who, frightened by the possible economic consequences of the collapse of the *Kreditanstalt*, started withdrawing their money. On 13 July the *Darmstädter und Nationalbank* (DANAT) had to stop all payments to their customers. On 14 and 15 July the other German banks also closed to stop a run on their deposits. When they re-opened, customers were permitted to withdraw only small amounts of money. The government was forced to come to the rescue of the German banking system with a sum of one billion marks

Why was Brüning dismissed?

Brüning was dismissed from office by Hindenburg on 29 May 1932. Why was he so abruptly removed when he was about to achieve the cancellation of reparations?

1 The most important reason was that the depth and intensity of the Depression inevitably caused his government to lose popular support and played into the hands of the Nazis and Communists. Brüning made no secret of the fact that he believed that the Depression would last until 1935! His deflationary policies of reducing the salaries of the civil servants, freezing wage levels and making unemployment payments ever more difficult to secure were so unpopular that he became known as the 'Hunger Chancellor'. When he travelled on a train, the window-blinds of his carriage were permanently drawn to stop crowds catching sight of their Chancellor and hurling stones at him.

2 Both the Nationalists who were influential with Hindenburg and the Nazis were bitterly opposed to him. His continued cooperation with the SPD, who now supported him as the only alternative to a Nationalist-Nazi regime, also annoyed the industrialists and businessmen who had previously backed him. It was significant that it was Hitler who was invited to speak to their representatives at the Industry Club in Düsseldorf in January 1932.

3 A key figure in the intrigue leading up to Brüning's replacement was **General von Schleicher**, who was the army's chief political adviser in the War Ministry. Schleicher repeatedly informed Hindenburg that the army felt that Brüning's economic policy was damaging the arms industry and that his ban on 13 April 1932, on the *Sturmbteilung* or SA (the Nazis' assault troops) would prevent the army from enrolling them as auxiliary troops in an emergency.

4 Brüning planned to break up the large bankrupt estates in east Germany and turn them into smallholdings for the unemployed. The great landowners described this to Hindenburg as Communist policies. Hindenburg, who had an estate of his own, was very alarmed.

von Schleicher hoped to convince Hindenburg to replace the Brüning government with a predominantly Nationalist Party (DNVP) government led by **Franz von Papen**, which he thought would be supported by the Nazis. Hitler did not agree to this, however, as he was determined not to enter a coalition in a subordinate position. He was convinced that the Nazis were capable of winning an overall majority in an election and consequently initially agreed to support von Papen provided that the SA ban was lifted and a general election was held within weeks. Hindenburg and Schleicher accepted these conditions, and on 29 May Brüning was dismissed and the government entrusted to von Papen.

BIOGRAPHY

Franz von Papen (1879–1969)

Von Papen was a regular army officer who joined the General Staff in 1911 and then became a **military attaché** in Washington. He was recalled from this post because the US government suspected him of contacts with German spies. In 1919 he was elected to the Prussian ***Ländtag*** and represented the right wing of the Centre Party. He owned the majority of shares in the Catholic newspaper *Germania*. After serving as Chancellor in May–November 1932 and then Vice Chancellor under Hitler in 1933–34, von Papen served as ambassador to Austria between 1934 and 1938 and then to Turkey in 1939–44. He was acquitted by the Nuremburg War Crimes Tribunal in 1946, but sentenced to eight years' hard labour by a German de-Nazification court. He was released in 1949.

Military attaché

A military representative who is part of a diplomatic mission in an embassy.

Ländtag

Local assembly or parliament.

BIOGRAPHY

General Kurt von Schleicher (1882–1934)

Schleicher was head of the Ministerial Bureau in the German Defence Ministry and played a key role in advising Hindenburg during the years1930–32. He was appointed Chancellor in December 1932 but was replaced by Hitler on 30 January 1933. He was murdered during the Night of the Long Knives (see page 71), 30 June/1 July 1934.

ACTIVITY

Period Studies

Assess Brüning's role in the collapse of the Weimar Republic.

Conclusion

Despite failing to gain a majority in the election of September 1930, Brüning remained Chancellor until May 1932. He had Hindenburg's backing, and in the *Reichstag* the SPD supported his government because it realised that its collapse would open up the way to Hitler coming to power.

Brüning made himself very unpopular by pursuing a policy of deflation in an attempt to make German exports cheaper and to convince the wartime Allies that Germany could not pay reparations. He nearly succeeded in his aims, but he was removed from office by Hindenburg in May 1932. His deflationary policy increased unemployment and so played into Hitler's hands.

How did the Nazi and Communist parties exploit the Depression, 1930–32?

The Communist Party

The German Communist Party (KPD), led by **Ernst Thälmann**, managed to recruit and mobilise the unemployed. They turned the working-class areas of the big cities into no-go areas or 'red districts' where they organised rent strikes and set up their own paramilitary force, the Red Front Fighters League. As unemployment climbed, their membership increased: from 117,000 in 1929 to 360,00 in 1932. They appealed especially to young men who had been made redundant and who had no hope of gaining any job in the foreseeable future, but these young men were just as likely to change their allegiance and join the SA.

The Communists, who took their orders from Stalin in Moscow, were convinced that capitalism was about to collapse in Germany and that a revolution would soon install them in power. Their main enemies were not so much the Nazis as the SPD, whom they saw as traitors to the working class as they were ready to cooperate with Brüning.

The Mittlestand, the professional classes and the industrialists all feared that the Communists would eventually be strong enough to seize power and establish a dictatorship which would abolish the private ownership of industry, land and capital.

BIOGRAPHY

Ernst Thälmann (1886–1944)

Thälmann had originally been a Social Democrat but in 1919 became the leader of the Independent Socialists in Hamburg, moving over to the Communists in 1922. He was no intellectual, working as a ship-breaker in the docks and he followed the party line laid down by Moscow unquestioningly. He stood for the presidency in 1932 against Hindenburg (see page 49) and was arrested when Hitler came to power. He died in the Buchenwald concentration camp in 1944. He was commemorated after his death in post-war Germany through the formation of SED youth groups and seen as a hero by the DDR. (See page 152.)

The Nazi Party

The Nazi Party had become the second largest party in the *Reichstag*. Over the next two years it continued to attract votes. It was essentially a movement rather than a political party. It had its symbols (particularly the swastika) and martyrs such as **Horst Wessel**, while Hitler himself was portrayed as the bearer of a new political 'religion'. The Nazis had no detailed political programme, but managed to project a powerful image of dynamism and energy that no other party possessed, with the possible exception of the Communists. The Nazi Party was a 'rainbow coalition' of the discontented and fearful. Voters were essentially protesting against the Weimar Republic, and the vagueness of the Nazi programme allowed voters to read into it virtually any message they wished to. As the Communist threat grew, the *Sturmbteilung* (SA) was increasingly seen by many as the only force that could push the Communist *Rotfront* off the streets, and prevent a Communist takeover of Germany.

BIOGRAPHY

Horst Wessel (1907–30)

Wessel was the son of a Berlin pastor and had studied at university, but had become an SA activist. At the end of 1929 he had moved into an apartment with his girlfriend, an ex-prostitute, which was owned by the widow of a Communist. When arguments arose between the landlady and Wessel, she asked for help from the Communist Red Front Fighters' League, who had Wessel shot as he opened the door of his apartment. Goebbels seized on his death to create a martyr.

Figure 2.4 Hitler and Hindenburg

Hitler and the presidential elections

In March 1932 Hindenburg had to stand for re-election. He had hoped that the *Reichstag* would pass legislation allowing him to continue in office without an election but this was blocked by the Nazis. The subsequent election was turned into a contest between Thälmann, Hitler and Hindenburg. The Centre Party, the DVP, the State Party (formerly the DP) and the SPD all backed Hindenburg even though he had previously been hostile to the idea of parliamentary democracy, while the Communists nominated Thälmann.

The Nazis launched a massive campaign on behalf of Hitler with all the usual marches, parades, public meetings and posters. It focused on Hitler as the candidate who could save Germany, and Goebbels targeted particular groups of voters from the middle classes with even greater accuracy than in September 1930. He stressed the Party's determination to help farmers and small businessmen, while also making a broader appeal to all classes by claiming that only the Nazis could create a united, prosperous and strong Germany. Hitler only won 30 per cent of the vote, but there had to be a second round because Hindenburg failed by 0.4 per cent to win an outright majority. Again Goebbels showed the effectiveness of the Nazi propaganda machine and Hitler made an enormous impact by flying from city to city delivering speeches. A striking Nazi poster of the time showed Hitler in a plane with the caption 'Hitler over Germany'. This time Hindenburg won outright, but Hitler managed to push his own vote up by over two million.

ABERGELE COMMUNITY COLLEGE
CANOLFAN ADNODDAU DYSGU
LEARNING RESOURCE CENTRE
131891
COLEG LLANDRILLO COLLEGE
LIBRARY RESOURCE CENTRE
CANOLFAN ADNODDAU LLYFRGELL

ACTIVITY
Period Studies

Assess the reasons for the rise of the Nazi and Communist parties, 1930–32.

Conclusion

The Nazis and Communists both benefited from the Depression and Brüning's policy of deflation. Young unemployed men were particularly attracted to the Nazi SA and the Communist *Rotfront* paramilitary organisations.

The Nazi Party steadily built up support during the years 1930–32. It continued to appeal to a wide cross-section of the German population, and by the time of the presidential elections attracted nearly 37 per cent of the German vote. The Nazi Party was a dynamic political movement, but there was tension between Hitler and the SA. Hitler hoped to achieve power through the ballot box while the SA were ready to seize it by force.

Why could neither von Papen nor von Schleicher stabilise the situation in Germany in 1932?

Von Papen's regime marked the end of parliamentary democracy in Germany. His new Cabinet was filled with men who were determined to create a new state, which would be much more authoritarian than anything that Brüning had planned. The ending of the ban on the SA (part of the deal with Hitler) immediately led to an escalation of street violence. On 17 July 1932 large-scale fighting between the SA and the Communists in Altona, a suburb of Hamburg, gave von Papen the chance to take over the Prussian state government on the grounds that it could no longer keep order on the streets. This was a devastating blow against the Social Democrats, whose power base was Prussia. The Reich Chancellor assumed the post of Prussian Minister-President, while a Reich Commissioner took over the Prussian Ministry of the Interior. The Prussian police now came under the direct control of the Reich. The historian Richard Evans has written that von Papen's coup 'was a mortal blow to the Weimar Republic. It destroyed the federal principle and opened the way to the wholesale centralisation of the state'.

Gestapo
The State Secret Police.

Why did the SPD not resist the takeover of the Prussian state by von Papen?

The odds were stacked against the SPD. Unlike the Kapp Putsch of 1920 (see pages 19–20), there was little chance of a general strike succeeding as there were large numbers of unemployed. The army was also ready to intervene to restore order and the divisions between the two left-wing parties prevented any united opposition against von Papen. The Communist Party viewed the SPD as class traitors, who had backed Brüning and were ready to cooperate with the bourgeois parties rather than overthrow the system.

The elections of 31 July 1932

The elections took place on 31 July. The Nazi propaganda was again the most effective, even though the Social Democrats tried hard to copy it. Goebbels' main attack was not directed against von Papen, but rather the record of the Weimar Republic. Through leaflets, films, speeches and meetings attended by thousands, voters were offered the stark choice of voting Nazi for a national rebirth and a glorious future or of decline and corruption under the Weimar regime. The Nazis again proved to be a 'catch-all' party of social protest, and more than doubled their vote to gain 230 seats, but this was still well short of an overall majority of 305, even though the Nazis were now the largest party in the *Reichstag*. Von Papen himself could only rely on the 37 members of the DNVP.

Table 2.3 Results of the election of 31 July 1932 (number of seats)

NSDAP (Nazis)	230
DNVP (Nationalists)	37
DVP (German People's Party)	7
Centre Party	75
State Party	4
SPD (Social Democratic Party)	133
KPD (Communist Party)	89
The Economy Party	2

Von Papen's failure to form a coalition with the Nazis and the election of 6 November 1932

As the leader of the largest party in the *Reichstag*, Hitler demanded the right to form a new government, which would give him the chance to use the forces of the state to create a dictatorship. However, Hindenburg was only ready to offer him the Vice-Chancellorship in von Papen's Cabinet. Having failed to bring Hitler into his Cabinet, von Papen, with the support of the President, was determined to dissolve the *Reichstag*. He would then hold fresh elections when he had drawn up a new constitution, which would drastically reduce the *Reichstag*'s powers.

The timing of his plans went wrong. **Hermann Göring** had been made the speaker of the *Reichstag* as the representative of the largest party and he ignored von Papen's attempts on 12 September to dissolve it, instead permitting a vote of no confidence in von Papen's government to take place. The government lost this by 512 votes to 42. At first von Papen was determined not to set a date for a new election, but retreated when the Centre Party and the NSDAP threatened to use **Article 59** of the Weimar constitution to take him to court for violating the constitution.

The elections of 6 November were a blow for the Nazis. This time round Hitler's main target was von Papen, but there was no longer sufficient money to pay for a dynamic electoral campaign. The Party also appeared to be moving sharply to the left, and it even took part with the Communists in the Berlin transport strike. This frightened off many of their middle-class supporters. As a result of increasing disillusionment with Hitler, the Nazis actually lost two million voters and their number of seats fell from 230 to 196.

Table 2.4 Results of the election of 6 November 1932 (number of seats)

NSDAP (Nazis)	196
DNVP (Nationalists)	52
DVP (German People's Party)	11
Centre Party	70
State Party	2
SPD (Social Democratic Party)	121
KPD (Communist Party)	100
The Economy Party	1

BIOGRAPHY

Herman Göring (1893–1946)

Göring, a Bavarian, was commander of the famous *Richthofen* squadron in the Great War. He joined the Nazi Party and became head of the SA in 1922. He was a Nazi *Reichstag* deputy in 1928 and in 1932 the President of the *Reichstag*. Then in 1933, he organised the ***Gestapo*** and set up the first concentration camps. During the Third Reich he built up the German air force and was put in charge of the Four Year Plan in 1936 (see pages 99–103). He was sentenced to death as a war criminal at Nuremberg, but managed to commit suicide before his execution.

Article 59

This gave members of the *Reichstag* the right to take legal action in the Supreme Court against any member of the government (President, Chancellor and Ministers) who violated the Reich constitution.

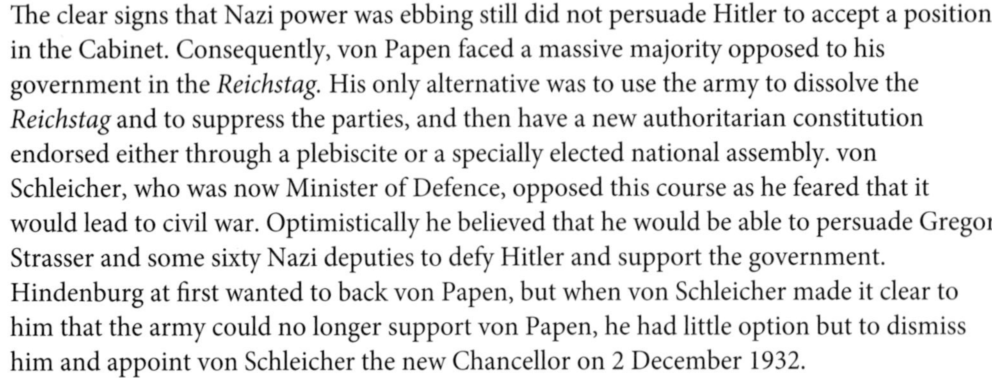

ACTIVITY

Examine the election statistics:

- who gained?
- who lost?
- and why?

The clear signs that Nazi power was ebbing still did not persuade Hitler to accept a position in the Cabinet. Consequently, von Papen faced a massive majority opposed to his government in the *Reichstag*. His only alternative was to use the army to dissolve the *Reichstag* and to suppress the parties, and then have a new authoritarian constitution endorsed either through a plebiscite or a specially elected national assembly. von Schleicher, who was now Minister of Defence, opposed this course as he feared that it would lead to civil war. Optimistically he believed that he would be able to persuade Gregor Strasser and some sixty Nazi deputies to defy Hitler and support the government. Hindenburg at first wanted to back von Papen, but when von Schleicher made it clear to him that the army could no longer support von Papen, he had little option but to dismiss him and appoint von Schleicher the new Chancellor on 2 December 1932.

The von Schleicher government, December 1932–January 1933

The following day (3 December 1932), von Schleicher offered Gregor Strasser the posts of Vice-Chancellor and Minister-President of Prussia. Hitler immediately vetoed von Schleicher's proposal, and Strasser then resigned in protest. Hitler managed to prevent a split in the Party by appealing successfully to the Führer principle (see page 76). Schleicher also tried unsuccessfully to persuade both the SPD and the trade unions to support his government by offering them a package of economic reforms and work creation projects, which would create jobs for the unemployed. This offer did, however, frighten both the industrialists and the East Elbian landowners and make them more sympathetic to supporting a possible von Papen-Hitler government, which would keep the SPD out of power.

Tariff duties

Taxes on imports.

Did Hitler come to power as a result of 'back stairs intrigue'?

Von Papen, angry at being outmanoeuvred by von Schleicher, was anxious to reopen negotiations with Hitler. As early as 10 December 1932 he made contact with him through Kurt von Schröder, a banker from Cologne, with whom Hitler was also in contact. On 4 January 1933 Schröder arranged a meeting between Hitler and von Papen. Hitler was ready to accept a Nazi-Nationalist coalition, as long as he controlled the Defence and Interior Ministries. Over the next two weeks his bargaining position was strengthened by the Nazi electoral success in the *Land* election of Lippe (where the Nazi Party won 39.5 per cent of the vote) and by the increasing difficulties facing the government. von Schleicher had no majority in the *Reichstag* and had even managed to anger the East Elbian landowners by refusing to increase **tariff duties** on imported food because he did not wish to make food prices more expensive for the unemployed.

By mid-January, Hindenburg had lost confidence in von Schleicher and instructed von Papen 'personally and in strict confidence' to go back to Hitler and see if he could form a government with the Nazis. Despite the Lippe election, Hindenburg and his advisers suspected that the Nazi Party was in decline. Consequently, if a Nazi–Nationalist coalition was to be formed, now was the right moment. Otherwise, if Nazi strength evaporated, there might be no alternative to the restoration of parliamentary government.

BIOGRAPHY

Wilhelm Frick (1877–1946)

Frick worked in the Munich police offices from 1904 to 1924, when he was elected to the *Reichstag* representing the Nazi Party. In 1930 he became Minister of Interior in Thuringia, and in January 1933 he was promoted to Reich Minister of the Interior. In 1943 he was replaced by Himmler and given the post of Protector of Bohemia and Moravia. In 1946 he was hanged at Nuremberg.

Hindenburg withdrew his support from von Schleicher, who resigned on 28 January 1933. Hitler was now in the position to demand the Chancellorship for himself and the key Ministries of the Interior in both the Reich and Prussia for **Dr Wilhelm Frick** and Hermann Göring respectively. Von Papen agreed, as he was sure that by appointing reliable Nationalists to the other nine posts he would be able to control Hitler and the other two Nazis in the Cabinet. On the evening of 28 January Hindenburg gave his consent and the

new Cabinet with Hitler as the new Chancellor came into office on 30 January 1933. The secret negotiations which took place were described by historian Allan Bullock as 'back stairs intrigue'.

ACTIVITY **Period Studies**

1 Hitler was manoeuvred into power by 'back stairs intrigue'. How far do you agree with this view of Hitler's success in January 1933?

2 'Hitler came to power just at the moment when the Nazi Party was in decline'. How far do you agree with this view?

Could Hitler's appointment as Chancellor have been avoided?

The Nazi party was mainly a party which attracted protest votes against unemployment and Brüning's policy of deflation. One commentator writing in 1930 observed that 'if the sun shines once more on the German economy, Hitler's voters will melt away like snow'. By the end of 1932 the Party was in steep decline for several reasons:

- It was nearly bankrupt as it has spent all its money on elections.
- It had been unable to gain power and therefore could not carry out any of its promises.
- There were even some slight signs that the economy was beginning to recover.

Even though support for the Nazis was draining away, Hitler's appointment as Reich Chancellor became more rather than less likely. Neither the army nor the traditional elites around von Papen and Hindenburg were strong enough to set up an authoritarian regime themselves. If they were to seize power, they had no alternative but to negotiate a coalition with Hitler.

Von Papen wrote in his memoirs in the early 1950s, that his 'own and von Schleicher's Cabinets and Hitler's government were only part of a logical sequence of events'. Up to a point this was true. All three governments wanted an authoritarian constitution and the restoration of Germany's power. The fact that the Nazis had only three Cabinet seats seemed to be a guarantee that, in the words of von Papen, within two months 'we will have pushed Hitler so far into a corner that he'll squeak', but this ignored the dynamism of the Nazi movement and Hitler's own determination to outflank his conservative 'minders', as we shall see in the next chapter.

How much of a victory was the March 1933 election?

The election of 5 March 1933

The intention of not just Hitler but of von Papen and the whole Cabinet was to eliminate the *Reichstag* as an effective force in the German constitution. Hitler therefore rejected the offer of a pact with the Centre Party that would have given him a majority in the *Reichstag*. Instead, with the Cabinet's consent, he decided to fight yet another election. This was because he wanted to achieve power legally and then exploit the constitution to create a dictatorship. After the failure of the Munich Putsch (see pages 26–27), he realised that any attempt to seize power by force would meet with opposition from the army.

In the subsequent election campaign Hitler appealed to the nation's longing for unity, economic recovery and the restoration of German power in Europe. He constantly stressed the total failure of the **'November parties'**, even by implication associating his allies in the

November parties

The parties that formed the Weimar coalition – the first government of the Weimar Republic in 1919: the SPD, the Democratic Party and the Centre Party (see page 10).

Cabinet with them. He reassured those voters who feared that the Nazis might be as revolutionary as the Bolsheviks in Russia that he would 'take under its firm protection Christianity as the basis of our morality and the family as the nucleus of our nation and state'. He also promised both to revive agriculture and to launch 'a massive and comprehensive attack on unemployment', but he did not say how he would do this.

Hindenburg allowed Hitler to use the emergency powers under Article 48 (see pages 17–18) to forbid political meetings and to ban opposition newspapers. The abolition of the Prussian government in June 1932 also allowed Hermann Göring, as Prussian Minister of the Interior, to control the Prussian police and reinforce them with auxiliary SA men.

Coup d'état

The overthrow of a government and the seizure of power illegally.

The Nazi campaign was helped by the *Reichstag* fire on 27 February 1933. Although the fire was not the work of the German Communist Party but that of an unemployed Dutch building labourer, **Marinus van der Lubbe**, it presented Hitler with an excellent opportunity to play on the fears which so many Germans had of a Communist uprising. He immediately announced the 'Decree for the Protection of the people and the state' which not only gave the central government the powers to order the arrest of individuals, censor the post and have private houses searched, but also to dismiss *Länd* governments if they refused to carry out the necessary 'measures for the restoration of public security'. This decree presented Hitler with wide-ranging powers and has been described by the historians J. Noakes and G. Pridham as 'a kind of **coup d'état**'.

BIOGRAPHY

Marinus van der Lubbe (1909–34)

Marinus van der Lubbe had been a member of the Communist Party but, disliking its discipline, he had become an anarchist. He had already attempted to burn down public buildings in Berlin, as he was convinced that this would inspire the unemployed to revolt. He managed to force his way into the *Reichstag* early on 27 February 1933 and start a fire in the debating chamber. Alerted by Goebbels, Hitler attended van der Lubbe's interrogation by the police and decided to use the fire to justify arresting the Communists and their sympathisers in Berlin. It was Göring's adviser, Ludwig Grauert, who suggested that an emergency decree would provide the necessary legal cover for the arrests

Figure 2.6 The Reichstag fire was to serve as Hitler's initial excuse for taking on such wide-ranging powers

Throughout Germany the SA were let off the leash to attack their enemies. They now no longer had to worry about public opinion and both Socialists and Communists were seized and beaten up. The election campaign was conducted in an atmosphere of terror. Active campaigning by the Social Democrats and Communists was forbidden. Yet when the German people voted on 5 March 1933 the Nazis won only 43.9 per cent of the votes and had to rely on their alliance with the Nationalist Party, which was supported by just 8 per cent of the electorate, for a majority in the *Reichstag*. While the results were disappointing for Hitler they also showed that there was little desire for the return of the Weimar Republic. Unlike 1919 (see page 10), three-quarters of the voters supported parties which did not support the Republic. Even the Centre Party had moved strongly to the right.

Table 2.5 Results of the election of 5 March 1933 (number of seats)

NSDAP (Nazis)	288
DNVP (Nationalists)	52
DVP (German People's Party)	2
Centre Party	73
State Party	5
SPD (Social Democratic Party)	120
KPD (Communist Party)	81
The Economy Party	0

ACTIVITY

Period Studies

Assess the reasons for an increase in the Nazi vote in the election of 5 March 1933.

Review questions

1 Assess the importance of the Great Depression in Hitler's rise to power.

2 Assess whether Hitler's rise to power could have been prevented at any point in the period March 1930–January 1933.

3 To what extent was Hitler put into power by a 'back stairs' intrigue?

4 'In the period 1930–33 Hitler showed himself to be a skilful politician.' How far do you agree with this view?

5 Assess the view that the Weimar Republic effectively came to an end in March 1933.

6 To what extent did Hitler use the Communists?

Exam Café

Relax, refresh, result!

Relax and prepare

Hot tips

Laura

I studied Hitler for GCSE so I thought I wouldn't have to work so hard. It turns out that my knowledge wasn't deep enough to do well at AS. For example, I hadn't considered the different interpretations for his coming to power. I soon realised that I could use my knowledge from GCSE as a basis, but that I had to build on this.

Jemail

For this topic it is so easy to get the order of events and dates wrong: apparently that is a really common mistake in exams. For some reason sorting things out on a timeline helped me remember much better. A really tricky period is from January 1933, when Hitler became Chancellor, through to the Army Oath in 1934 – if you can draw yourself a timeline for that you'll be sorted!

Maisie

I remember my teacher saying people often write too much about the period before 1929 when answering a question on Hitler's rise to power in 1933. She'd always say 'Nazis and Depression go together.' Until the Depression in 1929 the Nazis had almost no electoral support at all. And their anti-Semitism wasn't getting them votes then either.

Omar

The Nazi Party never won a majority in elections to the Reichstag in this period, even in March 1933. Lots of students get that wrong, apparently. The Nazis were the largest single party but needed the support of other nationalist groups to command a majority.

Hailey

Everyone remembers how the Nazis used cheap radios to help spread propaganda, right? Well, it's no good giving this example for propaganda in the rise to power: the Nazis only issued cheap radios after they came to power. Think of it like this: you need power for radios to work. Got it? Make sure your examples are from the correct time period.

Refresh your memory

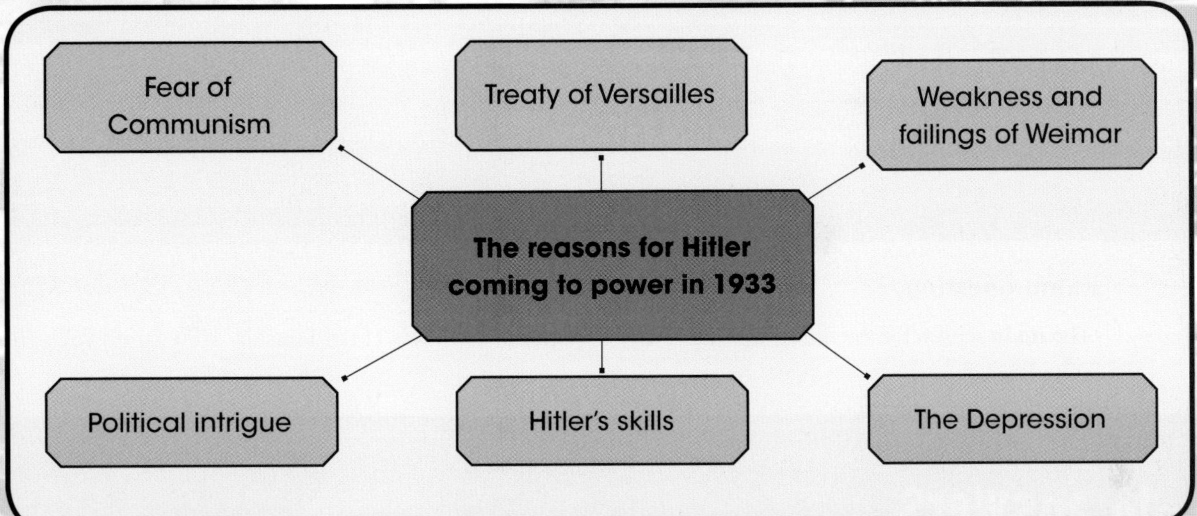

Hitler's rise to power

- Understand that events from 1929–33 were crucial.
- Be able to support this point with precise examples from the election results to the Reichstag. You must know the details of the Nazi performance from before the Depression through to March 1933.
- Be able to explain how and why the Depression helped the Nazi Party gain support.
- Understand and be able to explain the role played by political intrigue in the period from November 1932 to January 1933.
- Explain that the weakness of Weimar was a precondition for the Nazi rise to power, but that any party could have taken advantage of its weakness.
- Explain that the long-term weaknesses of Weimar did not guarantee that the Nazi Party would come to power; they had to be able to take advantage of the situation.
- Be able to explain the role of Hitler in exploiting the situation.
- Ensure you can explain links between these factors.

Get the result!

Prioritising factors

Instead of just explaining the factor, which in this example is the Depression, it is important that you consider its relative importance. This is done by weighing it up against other factors and also making links between factors. Here we will focus on one paragraph from an answer to the following question.

You can find the rest of the answer on the CD-ROM. 

Exam question

'The **main** reason for the rise of the Nazi Party to power in 1933 was Hitler himself.' How far do you agree with this view?

Sample answers

Examiner says:

Laura's answer hints at the Depression being a very important factor, but she needs to further explain why it was so important. This is hinted at when Laura considers the election result; she should try to take this analysis further. The factual knowledge Laura uses in this paragraph is good. Not many candidates use the election results to support their arguments.

Laura's answer:

The Depression was very important in the rise of Hitler because it further weakened the Weimar government. The German economy depended upon loans from America so following the Wall St. Crash the USA recalled all its loans. This meant that the German economy went into decline and millions became unemployed; by 1932 the numbers unemployed had reached six million. The government appeared to do nothing to help them and so they started to look for other parties who might offer a solution to their problems and many turned to the Nazis. This is reflected in the election results as the Nazi Party went from having 12 seats in the Reichstag in 1928 to 230 by July 1932 and being the largest party. The other party that did well during the Depression was the Communist Party, but their growth worried the middle classes who had seen what had happened in Russia and feared that a similar thing would happen in Germany and so they turned to the Nazi Party.

Laura's improved answer:

The Depression was the turning point in the fortunes of the Nazi Party. This is evident from their changing fortunes in elections to the Reichstag, before the Depression the Nazis had won 12 seats in the 1928 election, but in July 1932 they won 230 seats and became the largest party. The Depression led to deep social and economic hardship and created an environment of political discontent, which Hitler was able to exploit. Weimar governments appeared unable to deal with the crisis as the scale of unemployment, reaching 6 million in 1932, overwhelmed the unemployment scheme and forced many out of their homes. With the failure of Weimar many looked for alternatives and turned to extremist parties. This situation was cleverly exploited by the Nazi Party, as was seen in their election poster of 1932 that proclaimed Hitler was 'Our last hope'.

Examiner says:

The opening sentence is well focused and raises the relative importance of the Depression. Laura now supports the point with clear and relevant knowledge and she is also able to draw links between a variety of factors, such as the Depression, the failure of Weimar and Hitler's ability to take advantage of this. The focus of the whole paragraph is on the actual question set.

How to prepare for questions on Hitler's rise to power

It is likely that your essay answer will cover issues such as: the Treaty of Versailles, Hitler's skill, the weakness of Weimar, fear of Communism and political intrigue.

Devise an opening sentence for each of the above topics that directly answers the question:

Exam question

'The **main** reason for the rise of the Nazi Party to power in 1933 was Hitler himself.' How far do you agree with this view?

Remember, the sentence should introduce an **idea** that relates directly to the question. By reading just the opening sentences of each paragraph the examiner should know what your overall argument is.

How effectively did Hitler establish and consolidate Nazi authority, 1933–45?

Source

In 1938 Hans Frank, the head of the Nazi Association of Lawyers and of the Academy of German Law, said in a speech:

...as a result of five years government by the Führer there can be no ***juridical*** *doubts about the following absolutely clear principles of the Reich:*

1 *At the head of the Reich stands the leader of the NSDAP as leader of the German Reich for life.*

2 *He is, on the strength of his being leader of the NSDAP, leader and Chancellor of the Reich. As such, he embodies simultaneously, as Head of State, supreme state power and, as Chief of Government, the central function of the whole Reich administration. He is head of state and chief of government in one person. He is Commander in Chief of all the armed forces of the Reich.*

J. Noakes and G. Pridam (eds) (1984). *Nazism, 1919–45, Vol 2: State, Economy and Society, 1933–39* (p. 199). Exeter: University of Exeter Press.

Key Questions:

To understand how effectively Hitler established and consolidated Nazi authority, 1933–45, the key questions that need to be answered are the following:

- How was the Enabling Act passed and why was it so important?
- What was the process of coordination (*Gleichschaltung*) and how did it enable Hitler to set up the one-party state?
- Why did the SA threaten Hitler's Power, 1933–34?
- How well organised was the system of government and administration in the Third Reich?
- How successful was the Nazi machinery of terror at controlling the Third Reich?
- How did Nazi censorship and propaganda work?

Hitler was legally appointed Chancellor on 30 January 1933. Including himself, there were only three Nazis in the Cabinet. Nevertheless, he secured Cabinet agreement for a general election so that his government could gain an outright majority, and exploited the *Reichstag* fire to issue the decree for Protection of People and State on 28 February. After the election the Nazis emerged as the largest party in the *Reichstag* and, together with the Nationalists, had just over 51 per cent of the votes. Hitler's immediate aim was to pass through the *Reichstag* the Enabling Bill, which would legally grant sufficient powers to establish a dictatorship.

How was the Enabling Act passed and why was it so important?

The election results of 5 March 1933 were celebrated by the SA with a fresh wave of violence throughout Germany. This was potentially dangerous for Hitler. It threatened to spiral out of control and turn against him both his coalition partners and Hindenburg, the Reich President, whose support at this stage was still vital. Hitler therefore made repeated appeals to the SA to control the violence and particularly the 'obstruction or disturbance of business life'.

Case study: SA violence

In Wuppertal in the Ruhr a Brownshirt detachment raided the home of Heinrich B, a former Communist, and murdered him – his body was found on an allotment the following day. In the same area eight stormtroopers ambushed August K, a former leader of the local Communist band, and shot him dead.

To reassure his coalition partners, Hitler invited the **Crown Prince**, the generals and the President to a ceremony in the Military Church in Potsdam on 21 March where he pledged allegiance to the traditions and values of the past and cleverly reawakened memories of the **unity of August 1914**. The ceremony conveyed the message that Hitler was a conservative statesman who was aiming to restore the old pre-1914 regime.

On 23 March the *Reichstag* met in the Kroll Opera House in Berlin to debate the Enabling Bill, the aim of which was to hand over full legislative and executive powers to the Cabinet for a period of four years, which effectively gave power to Hitler. The Cabinet was to be given the legal power to introduce budgets and to revise the constitution independently of the *Reichstag* (the parliament). However, as it involved a change in the constitution, the *Reichstag* had to approve it by a two-thirds majority. Although the KPD deputies and twelve of the SPD members had already been arrested, to gain the necessary majority Hitler needed to win over the Centre Party. He managed to do this when he reassured their leaders that he would protect the rights and privileges of the Catholic Church. Mistakenly, the Centre Party also believed that it would be able to influence Hitler 'from the inside', as it had successive governments since 1919, and therefore decided to vote for the bill. Hitler told the **bourgeois parties** that the *Reichstag* and *Reichsrat*, the Presidency, and the *Länder* would eventually regain their powers, but significantly he made it brutally clear that if the *Reichstag* did not give him the necessary majority, he would still 'go ahead in face of the refusal and the hostilities which will result from that refusal'.

To reinforce the threat, the SS surrounded the Opera House outside and the SA lined the corridors inside. The law was passed by 444 votes to 94. Only the SPD opposed it. The Enabling Law was crucial for Hitler as it removed any doubts the civil service or the **judiciary** had as to the legality of the Nazi takeover. The law greatly strengthened Hitler's position in the Cabinet as the President's signature was no longer needed for passing any decrees or legislation. On 22 April Joseph Goebbels observed that 'the *Führer's* authority in the Cabinet is absolute'.

BIOGRAPHY

Crown Prince

This was Prince Wilhelm, who would have been the heir to the German throne had the Kaiser not abdicated.

Unity of August 1914

The spirit that united Germany when war broke out in August 1914.

Bourgeois parties

The middle-class political parties of Germany.

Judiciary

The German system of courts in which judges and magistrates administer justice on behalf of the state.

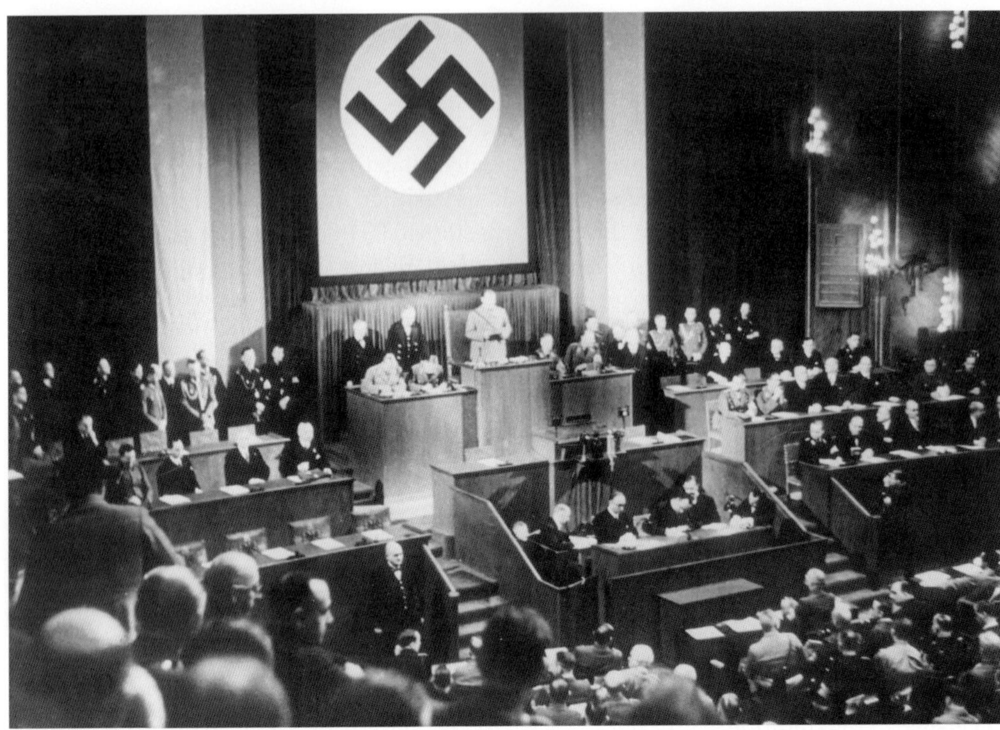

Figure 3.1 Potsdam Day: Göring opening the first Reichstag session in the Kroll Opera House, Berlin, 21 March, 1933

ACTIVITY ***Period/Enquiry Studies***

1 Assess the importance of the Enabling Act in establishing Nazi power.

2 Study Sources A and B. Compare these sources as evidence for why the Centre Party voted for the Enabling Law.

Sources

(A) Carl Bachem, who was the historian of the Centre Party, reflects on whether the Centre Party should have voted for the Enabling Bill:

If the Centre had voted against it, it would, given the current mood of the National Socialists, probably have been smashed at once just like the Social Democratic Party. All civil servants belonging to the Centre would probably have been dismissed. There would have been a great fracas in the Reichstag, and the Centrists would probably have been beaten up and thrown out. The parliamentary group would probably have made an heroic exit, but with no benefit to the Catholic cause or to the cause of the Centre Party. The links between the Centre and National Socialism would have been completely cut, all collaboration with the National Socialists and every possibility of influencing their policy would have been out of the question. Perhaps, then, it was right to make the attempt to come to an understanding and cooperate with the National Socialists, in order to be able to participate in a practical way in the reshaping of the future... .

J. Noakes and G. Pridham (eds) (1998). *Nazism, 1919–45, Vol. 1: The Rise to Power, 1919–34* (2nd edn) (pp. 157–58). Exeter: University of Exeter Press.

(B) An SPD deputy described the atmosphere in the Kroll Opera House, in which the *Reichstag* met on 23 March 1933 after the fire of 27 February had made the *Reichstag* building unusable:

... The wide square in front of the Kroll Opera House was crowded with dark masses of people. We were received with wild choruses; 'We want the Enabling Act!' Youths with swastika on their chests eyed us insolently, blocked our way, in fact made us run the gauntlet, calling us names like 'Centre pig', 'Marxist sow'. The Kroll Opera House was crawling with armed SA and SS men. In the cloakroom we learned that Severing (former SPD Prime Minister of Prussia) had been arrested on entering the building. The assembly hall was decorated with swastikas and similar ornaments. When we Social Democrats had taken our seats on the extreme left, SA and SS men linked up at the exits and along the walls behind us in a semi-circle. Their expressions boded no good.

J. Noakes and G. Pridham (eds) (1998). *Nazism, 1919–45, Vol. 1: The Rise to Power, 1919–34* (2nd edn) (p. 159). Exeter: University of Exeter Press.

What was the process of coordination (*Gleichschaltung*) and how did it enable Hitler to set up the one-party state?

Hitler was empowered by the Enabling Act, strengthened by the SA and he also enjoyed considerable support from the public who desired an end to unemployment and the bitter divisions of the Weimar years. This enabled Hitler through the process of coordination (***Gleichschaltung***) to create a **one-party centralised Reich** by early 1934. Through various different means and with varying degrees of success, the Nazis attempted to control every aspect of life in the Reich.

Case study: Coordination in Bavaria

In Bavaria the legal government resigned on 16 March and the newly installed Reich commissioner appointed Nazis for the senior ministerial posts. The Chief of Staff of the SA, Ernst Röhm, was made State Commissioner for Special Duty, and Himmler was made head of the Munich Police Administration. Himmler immediately ordered a large-scale round up of Social Democrats, Communists and other enemies of the Nazis. He also set up an unofficial concentration camp in Dachau, which was built around a disused factory on the outskirts of the town. On 22 March 200 prisoners were brought to the camp for 'protective custody'. In early April the camp was handed over to the SS. By the end of May at least twelve inmates had been murdered or tortured to death.

Gleichschaltung

This literally means synchronisation or 'making the same'. In Germany at this time it meant controlling all aspects of life so that the way people thought and behaved was in line with or synchronised with Nazi ideology.

One-party centralised Reich

A form of government in which only one political party is allowed to stand for election or form the government.

How were the federated states put under control of the Nazi Party?

The ***Länder*** governments lost all their independence under heavy pressure in the 1920s. Through a combination of pressure from the SA and action from the government in Berlin, they were brought under the control of the National Socialist regime. Under the Coordination Law of 31 March 1933, the ***Länder* Diets** were reconstituted to reflect the share of the different parties in the *Reichstag.* Under a second law announced on 7 April, Reich governors, who were usually the local Nazi ***Gauleiter***, were appointed with powers to make their own laws. The *Länder* diets were dissolved in January 1934 and the state governments were subordinated to the Reich government.

Länder

The federated states independent from the central government.

***Länder* DIETS**

The local parliaments of the federated states.

Gauleiter

A regional party leader in charge of a *Gau*, a regional territorial division of the Nazi Party.

Anti-socialist laws

These are laws aimed at restricting or banning the activities of political parties and groups whose beliefs are founded on socialist principles. In Germany this applied to the SDP and trade unions, for example.

Job creation schemes

To help solve the unemployment problem, and to gather support from workers, the Nazi Party set up a scheme to create jobs through public works programmes.

ACTIVITY

What was the significance of the coordination of the individual *Länder* for the establishment of Nazi power in Germany?

ACTIVITY

Why did Hitler meet with so little opposition in banning the political parties.

How did the Nazis ban the SPD and the trade unions and create the Reich Labour Front?

Both the SPD and the unions had survived the **anti-socialist laws** of Bismarck in the 1880s and at first thought that with some concessions to the Nazis, they would be able to survive. The trade unions were impressed by Hitler's willingness to set up **job creation schemes** and believed at first that they had a part to play in the new Nazi Germany. They therefore agreed to support Goebbel's decison to declare 1 May a holiday in honour of National Labour and to take part in the planned procession in Berlin. However, these concessions failed to save the unions. Hitler moved quickly to decapitate the movement, preventing it from acting. On 2 May the SA and SS occupied trade union offices throughout Germany, and leading trade union officials were beaten up and put into concentration camps. The unions were replaced by the German Labour Front (DAF), in which all workers and employers had to enrol (see page 112).

With the unions now liquidated, the government moved to close the SPD down. On 10 May its assets and files were seized and finally on 21 June it was banned. Again this was accompanied by a outbreak of savage violence against the SDP and Communists. About three thousand Social Democrat officers were rounded up and incarcerated in prisons or concentration camps. In the Berlin working-class suburb of Köpenick, the SA, after encountering armed resistance, seized 500 SPD members, who were so badly beaten and tortured that 91 died!

The dissolution of the Centre Party

In his approach to the Centre Party, which after the SPD was the largest political party in Germany, Hitler used different tactics. He was aware that using violence against the Centre Party could be self-defeating and might turn many German Catholics against the Nazi Party. The Pope and the German Catholic bishops saw Hitler as a defence against the dangers of Communism. They hoped they could negotiate an agreement, or Concordat, with the government that would give Catholicism the independence necessary to survive. To achieve this they were prepared to agree to a ban on the Centre Party. Once the Concordat was signed in July the Centre Party was dissolved.

The liquidation of the State Party, DVP and DNVP

The State Party and the DVP were so small that Hitler had no problem getting rid of them. The Nationalists (DNVP), on the other hand, were coalition partners of the Nazis and believed they would be able to control Hitler. However, this was an illusion, and they were quickly outmanoeuvred by Hitler. They came under increasing pressure to dissolve the party and amalgamate their paramilitary fighting groups with the SS. On 7 May 1933 their leader in the *Reichstag*, Ernst Oberfohren, who had already been forced to resign by the Nazis, was found dead in his home. Officially he committed suicide, but it was generally assumed that he had been murdered! By the end of June the party agreed to be dissolved. The *Stahlhelm*, the right-wing Ex-Soldiers' League, which was closely linked to the DNVP, was incorporated into the SA at the end of June.

Business and industry

Employers, business associations and agricultural interest groups were all forced into a single organisation under Nazi control. Businessmen and industrialists rapidly declared their loyalty to the regime, and were coordinated into the Reich Chamber of German Industry. They were, however, able to manage their own affairs and were not subordinated to the Nazi Party. On 1 June 1933 leading German industrialists recommended that German industry should pay a special 'Adolf Hitler donation' to express its gratitude for the elimination of the trade unions and in anticipation of the coming rearmament boom. The thinking behind this proposal was that by making voluntary donations they would be able to head off any attempts by the Nazi Party to demand more money. Big business was, as the historian Norbert Frei said, putting up 'a clear marker of its independence'.

ACTIVITY

Period Studies

To what extent were business and industry coordinated between 1933 and 1945?

Education, the media and culture

The Nazis had little difficulty in controlling education, the media and the cultural life of the Reich. By the spring of 1933 Goebbels, as Minister of Propaganda, controlled broadcasting and ensured that news coverage in newspapers and on the radio was favourable to the government (see pages 85–87). In May the Ministry of the Interior compelled the German states to introduce new syllabuses into the schools and universities. All teachers' and university lecturers' associations were affiliated to the National Socialist Teachers' Organisation. At the universities, gangs of Nazi students terrorised left-wing or independent-minded lecturers and forced them to resign or adopt a more pro-Nazi line in their teaching. In September all **'intellectual workers'** were forced to join the Reich Chamber of Culture, so that a rigorous check could be kept on their activities.

Intellectual workers

These are people who work with their intellect, such as teachers, lawyers, writers, etc.

ACTIVITY

Why was the army not coordinated?

Case study: Book Burning ceremonies

On 10 May 1933 students organised Book Burning ceremonies in Berlin and then in university towns across Germany. In Berlin it was attended by Goebbels, but it was organised by the students themselves with the help of Dr Wolfgang Hermann, a Nazi who had been appointed to 'reorganise the Berlin City and People's libraries'. The students drew up lists of books for burning that were considered offensive to the 'German spirit', such as being anti-war or written by Jewish or left-wing authors, and then burnt them in the squares and streets of the cities.

The army

The army escaped coordination and retained its own traditions. Indeed, **General von Blomberg** banned army officers from joining the Nazi Party. Hitler won over the army when he met its senior officers in early February 1933 and promised to respect the army's traditions and political neutrality. He also enthused them with the prospect of rearmament, the re-introduction of conscription and eventually the conquest of eastern Europe. On the other hand, by setting up the Reich Defence Council on which von Blomberg had a seat, under his own chairmanship, Hitler did in reality ensure that he, rather than the Commander-in-Chief of the Army, decided all key issues.

BIOGRAPHY

General Werner von Blomberg (1878–1946)

Blomberg was appointed Minister of Defence in January 1933. In 1935 he became War Minister, but was dismissed in January 1938 after he married Eva Grühn, a former prostitute. Hitler used his dismissal to abolish the War Ministry and replaced it with the OKW (High Command of the Armed Forces), which reported directly to him.

ACTIVITY

Research how the struggle continued for religious Youth groups (see also page 106).

ACTIVITY

Why was Hitler unable to effectively coordinate the churches in 1933–34?

ACTIVITY

Period Studies

1 'The Enabling Act, SA terror and *Gleichschaltung* were all vital in establishing Hitler's power in 1933.' How important were each of these and for whom?

2 Assess the effectiveness of the Nazi policy of coordination.

The churches

Catholic Church

Like the industrialists, the bishops were ready to negotiate an agreement with Hitler which would essentially preserve its independence at the expense of the Centre Party. The Concordat signed between the Vatican and the German government on 14 July 1933 appeared to make generous concessions to the Catholic Church. It was guaranteed:

- religious freedom
- the right to administer itself and appoint its own clergy
- the extension of privileges which previously had existed in only a few Catholic areas, to the whole of the Reich: throughout Germany parents would be able to demand Catholic faith schools, provided there were sufficient children to set up the school.

However, in Article 31 of the Concordat the government made a distinction between Catholic organisations which were purely ecclesiastical and 'those that serve other purposes, such as social or professional interests', such as youth clubs.

Why was Hitler ready to make these concessions? His plan was to end the Church's intervention in politics. In any case, he believed that the Concordat was only a temporary concession until he could coordinate the Catholic Church. Later he was determined to use Article 31 to coordinate Catholic Youth groups with the Hitler Youth (see pages 105–108).

Evangelical Church

Hitler assumed that the Protestant churches in Germany would be easier to deal with as they were not controlled, like the Catholic Church was, from outside the Reich. At first he hoped to reorganise the **Evangelical Church** into one united Reich Church under an elected Reich bishop, as this would enable the government to control them more easily, but these plans were unexpectedly opposed. The election of Otto Müller, a fanatical Nazi and former military chaplain, as Reich Bishop was challenged by a strong dissident group, the Pastors' Emergency League. Müller at first attempted to intimidate the opposition. In the autumn of 1934 there was a major crisis when two Protestant bishops were arrested. This led to the Pastors' Emergency League setting up an independent church – the Confessing Church – in October. In July the following year Hitler created a new Ministry of Church Affairs, but this also failed to coordinate the German Protestants, who remained divided into three main groups: the German Christians, under an increasingly marginalised Bishop Müller, the Confessing Church, and the mainstream churches, which tried to tread the tightrope between cooperating with the regime and preserving a degree of independence.

Evangelical Church

The Lutheran and Calvinist churches were united into the Evangelical Church in the 19th century, and by 1933 this consisted of 28 self-governing regional churches. Unlike the Catholic Church, the Evangelical Church owed no loyalty to a power outside Germany. Many of its members were ardent German nationalists.

Conclusion: How effective was coordination?

By the end of the summer all parties, trade unions and associations had been either abolished or taken over by the Nazis. On 14 July 1935 under the 'Law against the New Formation of Parties' all political parties except for the Nazi Party were banned. As the historian F. L. Carsten wrote, everything from 'bowling clubs to bee keeping was brought under National Socialist control'. Only at home, or perhaps with friends, could some privacy be found. Through coordination the Nazis not only eliminated opposition, but made possible the mass indoctrination of the German population. On the other hand the army, the Catholic Church and some of the Protestant churches had initially escaped the process, von Papen and Hindenburg remained in office and the 'conservative bearers of state', the **bureaucratic, military and big business elites**, were still intact.

Party monopoly

The sole control of political, economic etc. power in a country by one party, as in a dictatorship like that of the Soviet Union.

Bureaucratic, military and big business elites

The civil service, army and major industrialists and bankers.

Why did the SA threaten Hitler's power, 1933–34?

Hitler needed the support of the traditional elites if he was to solve the unemployment problem and rearm Germany. He therefore had to ensure that the violence of the SA, the demand from Nazi activists for the takeover of big business, the creation of a Nazi army and the elimination of the old elites did not turn them against him. Consequently, Hitler reassured the generals and the industrialists by stressing that the revolutionary period of the Nazi takeover was at an end, and that it was now more important to concentrate on reviving the economy.

Once Hitler announced the end to the 'legal revolution' in July 1933, the SA increasingly became, to quote the historian Alan Bullock, an 'embarrassing legacy of the years of struggle'. **Ernst Röhm** was a passionate believer in a more radical Nazi revolution, which would carry out the Nazi programme as outlined in the Twenty-Five Points. Above all, he wanted to turn the SA into the basis for a new mass Nazi army. It was this that threatened the regular army's role in rearmament and led to its growing rivalry with the SA. Hitler had already made it clear that the traditional army, rather than the SA, would be the basis of the new German army when in January 1934 he decided to reintroduce **military conscription**, once he was sure that France would not intervene.

Military conscription

The calling up of young men to serve for two years in the army. This had been the tradition in Germany since the 19th century. It was reintroduced in 1935.

BIOGRAPHY

Ernst Röhm (1887–1934)

Röhm, whose father was a Bavarian civil servant, had a distinguished war record as a captain in the Bavarian army. In the early post-war years he remained an army staff officer, and liaised with the Bavarian paramilitary groups, especially the Nazis, which he joined in 1923. He did, however, bitterly disagree with Hitler over the future shape of the SA and in 1928 emigrated to Bolivia as a military instructor, but was called back by Hitler in 1930 to become Chief of Staff of the SA. He reorganised the SA and expanded it into a mass organisation.

Figure 3.2 The revolutionary and violent SA and their leader Ernst Röhm (on the left) found themselves increasingly out of place in Hitler's Germany.

The problem of the SA became urgent by the spring of 1934 because of Hindenburg's ill-health. Hitler needed to succeed Hindenburg as President, otherwise, if a new non-Nazi President was appointed, there was the risk of a potential alternative leader emerging to whom the army and the DNVP could turn if they became disillusioned with him. Also, it was possible the generals would attempt to block Hitler's ambitions to succeed Hindenburg if they believed that the SA was threatening their role in rebuilding Germany's armed forces. There was even a danger that the army and the conservative elites might attempt to restore the monarchy after Hindenburg's death in an attempt to control the Nazi regime. Some Nationalists were already having second thoughts about Hitler. Edgar Jung, a leading right-wing intellectual and Papen's speechwriter, observed, for instance, that 'We are partly responsible that this fellow has come to power [and] we must get rid of him again.' However, as long as Hitler could control the SA, the army would continue to support him, as both General von Blomberg, the Defence Minister, and **General Freiherr von Fritsch**, the new Commander-in-Chief, as well as many other officers, were convinced that Hitler had the necessary drive to rearm Germany.

BIOGRAPHY

General Werner Freiherr von Fritsch (1880–1939)

From 1934 to 1938 Fritsch was Commander-in-Chief of the Army. He was critical of the risks Hitler ran in his foreign policy and was forced to resign in January 1938 as a result of being falsely accused of homosexuality. He was killed in the Polish campaign in 1939.

Hitler was also under pressure from Göring, Himmler and Hess who wanted to eliminate Röhm, as he was a dangerous rival to their own ambitions within the Party. Consequently, in the early summer of 1934, Hitler in the words of the historian Gordon Craig, 'moved erratically and with spells of doubt and indecision towards a showdown with the SA'. On 17 June Hitler was openly criticised by von Papen in a hard-hitting speech delivered at Marburg University. Von Papen warned against the dangers of a second revolution unleashed by the SA and even dared to criticise the growing *Führer* cult. 'Never again in the Third Reich', as the historian Ian Kershaw has observed, 'was such striking criticism at the heart of the regime to come from such a prominent figure'. When Hitler visited the President at his estate at Neudeck on 21 June, he was firmly told by von Blomberg that if he failed to control the SA, Hindenburg would hand over power to the army.

If the Nazi regime was to survive, Hitler now had to liquidate Röhm and the leading Brownshirts, but he was also determined to eliminate his critics on the Right. In the 'Night of the Long Knives' of 30 June/1 July, not only were the SA leaders murdered, so were the two conservative monarchists in Papen's office, Herbert von Bose and Edgar Jung, as well as other political enemies of Hitler, including Kurt von Schleicher and Gregor Strasser. At least 85 people were murdered, and the figure could have been much higher according to a list which was published in Paris by German émigrés; it claimed the number was as high as 401.

The Night of the Long Knives in Munich

On 29 June 1934 Hitler summoned a meeting of SA leaders for the following day at Wiessee in Bavaria. Both the army and the SS were put on alert, and Göring was given responsibility for overseeing the purge in Berlin. Hitler arrived at Munich airport at 4.30 on the morning of 30 June and drove with a group of SS bodyguards and police to Hanselbauer Hotel at Bad Wiessee, where Röhm and the senior SA leaders were staying. The Brownshirts were arrested and locked in the hotel linen room before being taken to Stadelheim prison in Munich. Here they were shot. Röhm was given the option of shooting himself, but refused and was shot dead by two SS officers.

Conclusion: How secure was Hitler by August 1934?

Once Röhm was eliminated, Hitler was able to consolidate his power without difficulty. Von Papen was dismissed from the Vice-Chancellorship and was lucky to escape with his life. When Hindenburg died on 1 August, there was no opposition from the army to Hitler combining the offices of Chancellor and President – a step which was confirmed by plebiscite on 19 August. As head of state, Hitler became the Supreme Commander of the Armed Forces, which now voluntarily swore a personal oath of loyalty to him. He had survived a crisis which could have led to civil war and the end of the Nazi regime, and had managed to eliminate the threat from the SA without becoming the prisoner of the conservative elites. Short of a disastrous war or the economic collapse of Germany, by the autumn of 1934 Hitler was securely in power.

ACTIVITY
Period Studies

Assess the reasons why the SA was a threat to the consolidation of Nazi power in 1934.

ACTIVITY
Period Studies

'Without the "Night of the Long Knives" Hitler might well have lost power.'

How far do you agree with this view of the significance of the Night of the Long Knives?

Figure 3.3 On Hitler becoming head of state the army swore an oath of allegiance to him *personally*, not to the office he held. For many German officers this was an unbreakable bond of honour.

Rival hierarchies

The rival power systems, the members of which are ranked according to power.

The dual state

This is state in which there appears to be two forms of government at work at the same time. In this case there were the existing pre-1933 organs of ministries, civil service, etc. existing alongside the Nazi Party and its organisations.

Civil servants

They are people employed in government ministries to carry out duties of the state, such as advising the government on policies and then carrying out these policies.

How well organised was the system of government and administration in the Third Reich?

Although Hitler had broken the opposition by the autumn of 1934, the Third Reich itself remained an unstable regime characterised by **rival hierarchies** and centres of power, as well as by a lack of a clear command structure. There were three overlapping centres of power:

- The central government together with its ministries and civil service.
- The Nazi Party and the SS.
- The charismatic dictatorship of Hitler, intervening at will.

Central government

Hitler had no detailed plans for creating a specifically Nazi state when he came to power. He was primarily interested in consolidating his grip on power, and at the same time needed to reassure the conservative elites that he was no revolutionary on the Russian scale. He was also anxious to emphasise that the new Nazi regime was in many ways linked to the great traditions of the German past. Consequently, the government of the Third Reich was a bewildering mixture of the old and new where freshly created Nazi institutions flourished side by side with the traditional German organs of state. It was what one exiled German observer called **'the dual state'**.

Up to March 1933 the Reich Cabinet met at regular intervals but once the Enabling Act gave Hitler the power to make laws independently of the *Reichstag*, its importance declined. It met only six times in 1937 and its last meeting was on 5 February 1938. Although Hitler appointed an increasing number of Nazi ministers up to the winter of 1937–38, seven important ministries of state were still in the hands of Conservative-Nationalist ministers. In many ways the power of the central departments of state was increased because the Nazis had greatly weakened the power of the federated states.

The **civil servants** who ran the government departments and their branches throughout the Reich retained much of their traditional independence. In April 1933, under the Law for the Restoration of the Professional Civil Service, the civil service was purged of Jews, unless they had fought in the war, Socialists and Communists, but this made up just 2 per cent of the 1,500,000 civil servants in the Reich. It was not until February 1939 that all new entrants into the civil service had to be members of the Nazi Party.

BIOGRAPHY

Fritz Todt (1891–1942)

Todt studied civil engineering and joined the Nazis in 1922. Eleven years later he was an SS colonel. He was made Inspector-General of German Roads in 1933, making him responsible for the construction of the motorways and military fortifications along the frontiers. In 1940 he was made Armaments Minister, but was killed in an air crash in January 1942.

Supreme Reich authorities

Parallel to the traditional departments of state Hitler created several new departments which combined both party and state responsibilities. Their leaders were prominent Nazis who reported directly to Hitler. In that way they could force through their own policies independently of the other departments. Thus **Fritz Todt**, Hitler's road-building expert, was given the necessary power to implement the *Autobahn* programme, despite opposition from the Ministries of Interior, Finance and Transport. As Inspector-General of German Roads, his office formed what the historian Martin Broszat has called 'an element of direct *Führer* authority ... alongside the normal state government and administration'. Other supreme Reich authorities were the Labour Service (see page 96), the Hitler Youth and the Four Year Plan. The supreme Reich authorities challenged the existing ministries and contributed to the intense rivalries that so undermined the effectiveness of the Reich government.

Figure 3.4 Hitler inaugurates a segment of the autobahn, May 1935.

Cadre party

A party composed of a relatively small number of people who are trained to be the future leaders of Germany.

National Socialist Senate

An influential body which would have served as the Upper House of the *Reichstag*. It would have consisted only of senior members of the Nazi Party and acted in an advisory capacity.

The Nazi Party

What was the role of the Nazi Party, 1933–37?

In March 1933 the role of the NSDAP in the new Nazi Germany was far from clear. Röhm and many of the veteran Nazis, who joined the party before 1923, passionately believed that the Party and the SA should completely change the social and political structure of Germany, but this view was not shared by Goebbels, Göring, and Wilhelm Frick, who had become immensely powerful by taking over existing government departments and becoming ministers. Nor was there any agreement on whether the NSDAP should become an elite **cadre party** which would train the future leaders of the regime, or merely a large mass movement which would both mobilise and brainwash the masses.

In the summer of 1933 Hitler considered setting up a **National Socialist Senate** which would give the Party a say in running the state, but he rapidly dropped the idea for fear that it might undermine his own position. In July 1933 he ambiguously observed that the 'party had now become the state' and that all power lay with the Reich government. What that really meant is hard to say! In practice, as Hitler made clear to the regional Nazi leaders (*Gauleiters*), its role was to carry out propaganda activities and in general 'to support the government in every way'.

On the whole, up until 1938 the influence of the Nazi Party within the government remained relatively weak. Although some ministers, like Wilhelm Frick, the Minister of the Interior, were Nazis, they nevertheless vigorously blocked Party attempts to interfere in their departments. As long as the wishes of the *Führer,* as far as they could be understood, were carried out, it was usually possible to stop the Party from interfering, and civil servants quickly learned to see, as the historian Dietrich Orlow observes, "the Party as a rival but not necessarily as an invincible one'. The Nazi Party and the state appeared to settle down to an uneasy coexistence. Nevertheless the Party's desire to interfere in government ensured that State-Party rivalries had a potentially destabilising impact on the government.

ACTIVITY

To what extent can one argue that calling the Third Reich a 'dual state' is in fact a simplification of a complex situation?

Why did the influence of the Nazi Party revive, 1938–39?

In the winter of 1937–38 the influence of the Nazi Party on the state began to increase. First of all **Ribbentrop**, a Nazi, was appointed to the Foreign Ministry, specifically to weaken the power of the **professional diplomats**. In February 1938 the independence of the army was also weakened when Hitler sacked both General von Fritsch, the Commander-in Chief and the Defence Minister, General von Blomberg, over alleged scandals. The Defence Ministry was abolished and in its place the new High Command of German Armed Forces (OKW) was set up, which reported directly to Hitler.

Professional diplomats

These were full-time officials in the German Foreign Office who represented the government in its relations with other governments.

BIOGRAPHY

Joachim von Ribbentrop (1893–1946)

Ribbentrop joined the NSDAP in 1932 and acted as Hitler's foreign affairs adviser in 1933. In 1936 he was appointed ambassador to Britain and in 1938 he became Foreign Minister. His main success was the Nazi–Soviet non-aggression treaty of August 1939, which ensured that the USSR remained neutral when Germany attacked Poland. He was condemned to death at Nuremberg and executed in 1946.

The **Anschluss** of Austria in March 1938, the **annexation of the Sudetenland** (October 1938) and of **Bohemia** (March 1939) also strengthened the Nazi Party. In Austria the Nazis seized power by armed force and therefore did not have to make concessions to the old ruling elites, which had been politically necessary in Germany in 1933. Consequently, **Josef Bürckel**, the Nazi Commissioner, was able to govern Austria without any interference from the traditional authorities as was soon also the case in the Sudetenland and Bohemia. This gave the Party a new lease of life in the **Old Reich**, and it began to interfere more vigorously in church affairs and the legal system and demand that tougher measures should be taken against the Jews. Inevitably this heightened the rivalry between the Party and the State and contributed to the chaotic system of government under Hitler.

Anschluss:

The annexation of Austria by Germany in March 1938. Literally it means the 'joining on to', in this case the joining of Austria on to Germany.

Old Reich

The parts of Germany that lay within the frontiers of 1933.

BIOGRAPHY

Josef Bürckel (1894–1944)

Burkel was the *Gauleiter* of the Rhineland Palatinate in 1938, the Reich Commissioner for the Saarland in 1935–38 and then for Austria in 1938–40. He committed suicide in 1944.

Figure 3.5 The Anschluss greatly increased the territory and people Hitler had control over. Here is Göring visiting the city of Wels in northern Austria, March, 1938

ACTIVITY

Period Studies

To what extent did the influence of the Nazi Party revive after 1938–39?

Annexation of the Sudetenland (October 1938) and Bohemia (March 1939)

In October 1938, with British and French support, the Germans occupied the German-speaking Sudetenland in Czechoslovakia. In March 1939 Hitler seized Bohemia. In response to this Britain and France guaranteed Poland against German aggression.

Civil authorities

These are the non-military bodies that have authority over civilian affairs, such as the police and local government.

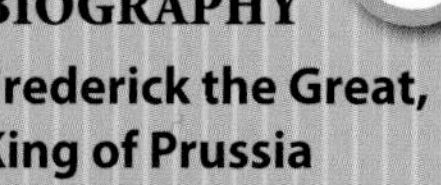

What was the impact of the Second World War on the Nazi Party, 1939–45?

The Second World War greatly increased the Party's responsibilities. It had the key role of maintaining the morale of the civilian population. The *Gauleiters* were also made Reich Defence Commissioners in September 1939. In the case of an emergency, such as an invasion, they were given the authority to take complete charge of the **civil authorities** within their *Gaue*. Later, in 1944, they were also made responsible for organising the citizen's militia, the *Volkssturm*.

The war also provided the Nazi Party with many opportunities to increase its influence:

- To escape the impact of the Anglo-American bombing offensive on Germany, children were evacuated from the towns to the countryside. As they were often not accompanied by their parents, Hitler Youth leaders were responsible for their welfare and had valuable opportunities for indoctrinating them in Nazi ideology;
- After the **Battle of Stalingrad** Nazi influence within the army increased. By the end of 1943 Party officials took part in the selection and training of new officers. In 1944, after the **plot of 20 July,** Joseph Goebbels also set up a special post office box address to which any soldier in the ranks could write if he believed that any of his officers were potential traitors to the regime.

BIOGRAPHY

Frederick the Great, King of Prussia (1712–86)

Frederick II, King of Prussia, was a brilliant military leader whose success on the battlefield considerably increased Prussia's power and influence in Europe. He also modernised the way his country was governed and had a keen interest in the arts.

Battle of Stalingrad

This was the battle between German and Soviet forces for the Soviet city of Stalingrad which was fought between September 1942 and February 1943. The German army was eventually surrounded and heavily defeated by the Soviet forces. This defeat for Germany was the turning point of the war.

Plot of 20 July

This was the plot to assassinate Hitler. It was planned by officers in the German army and carried out on the 20 July 1944. It failed and thousands of suspects were arrested (see pages 83–84).

ACTIVITY

Period Studies

Assess the role of the Party in establishing and consolidating Nazi authority in Germany, 1933–45.

What was Hitler's role as Führer?

In the Third Reich the cult of Hitler was all-pervasive. The charismatic image of Hitler, the *Führer*, was projected across Germany. He was regularly compared to **Bismarck** and **Frederick the Great**. His birthdays were celebrated with parades and torchlight processions. He was portrayed, as the historian Richard Evans observed, as a 'soldier artist, worker, ruler, statesman, … as a man with whom all sectors of German society could identify'. Like Stalin in

BIOGRAPHY

Otto von Bismarck (1815–1898)

Bismarck was a German statesman who was responsible for the unification of Germany and became its first Chancellor in 1871.

Russia, Hitler's actions and gifts were often celebrated in religious language, with Biblical echoes. This constant stream of propaganda portraying Hitler as a wise statesman who could do no wrong had a considerable impact on the population. Even though the Nazi Party became increasingly unpopular, Hitler himself remained genuinely popular.

***Führer* principle**

The principle that the *Führer* cannot be wrong and must be obeyed at all times.

The key to the Hitler dictatorship was *Führerprinzip* or the *Führer* **principle**. This meant that the Führer's will was law throughout the Party, and after 1933, theoretically at least, throughout Germany. Any decision made by him was final.

Arguably, it was Hitler who held the Third Reich together, which was bitterly divided at every level. Theoretically, he was all-powerful. As *Führer* he was: 'supreme legislator, supreme administrator, and supreme judge', as well as being 'the leader of the Party, the Army and the People'. However, despite these powers, he played virtually no part in the day-to-day government of the Reich. The American historian E. N. Peterson called him a 'remote umpire handing down decisions from on high', but this actually exaggerates his role in government. He avoided making decisions, stood back and let events take their course. Sometimes he made vague declarations of intent or principle. Only rarely in peacetime did he issue unambiguous orders.

Ministers and officials had little contact with him, especially when he had retreated to his isolated chalet in the Berghof in Bavaria. Consequently, they were compelled to interpret his intentions for themselves, often coming to contradictory conclusions. Werner Willikens, the State Secretary in the Prussian Agriculture Ministry, accurately described this process of interpreting Hitler's will as 'working towards the *Führer*'. This lack of leadership and contact, combined with the *Führer* principle was one of the key reasons for the Third Reich's chaotic system of government.

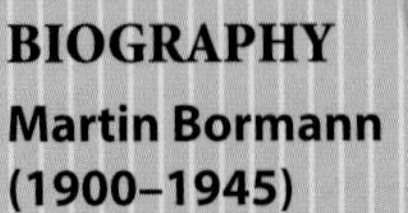

BIOGRAPHY

Martin Bormann (1900–1945)

Before serving with the artillery in the Great War, Bormann worked on a farm. After the war he was recruited by the *Freikorps* and was imprisoned for a political murder in 1924. He joined the Nazi Party in 1927, and after 1933 became deputy to Rudolf Hess. He also managed the 'Adolf Hitler fund of German Business'. He replaced Hess when the latter flew to Scotland in 1941 and became Director of the Party Chancellery. As he was always at Hitler's side, he amassed enormous powers and controlled access to the *Führer*. He was killed in May 1945 trying to escape from Berlin.

Hitler in the Second World War

The need 'to work towards the *Führer*' became even more necessary in the Second World War. From June 1941 until November 1944 Hitler was encamped in his headquarters in East Prussia and the Ukraine. As Supreme Commander of the Army, he took on a heavy workload, which left him little time for matters affecting the home front. Consequently, the Reich government became ever more chaotic, despite repeated attempts by ministers to create an effective War Cabinet. Hitler stubbornly opposed setting up any committee with real powers because these might eventually be used to challenge him. He vetoed all attempts to reintroduce regular Cabinet meetings and even disapproved of ministers meeting unofficially. Decisions could only be reached by seeing Hitler in person, but increasingly access was controlled by **Martin Bormann**, who was Chief of the Party Chancellery at the *Führer* headquarters. The historian Ian Kershaw has come to the conclusion that the regime was incapable of being reformed, as it 'was both the inexorable product of Hitler's personalised rule and the guarantee of his power'.

Was Hitler a weak dictator?

Was the chaos at the centre of the Nazi regime a sign that Hitler was actually a 'weak dictator'? According to the German historian Hans Mommsen, Hitler was 'reluctant to take decisions, often uncertain, concerned only to maintain his own prestige and personal authority, and strongly subject to the influence of his environment – in fact, in many ways, a weak dictator'. Like any politician, Hitler was not immune to the pressure of events. Party members, for instance, put him under pressure to intensify the persecution of the Jews (see pages 118–119), and he also faced difficult economic problems, such as the worsening balance of payments deficits (see page 98). On the other hand, by August 1934 he had destroyed most potential centres of opposition to his regime. He was most interested in foreign policy and rearmament and here he was able to carry out his policies successfully and override opposition.

There is little evidence that Hitler ever desired a different system. His charisma depended on distancing himself from the everyday decisions of government, so that his image would not be damaged by politically unpopular measures. So arguably he was not as such a weak dictator, but he had created a chaotic system of government that inevitably weakened Germany.

ACTIVITY ***Enquiries***

1 Study Sources A and B. Compare these sources as evidence for Hitler's style of government.

2 Study all the sources (A–E). Use your own knowledge to assess how far these sources support the view that Hitler deliberately created a disorganised and chaotic system of government to defend his own position as *Führer.*

ACTIVITY
Period Studies

In both his role as Party leader from 1925 onwards and as Chancellor and *Führer* of the German Reich, Hitler acted as a 'remote umpire handing down random decisions from on high, 1933–45'.

How far do you agree with this assessment?

Sources

(A) The State Secretary in the Prussian Agricultural Ministry, Werner Willikens, in a speech on 21 February 1934 to representatives from the agricultural ministries in the federal states, advised them on the art of interpreting the will of the *Führer* when no precise guidelines were given by him:

Everyone with opportunity to observe it knows that the Führer can only with great difficulty order from above everything that he intends to carry out sooner or later. On the contrary, until now everyone has best worked in his place in the new Germany if, so to speak, he works towards the Führer... .

Very often, and in many places, it has been that individuals, already in previous years, have waited for commands and orders. Unfortunately, that will probably also be so in the future. Rather, however, it is the duty of every single person to attempt, in the spirit of the Führer, to work towards him. Anyone making mistakes, will come to notice it soon enough. But the one who works correctly towards the Führer along his lines and towards his aim will in future as previously have the finest reward of one day suddenly attaining legal confirmation of his work.

J. Noakes and G. Pridham (eds) (Revised edition, 2000). *Nazism 1919–1945, Vol. 2: State, Economy and Society, 1933–39*. Exeter: University of Exeter Press.

(B) Carl Schmitt, a leading constitutional lawyer, and the diplomat Ernst von Weizsäcker recalled after the war how difficult it was to obtain a decision from Hitler:

Ministers ... might for months on end and even for years, have no opportunity of speaking to Hitler... Ministerial skill consisted in making the most of a favourable hour or minute when Hitler made a decision, this often taking the form of a remark thrown out casually, which then went its way as an 'order of the Führer'... .

J. Noakes and G. Pridham (eds) (1984). *Nazism 1919–45, Vol. 2: State, Economy and Society, 1933–39* (p. 197). Exeter: University of Exeter Press.

(C) Hans Mommsen writing on Hitler's style of government:

As Chancellor ... Hitler personified the specific political style which ensured the movement's success. One aspect of this was the postponement of decisions on political priorities for the sake of tactical flexibility: even after 1933, Hitler did his utmost to avoid hard and fast political rulings wherever possible. A side-effect of this tendency was to obscure the real intentions of the National Socialist leadership, however often they might be displayed in all their ambiguity. As dictator, Hitler still obeyed the maxims of the successful publicity man: to concentrate on the aims of the moment, to profess unshakable determination to achieve them, and to use parallel strategies, heedless of the political consequences resulting from the inevitable inter-institutional friction entailed.

Hans Mommsen (1976). 'National Socialism: Continuity and Change' in Walter Laqueur (ed.), *Fascism* (pp. 175–76). London: Penguin.

(D) The classic analysis of Hitler's calculated attempt to divide and rule is given by Otto Dietrich, Hitler's former press chief, in his memoirs written in 1955:

In the twelve years of his rule in Germany Hitler produced the biggest confusion in government that has ever existed in a civilised state. During his period of government he removed from the organisation of the state all clarity of leadership and produced an opaque network of competencies. It was not laxness or an excessive degree of tolerance which led the otherwise so energetic and forceful Hitler to tolerate this real witch's cauldron of struggles for position and conflicts over competence. It was intentional. With this technique he systematically disorganised the upper echelons of the Reich leadership in order to develop and further the authority of his own will until it became a despotic tyranny.

J. Noakes and G. Pridham (eds) (1984). *Nazism, 1919–45, Vol. 2: State, Economy and Society, 1933–39* (p. 205). Exeter: University of Exeter Press.

(E) As Hitler's architect, Albert Speer had a unique chance to observe the *Führer*'s inefficient work patterns:

When, I would often ask myself, did he really work? Little was left of the day; he rose late in the morning and conducted one or two official conferences; but from the subsequent dinner on he more or less wasted his time until the early hours of the evening... .

In the eyes of the people Hitler was the Leader who watched over the nation day and night. This was hardly so... According to my observations, he often allowed a problem to mature during the weeks when he seemed entirely taken up with trivial matters. Then after the 'sudden insight' came, he would spend a few days of intensive work giving final shape to his solution... .

Once he had come to a decision, he relapsed again into his idleness.

A. Speer (1970). *Inside the Third Reich*. London: Weidenfeld and Nicolson.

Conclusion: Was Nazi Germany a divided and chaotic state?

From 1925 onwards Hitler's approach to power was ambiguous. The failure of the Munich Putsch in 1923 convinced him that he must seize power legally so that the Nazi revolution would be legitimate (see page 26–27). When he was appointed Chancellor and consolidated his grip on Germany, he did not act as a conventional head of government. He grafted his role of *Führer* of the Party onto the structure of the German state. Therefore, from the start of the Third Reich there was a dualism between Party and state. Yet the Party itself was bitterly divided and the rivalry of the local *Gauleiters* and party officials was only held in check by the *Führer* principle.

ACTIVITY

Period Studies

Assess Hitler's contributions to establishing and consolidating Nazi authority in Germany, 1933–45.

How successful was the Nazi machinery of terror at controlling the Third Reich?

Crucial to the survival of the Nazi regime was its ability to eliminate its enemies and to terrorise the population into obedience. Up to a point the Nazi government had to rely on the existing courts to sentence the enemies of the People's Community (*Volksgemeinschaft*) according to the new laws and instructions sent to the judges, but these were backed up by a machinery of terror: the SS, the *Gestapo* and the concentration camps.

The Nazis used a variety of ways to ensure that the courts carried out their wishes:

- They introduced new laws to deal with political offences. For instance, in December 1934 anyone convicted of making 'hateful' remarks about the Nazi state and its leaders could be executed.
- Parallel to the traditional courts, 'people's courts were set up to try communists and other enemies of the regime.
- Judges were instructed to be much tougher in sentencing criminals.
- Pressure was brought to bear on lawyers and judges to carry out the wishes of the government. By 1939 in order to qualify as a judge it was necessary to make 'a serious study of National Socialism and its ideological foundations'.

It was not, however, until the Second World War that the remaining independence of the judges and the courts was destroyed. In April 1942 the government announced that it would remove from office 'judges who clearly fail to recognise the mood of the hour' – in other words to carry out what the government ordered them to do. This enabled the Nazis to interfere directly in trials. In August 1942 **Otto Thierack**, an SS Group Leader and President of the People's Court, was appointed Minister of Justice, and the senior officials at the ministry were replaced by men who were more loyal to the Nazis. From now on it became the norm for the public prosecutors, who represented the Nazi state, to indicate to the judges beforehand what their verdicts should be.

ACTIVITY

What was the role of the courts in consolidating Nazi authority, 1933–45?

BIOGRAPHY

Otto Thierack, (1889–1946)

Thierack joined the Nazi Party in the early 1920s. He was Minister of Justice in Saxony and President of the People's Court from 1936 to1942.

The SS

Heinrich Himmler by building up the SS into a 'state within a state' created an independent organisation which was responsible only to Hitler. The SS had been created in 1925, initially as a small force to protect Hitler and the leading Nazis. Under Himmler, who became its head in 1929, it took over responsibility for the party's intelligence and espionage section (**SD**). Himmler hoped that in the SS he would be able to create a new racial elite, and from 1935 only those who were of pure Ayran ancestry could join its ranks.

BIOGRAPHY

Heinrich Himmler *(*1900–45)

Himmler took part in the Munich Putsch, but did not join the Nazi Party until 1926. In 1929 he was made head of the SS. In 1933 he was appointed Chief of the Police in Bavaria and by 1936 had consolidated his grip on the entire police apparatus in Germany. In 1943 he became Reich Minister of the Interior, and in 1944 Commander of the Reserve Army, and then in quick succession Commander-in-Chief of the Rhine Army Group in December 1944 and of the Vistula Army Group in January 1945. His unsuccessful attempt in April 1945 to end the war through neutral contacts in Stockholm led to Hitler ordering his arrest. He was captured by British troops in May, but committed suicide before he could be tried by the Nuremberg tribunal.

SD

This is the security service of the SS (*Sicherheitsdienst).* It was created in 1932 and in July 1934 became the sole political intelligence agency of the Reich.

BIOGRAPHY

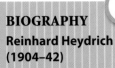

Reinhard Heydrich (1904–42)

Heydrich became Himmler's deputy in 1933. He organised the deportation of the Jews to occupied Poland and in 1941 briefed the Operation Groups (*Einsatzgruppen*), whose mission it was to hunt down and kill Jews and Communist officials in Russian territory once it was occupied by the German army. He was assassinated by Czech resistance fighters in 1942.

Once the Nazi government was formed, the SS rapidly expanded its power and became a key instrument in the machinery of terror:

- Himmler had loyally supported Hitler against Röhm (see pages 67–71). The SS was rewarded by being made independent of the SA and given responsibility for the concentration camps.
- To carry out this task the notorious Death's Head Units (*Totenkopfverbände*) were formed. Those recruited for the units were mostly young peasants who were trained to treat the inmates of the camps brutally.
- In February 1936 Himmler also took control of the ***Gestapo***. It now worked closely with both the SS and the SD under the direction of **Reinhard Heydrich**.
- In June 1936 Himmler took over the command of all the German police forces.
- Himmler's power potential was further increased by the formation of a small number of armed regiments based on the SS squads. These squads had operated together with the SA as a 'revolutionary strike force' in the early months of the takeover of power. By 1944 these had increased to 35 divisions.

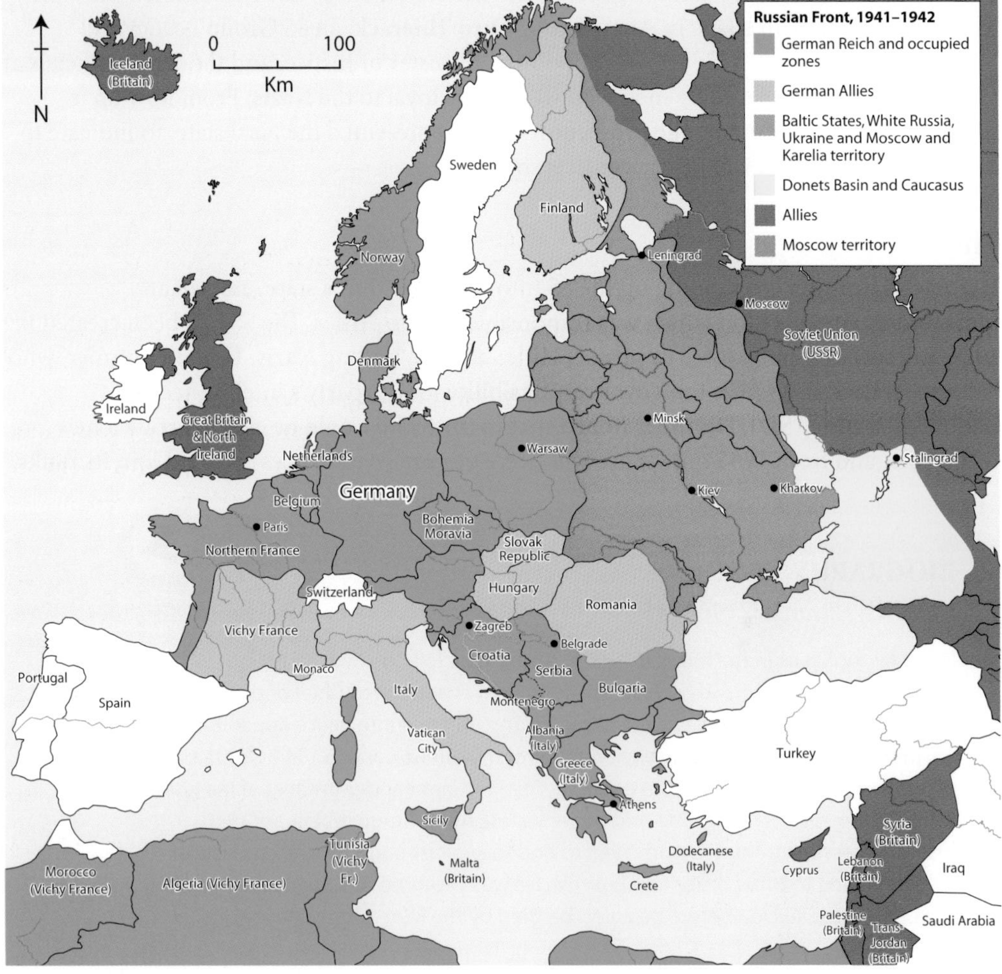

Figure 3.6 The large amount of territory occupied by Nazi Germany at the height of the war also led to a vast increase in the SS sphere of influence

Gestapo

During the Weimar Republic, Department 1a of the Berlin Police *Praesidium* ran the Prussian political police. In April 1933, Göring, as acting Prussian Interior Minister, set up a new Secret State Police Office (Gestapo, *Geheime Staatspolizei* – Secret State Police). Its task was to maintain discipline in the factories and keep political and ideological opponents of the regime under surveillance.

The influence of the SS increased hugely during the Second World War. Himmler was appointed Commissioner for Consolidating German Nationhood (RKFDV), which gave him responsibility for the resettlement of **ethnic Germans** from Poland and elsewhere back into Germany. He was also responsible for eliminating 'the harmful influences of such alien parts of the population as constitute a danger to the Reich and the German community' in the **occupied and incorporated territories**. Effectively, he had a free hand to deport and, later, to murder Jews, gypsies, Poles and Russians in the concentration camps. The control of the concentration camps gave the SS the chance to use prison labour in the operation of their business enterprises, which in 1944 consisted of about 150 firms, ranging from quarrying to the manufacture of armaments and textiles.

Ethnic Germans

These were people of the German race who lived mainly in Poland as a result of the new frontiers drawn in 1919.

Occupied and incorporated territories

These were territories which had either been occupied by the German army in the war or else annexed by Germany.

The *Gestapo*

The defence of the People's Community was in the hands of the political police – the *Gestapo* – the criminal police – the Kripo (*Kriminalpolizei*) – and the uniformed police. The aim of both forces was to wage 'war' against the political and **asocial** enemies of the state. The duty of the police in the words of Werner Best, the legal expert at Gestapo headquarters, was to watch over 'the health of the German body politic', to recognise 'every system of sickness' and destroy all 'destructive cells'. The *Gestapo* ensured that their role as the defenders of the People's Community was well publicised in the German press. Invariably, the impression created by the *Gestapo* through the mouthpiece of the press was that the Jews were behind Communism, embezzling, swindling, smuggling and virtually every crime it looked into. Its power was such that it had complete freedom to operate outside the law.

In September 1939, shortly before he left Berlin for his new headquarters on the **Polish front**, Hitler instructed Himmler to keep order on the home front 'with all means'. Himmler's response was to amalgamate the SD, the *Gestapo* and the Reich Criminal Police Department into the Reich Security Head Office. Its powers were increased by the 'Ordinance against Parasites on the Body Politic' and the newly drafted War Penal (Punishment) Code. These wide-ranging powers entitled the *Gestapo* to arrest not only criminals but anyone who dared voice doubts about the war or who listened secretly to the BBC's foreign broadcasts.

As the historian Richard Evans has written, the '*Gestapo*... quickly attained an almost mythical status as an all-seeing, all-knowing arm of state security and law enforcement', but in reality it was a very small organisation. In 1939 it consisted of about 20,000 men of whom 3000 were also members of the SS. Most of the *Gestapo* officials were office workers who spent their time creating and then updating card indexes in which the particulars of Communists, Social Democrats, 'deviants' and grumblers were kept. The *Gestapo* were dependent on informers for most of their information. These informers could be dedicated Nazis or simply those with a desire to get even with difficult neighbours, or colleagues at work.

Asocial

A category of people, such as criminals, tramps, etc., considered by the Nazis to be 'biologically criminal' (see page 116).

Polish front

Where the German and Polish armies were fighting against one another during the German invasion of Poland.

ACTIVITY

Period Studies

To what extent did the SS play a vital role in establishing and consolidating Nazi authority?

Block wardens and the Gestapo

The block wardens were one of the *Gestapo's* most reliable sources of information. Each local branch of the Nazi Party was divided into eight cells, which in turn were divided into about 50 blocks containing approximately 50 houses or apartments. These were run by block wardens. By 1939 there were nearly two million of them, their job being to make sure that everyone displayed Nazi flags outside their homes or attended mass rallies on special occasions. They wore brownish-gold tunics with red collar epaulettes and were known as 'golden pheasants'. In working-class areas they were extremely unpopular as they kept surveillance on 'politically unreliable' people, who were usually Jews, ex-Communists, or Socialists, and reported rumour-mongers. Those prepared to denounce someone they suspected as being unreliable would usually make their accusations to the block warden first.

ACTIVITY

How effective were the *Gestapo* in crushing opposition to Nazi authority, 1933–45?

BIOGRAPHY

Theodor Eicke (1892–1943)

Eicke joined the Nazi Party in 1928 and the SS in 1930. As a reward for his 'execution' of Ernst Röhm (see page 71), he was made Inspector of the Concentration Camps. He was killed when his plane was shot down by the Russians in 1943.

Political prisoners

Those who are imprisoned because of their political ideas.

The concentration camps, prisons and the treatment of opposition

In the early months of 1933 concentration camps and torture chambers were set up in various parts of Germany. They were used in the SA's brutal campaign of violence against Socialists and Communists. However, the camps were offensive to many Germans, in particular to Hitler's Nationalist allies. To reassure them that the Nazi revolution was over he ordered the closure of many of the camps over the following year. Some SA officers, including Hilmar Wackerle, the Camp Commandant of Dachau, were charged with murdering prisoners. In June 1933 Himmler replaced him with **Theodore Eicke** of the SS, who introduced a more disciplined regime and turned Dachau into a model for all future concentration camps in Germany. The new punishment regulations were aimed at stopping random personal violence by the guards and instituting a disciplined bureaucratic system which ensured that all punishments were recorded and carried out by several SS men rather than by an individual.

By the time Himmler took over responsibility for all the concentration camps in Germany there were only 3000 inmates, which indicated that the Nazis had virtually eliminated the Communist and Socialist opposition. Only hard-core opponents like Ernst Thälmann now remained in the camps. Himmler was therefore able to close down all but Dachau, Sachsenhausen, Buchenwald and Lichtenburg, the latter being a camp for women. There were, however, still 14,000 **political prisoners** in the state prisons.

Besides preventing any revival of Communist and SPD resistance, in February 1936, on Hitler's orders, the SS and *Gestapo* turned to rounding up habitual criminals, asocials and homosexuals. As a result, the composition of the camps began to change and the numbers of inmates increase. By July 1937, 57 per cent of the inmates in Dachau were not political prisoners, but tramps and professional criminals. In December that year a law was passed permitting the arrest and imprisonment of anyone whom the police or any official agency believed did not fit into the People's Community. Besides beggars, gypsies and homosexuals, this could include the long-term unemployed and even traffic offenders! By 1939 the concentration camp population had grown to 21,000. Two new camps at Flossenburg and Mauthausen were opened especially for asocials and criminals. These were sited near quarries to enable the SS-run German Quarrying Company to exploit the concentration camp labour.

Life in the concentration camps

Life in the camps was brutal. The prisoners were at the mercy of the SS. Inmates were woken at four or five in the morning and paraded for roll call. Those lucky enough to have a practical skill, were put to work in small workshops. Most, however, had to work in quarries manually excavating stones, chalk or gravel. On returning from a day's labour, they again had to attend roll call and stand at attention, often in the bitter cold, for hours on end. The SS exploited the detailed regulations to hand out punishments. These ranged from being beaten by a cane, dog whip or even a steel rod, to solitary confinement in a small, unheated cell for weeks.

During the war the concentration camp system in Germany expanded greatly. There were four main developments in this process:

- There was an enormous expansion in numbers: between September 1939 and December 1942 numbers increased from 25,000 to 88,000; by January 1945 there were about 714,211 inmates.
- An increasing number of foreigners were sent to the camps, who soon outnumbered the original German inmates. In December 1941 Hitler ordered that all resistance fighters in Nazi-occupied Europe should be sent to the camps.
- The camps were increasingly used as sources of labour. In September 1942 prisoners from the regular prisons in Germany were transferred to them, and foreign workers in Germany who were guilty of even the most minor crime were also dispatched there.
- In Poland from 1942 onwards the camps were also being used to exterminate on a large scale the Jews from different parts of Nazi-occupied Europe (see page 119–120).

ACTIVITY

Period Studies

To what extent did the concentration camps help Hitler establish and consolidate Nazi authority, 1933–45?

Figure 3.7 Prisoners pulling a trailer in Dachau. Although the concentration camps were at first a method of imprisonment, during the war they became the focal point for Hitler's own 'race war' against the Jewish people

BIOGRAPHIES

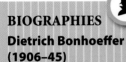

Dietrich Bonhoeffer (1906–45)

A Lutheran pastor and a founding member of the Confessing Church, Bonhoeffer belonged to the resistance movement against the Nazis and was involved in plots to assassinate Hitler. He was arrested in 1943 and hanged in April 1945.

Alfred Delp (1900–45)

A Jesuit priest who was involved in the underground resistance to the Nazis. He was arrested in July 1944 and hanged after torture in February 1945.

Johann Georg Elser (1903–45)

After his attempt to assassinate Hitler failed he was arrested and imprisoned in Sachsanhausen concentration camp and later moved to Dachau. Esler, a carpenter by trade, was a committed Christian and former communist. He was murdered by the *Gestapo* in 1945.

ACTIVITY

'It was the machinery of terror that established and consolidated Nazi authority'.

How far do you agree with this view of Hitler's rule in Germany?

Conclusion: How effective was the machinery of terror?

The machinery of terror was a major factor in the consolidation of Hitler's power. In the first three years the *Gestapo* and SS broke the residual political opposition to the Nazi regime and were then able to move on and deal with the 'enemies' of the People's Community: criminals, the habitual unemployed, tramps, gypsies, homosexuals, etc. In reality there were few *Gestapo* agents and only four concentration camps in 1939, but their reputation cast a shadow over the German people. They represented what could happen to you if you were reported to the authority by your block warden or any other official. This atmosphere of fear and terror was the background to everything that happened in the Third Reich up to its collapse in 1945. On the other hand, as we shall see in Chapter 4, it was not just terror that kept Hitler in power. Full employment, foreign policy successes and a feeling of national unity were all factors that made the Nazi regime popular with many Germans.

Nor did the machinery of terror completely eliminate dissent and opposition:

- Historians have used the medical term *resistenz* or immunity to describe how some groups, such as Christians, were at times able to block out or partially restrict the penetration of Nazi ideas. There were many people who rejected elements of National Socialism and who tried for example, to avoid giving the 'Heil Hitler' salute, or who on saints' days would hang out a church banner rather than the swastika flag. In 1941 the Catholic bishop of Munster openly criticised the Nazi euthanasia programme (see page 116) and forced Hitler to suspend it temporarily.
- There were brave individuals, such as the priests **Dietrich Bonhoeffer** and **Alfred Delp**, and **Georg Elser**, a carpenter. The latter attempted to kill Hitler by planting a bomb in the Bürgerbräu beer cellar, where Hitler was due to speak in November 1939. Hitler was only saved because he left the meeting early. Altogether there were 27,367 German political prisoners held in custody.
- Amongst young people, such as the *Edelweiss Pirates*, were formed in rebellion against the Hitler Youth (see page 111). In 1914 a group of students at Munich University formed the White Rose Group and distributed anti-Nazi leaflets. They were arrested and executed in February 1943.
- Despite the efforts of the Gestapo, small KPD and SPD opposition groups managed to survive.
- In 1941 Kreisau Circle which met at Kreisau, the Silesian estate of Count Helmut von Moltke. It was composed of Germans from all opposition groups, except the Communists, and began to plan for a post-Nazi Germany, but it was broken up by the Gestapo in 1944.
- There were individuals who joined opposition groups within the army and the bureaucracy, convinced that Hitler would destroy Germany. One of these was Colonel Claus Schenk von Stauffenberg (1907–44), a German army officer who was awarded the German Cross for courage in battle. However, as a committed Catholic with strong religious and moral convictions, he lost faith with the Nazis and Hitler. Convinced that only the army could remove Hitler, he joined the resistance movement and plotted to assassinate him. On the 20th of July 1944 he placed a bomb in the conference room of Hitler's headquarters in East Prussia. It exploded but Hitler escaped with minor injuries and Stauffenberg was executed. The failure of this plot led to the virtual elimination of the opposition as 7,000 people were arrested, 5,000 of whom were executed.

How far did Nazi censorship and propaganda work?

The Third Reich did not rely only on fear and repression to consolidate its power and subdue its opponents. It also sought to win over public opinion and create a new Nazi culture which glorified war and the Aryan race. This involved projecting a positive image of Nazi culture and achievements and censoring hostile ideas and inconvenient facts in the media, art, literature and theatre.

The main responsibility for creating a new Nazi culture lay with Goebbels, who was appointed head of the Propaganda Ministry when it was created on 13 March 1933. His task, as he said, was 'to transform the very spirit itself to the extent that people and things are brought into a new relationship with one another'. This involved setting up within the Propaganda Ministry departments dealing with the press, film, radio, theatre and a programme of '**popular enlightenment**'.

Popular enlightenment

The use of propaganda to enlighten or brainwash the German people into accepting the Nazi ideology and in this way controlling what people knew and believed. The Ministry of Propaganda did this through the radio, newspapers, theatre, literature, art and film.

Radio

Hitler and Goebbels understood the importance of radio for influencing public opinion. In the summer of 1933 the staff of all radio stations were purged of left-wingers and Jews. In April 1934 regional radio stations were removed from the control of the *Länder* and formed into the Reich Radio Company. Its director, who worked closely with Goebbels, had to approve all important programmes. The news programmes were subordinated to the Ministry's press department. Goebbels realised that too much political propaganda on the radio would bore its listeners, so by 1939 two-thirds of radio time was given over to playing popular songs and music.

The government successfully encouraged radio ownership. Millions of cheap radios were produced and special local radio wardens were appointed to encourage *Volksgenossen* (national comrades) to buy them and to listen to the programmes. These radios were produced with a limited pick-up range so that they were unable to pick up foreign programmes beyond German borders.

The press

Communication through the written word was also controlled. All Socialist and Communist newspapers were closed down, and any that were allowed to continue were controlled by the Reich Press Chamber directed by the Nazi publisher, Max Amann. In October 1933 the 'Editors' Law' made it impossible for newspaper editors to take an independent stance on issues and they were compelled to accurately record the views and opinions of the regime. Jews were banned from working as editors or journalists. In April 1935 newspapers were forbidden to target any particular group of people, such as Catholics or young people, and businesses were banned from purchasing newspaper titles for commercial reasons.

BIOGRAPHY

Igor Stravinsky (1882–1971)

A Russian composer who is regarded by some as one of the most influential of the 20th century. One of his most admired works is the ballet *The Rites of Spring*. He left Russia in 1910 and lived successively in Switzerland, France and the United States.

Drama and music

The Propaganda Ministry laid down strict guidelines for the arts. All theatres and performances, even amateur productions, had to be licensed by the Ministry. According to the Theatre Law of 15 May 1934, plays were a 'public exercise' subject to 'police supervision'. The public was restricted to a cultural diet which conformed to Nazi ideology. Modern experimental plays were banned, but the German classics could still be performed.

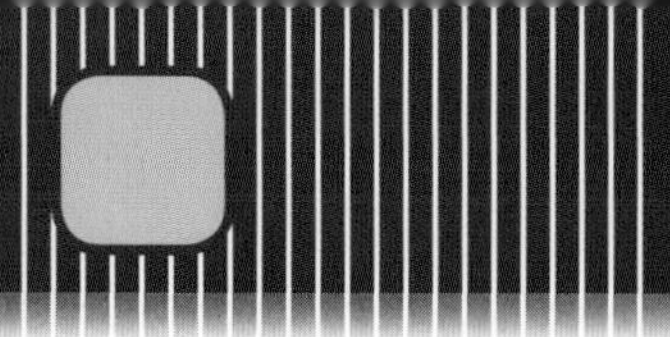

BIOGRAPHY

Igor Stravinsky (1882–1971)

A Russian composer who is regarded by some as one of the most influential of the 20th century. One of his most admired works is the ballet *The Rites of Spring*. He left Russia in 1910 and lived successively in Switzerland, France and the United States.

Libretti

This is the plural of libretto, which is the text of an opera.

BIOGRAPHY

Felix Mendelssohn (1809–47)

A German-Jewish composer and conductor, who was the grandson of the philosopher Moses Mendelssohn. His work includes symphonies, piano and chamber music.

Music

Experiments in modern music were also condemned. The work of the Russian experimental composer **Igor Stravinsky** was particularly ridiculed. Above all, jazz, as an Afro-American art form, was condemned as degenerate and banned. Jewish conductors and musicians were dismissed. The great German classics could, of course, still be played, but even these could be censored. For instance, in three Mozart operas the **libretti** had been written by Lorenza de Ponte, who was Jewish. These had to be rewritten in German translations! **Felix Mendelssohn's** music might at times still be played, but because he was Jewish his name never appeared on a programme.

Literature and art

As for German literature, Goebbels stressed that writers should depict the new Nazi Germany in a positive light. In effect this meant that books on war, the 'heroic' early days of the Nazi movement, Germany's historic mission in eastern Europe, and similar topics were the approved themes. The Reich Chamber of Literature drew up a list of 'damaging and undesirable literature'. The Gestapo and the SD could then raid libraries and second-hand bookshops to track down copies of banned books.

As something of an artist himself, Hitler had particularly strong views about art. He dismissed modern art as 'degenerate'. So all modernist art was banned in Germany. Modernist paintings were removed from galleries and their artists forced into exile, or at least prevented from selling and exhibiting their works. Exhibitions mocking 'degenerate art' were shown in German towns, and Hitler himself visited one of the largest of them in Dresden. Acceptable art included pictures of the German countryside showing virile peasants and blonde women, or compositions depicting heroic Germanic warriors. For the purpose of exhibiting such works, the House of German Art was opened in Munich in 1937.

Film

The Reich Film Chamber was set up in July 1933 by the Propaganda Ministry. Everyone employed in the film industry had to join. The Reich Cinema Law required all film scripts to be submitted to the censor and gave Goebbels the power to ban any film which he thought unsuitable.

As in the case of radio, Goebbels recognised that comedies and light entertainment were more popular with the German cinema-going public than political propaganda films. In1938 only 10 per cent of the films made were classified as political. On the other hand, the news feature *Weekly Review* (*Wochenschau*), half the coverage of which was devoted to politics, had to be included in the every film programme.

Propaganda during the Second World War, 1939–45

Nazi propaganda had been preparing the German people for war since 1933. Hitler was convinced that the Great War had been lost in 1918 because the German people gave up the will to fight. Consequently, the aim of Nazi wartime propaganda was to mobilise the German people and to sustain its morale. 'Never again will there be a November 1918' was a constantly repeated slogan. To achieve this it was vital to persuade the Germans that the war was necessary and that the enemy was intent on destroying Germany.

The Propaganda Ministry also had the task of providing the population with practical advice on air-raid precautions, the recycling of scarce materials, the economic use of food, and warning against revealing important information through 'careless talk'.

Nazi propaganda was greatly helped by the brutality of the Red Army as it advanced into Germany and by the insistence of the Western Allies on unconditional surrender. The German people felt that they had no choice but to fight to the bitter end.

Conclusion: The role of propaganda

Propaganda was vital to establish and consolidate the Nazi regime. Terror was not enough. The population had to be won over and prepared psychologically for war. The newspapers, the arts, films and radio were all purged of those critical of the regime, and a system of control and censorship forced them to follow the line laid down by the Ministry of Propaganda. Modernism in music, theatre and art was banned. Goebbels, however, tried with some success to avoid boring the public with too much politics. Radio programmes and films provided plenty of light entertainment which aimed to amuse and relax audiences. However, in the privacy of their homes, there were still people who did tune into foreign radio stations, read banned books or listen to jazz on their gramophones.

ACTIVITY ***Period Studies***

1 Which do you think was more important – terror or propaganda in the establishment and consolidation of Nazi authority?

2 Assess the aims of Nazi propaganda.

Totalitarian state?

In the 1950s historians argued that Nazi Germany had been a totalitarian state. By this they meant that the Nazi regime controlled every aspect of behaviour in the Third Reich. Now, however, the term 'totalitarian' is seen to be exaggerated. The Nazi regime did not control everything. For instance the Church enjoyed considerable independence while the chaotic nature of the Nazi government inevitably limited its impact on the population.

Review questions

1 To what extent was the Third Reich based upon suppression and terror?

2 To what extent did Hitler manage to consolidate his power in Germany by 1939?

3 'Given the chaotic way the Nazis governed Germany, it is a miracle that the Nazi state survived until 1945.' How far do you agree with this assessment?

4 'The only time the Nazi regime was in danger from internal opposition was in the period April–July 1934.' How far do you agree with this view?

5 Assess the reasons for the survival of the Nazi regime until 1945.

ExamCafé

Relax, refresh, result!

Relax and prepare

Hot tips

Oliver

Everyone always thinks the Gestapo were everywhere in the Reich, controlling the population through fear. But in fact there were very few Gestapo agents before the war. Rember there were other factors as well as fear – including some 'benefits' from Nazi rule.

Rosie

Getting to grips with command words – the words in essays that tell you what to do – is really important. Make sure you understand 'assess', 'to what extent?' and 'how far?' for Period Studies questions.

Common mistakes – Laura

I often got stuck on the difference between the SA and the SS: the SA were the 'Brown Shirts', they were under the control of Röhm and were not well disciplined. Rohm wanted them to lead a 'Second Revolution', but the Army was worried about them and to win the support of the army Hitler had the SA purged on the Night of the Long Knives. The SS were the 'Black Shirts', who were much better disciplined. My trick was to link 'SA' to 'suspicious Army' and work back from there: why were they suspicious? – because the SA were undisciplined, etc. Well, it worked for me!

Getting started...

It is very difficult to assess the effectiveness of propaganda in a totalitarian society. Many people were too frightened to express their views and so simply conformed, but did not actually approve of or support the regime. There are concerns that oral evidence from later has exaggerated the extent of the opposition. You need to be careful as it is possible to argue that there was large-scale opposition; if that was the case why did the regime survive?

Refresh your memory

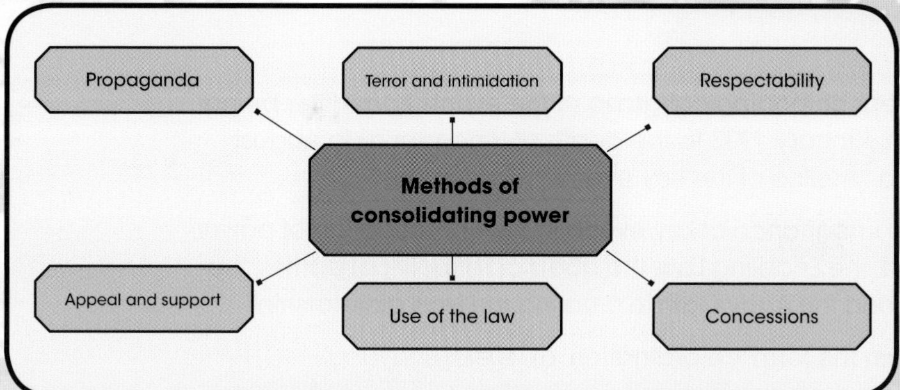

You can use this diagram as the basis of your revision. Make sure you have precise examples for each of the six points on the diagram. For example, with terror and intimidation this could include the SS, Gestapo, arrests, concentration camps, pressure exerted on the Reichstag to pass the Enabling Act, the March 1933 election.

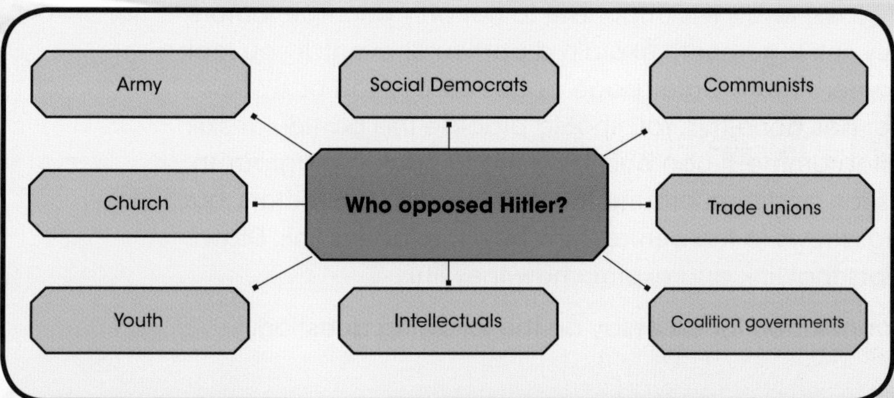

You should be able to explain why the above groups opposed Hitler, how Hitler dealt with them and why their opposition was so ineffective.

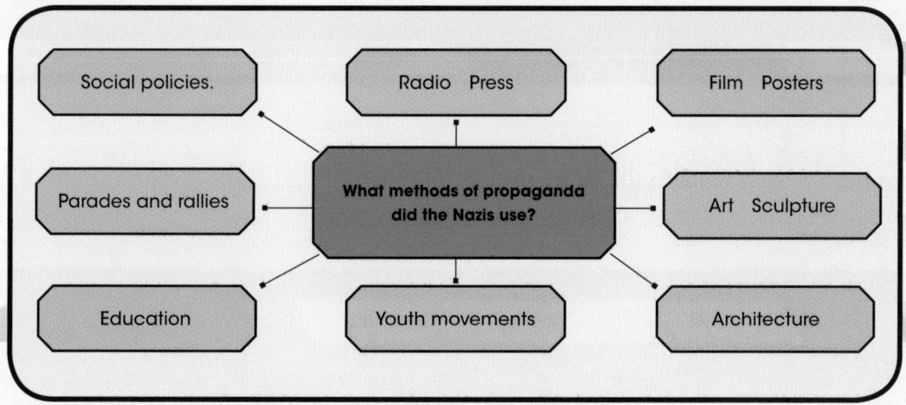

It is important that you have precise examples of each and can explain how far each method was successful.

Get the result!

Refresh your memory

▷ Ensure you have a clear chronological grasp of the events from Hitler being appointed Chancellor in January 1933 to the death of Hindenburg in August 1934. Construct yourself a timeline of the key events.

▷ Be able to explain the importance of key events in the consolidation of power, such as the Reichstag Fire, the Enabling Law, the abolition of political parties, the Night of the Long Knives and the Army Oath in creating the Nazi dictatorship.

▷ Ensure you can explain the term 'co-ordination' or '*Gleichshaltung*'.

▷ Ensure you know the main features of the Nazi police state: courts, Gestapo, SS and concentration camps. Can you explain how much repression there was in practice? Did the Gestapo really control people?

▷ Be able to explain who opposed the Nazis and why, and why their resistance was a failure.

In order to achieve the highest levels it is important to not only prioritise factors, but also to show how they link together to explain a particular event. If you look back to the previous chapter's Exam Café (page pages 60–61) you can see how the improved answer has done this. You should practise this particular skill as part of your revision programme. It can best be done through a diagram. In the centre write the question and then around the outside write the factors, but instead of simply drawing arrows to the centre think how the factors link. Draw arrows between the factors that link and explain how they link.

Now read the following conclusion for an essay on the following question.

You can find the rest of the answer on the CD-ROM.

Exam question

To what extent were the SS and Gestapo the **most** important reason for Hitler's consolidation of power?

Sample answers

Maisie's answer

It is fair to say that the SS and Gestapo were a major reason why Hitler was able to stay in power, however they were not the main reason. There were a number of reasons which included propaganda, SS, Gestapo, justice system and Gleichschaltung, which all played a major role and most of them are linked with each other. Propaganda played a part in informing people of how they should act and believe. The SS and Gestapo both struck fear into the public. The justice system also struck fear into the public – if you were arrested for anything, the judge would hand down a very severe sentence. It could range from imprisonment to concentration camps and death. Gleichschaltung was not necessarily a fear striking method, but it meant that Hitler had co-ordinated everything that the public participated in. As a result the public were unable to escape the Nazi regime.

Examiner says:

Maisie has identified a variety of reasons why Hitler was able to consolidate his power, including the SS and Gestapo, propaganda, the justice system and Gleichschaltung. However, although the answer suggests that these factors were linked together this is not demonstrated. Maisie needs to think how all these factors worked together to ensure that Hitler was able to consolidate his power. The answer might have suggested that different aspects of the system were used to deal with different groups; for example, terror was used to deal with and opposition who would never have conformed and needed to be silenced, whereas propaganda was used to win over doubters by portraying the successes of the regime. Therefore both aspects were essential in controlling the nation. Another way of establishing a link between terror and propaganda would be to show how propaganda was used to justify the terror and that therefore these two methods worked together.

How to take it further

You should now think of other possible links between the SS/Gestapo and the judicial system or perhaps between the Gestapo and informers. Try to construct a diagram like the one suggested above, draw in arrows showing the links and explain them.

Exam question

To what extent was the Enabling Act the most important reason why Hitler was able to consolidate his power in Germany in the period from January 1933 to August 1934?

As a starting point for this last question think how you could show links between the Reichstag Fire and the Enabling Act or the Enabling Act and the banning of other political parties.

4 Economy and society 1933–1945: To what extent did the Nazis transform German economic policy and society?

Sources: Two views of the People's Community

(A) In his speech to mark 1 May 1934, Hitler stressed that the new People's Community, which the Nazi movement was building, aimed to destroy class barriers and create a united society:

We want to destroy the arrogance with which unfortunately so many intellectuals feel that they must look down upon labour, and on the other hand we wish to strengthen their self-confidence through their consciousness that they too can perform manual labour. But beyond this we wish to contribute to the mutual understanding of the different classes in order to reinforce the tie which binds together the community of the people ... We all know that it is not words or outward professions that lead to the establishment of this community; that needs an inner unlearning, a new education of the people.

The gigantic organisations of our movement, their political bodies as well as the organisation of the SA and SS, the building up of the Labour Front just as much as the organisation of the army, these are all national and social melting-furnaces in which gradually a new German will be formed.

J. Noakes and G. Pridham (eds) (1991). *Nazism, 1919–45, Vol 2: State, Society and Economy, 1933–39* (p. 354). Exeter: University of Exeter Press.

(B) However, in 1938 Friedrich Reck-Malleczewen, a profoundly conservative landowner living deep in the country of Upper Bavaria, had a very different view of the Community the Nazis had constructed:

Mass-man moves, robot-like, from digestion to sleeping with his peroxide-blonde females, and produces children to keep the termite heap in continued operation. He repeats word for word ***the incantations of the Great Manitou,*** *denounces or is denounced, dies or is made to die, and so goes on vegetating ... But even this, the overrunning of the world with Neanderthals demands of the few full human beings, who are left that they shall also turn into cavemen; and then threatens them with physical extinction if they refuse.*

Richard J. Evans (2006). *The Third Reich in Power* (p. 415). London: Penguin.

The incantations of the Great Manitou

The spells of the great witchdoctor, by which he means Hitler.

These are both views as to the *product* of *Volksgemeinschaft*, rather than views on its effectiveness or success if defined in Nazi terms.

Key Questions:

To what extent did Hitler unite Germany into a People's Community? To assess this we need to look at how the Nazis transformed German economic policy and society, 1933–45, and consider the following key questions:

- How far did the Nazi government manage to create full employment?
- How did Hitler assist the *Mittelstand* and the farmers economically?
- How did Hitler rearm Germany and to what extent did he overcome the problems that rapid rearmament caused?
- How did the People's Community unite the German people?
- What groups were excluded from the 'People's Community?

How far did the Nazi government manage to create full employment?

In January 1933 the Hitler government was confronted with formidable economic problems:

- The German economy was practically bankrupt and the official unemployment rate was well over 6 million.
- Industrial production had declined to the levels of the1890s, while the volume of German trade had sunk by 50 per cent.
- Agriculture was burdened with debt and was uncompetitive internationally.

On the other hand, there were advantages:

- The Great Depression was easing, and the beginnings of economic recovery could already be detected.
- Hitler was able to build on plans put forward by von Schleicher (see page 48) to create work by building houses and roads and improving agriculture.
- Reparations were scrapped in 1932 and the *Reichsmark* was no longer tied closely to the **gold standard**, which enabled the government to inject much more money into the economy.
- The Voluntary Reich Labour Service, which in 1932 had enrolled nearly 300,000 men in short-term agricultural jobs, set up work for the unemployed.
- From 1932 onwards fewer young people were entering the labour market because of a dramatic decline in the birth rate between 1914 and 1918. Combined with this was a 40 per cent rise in the death rate of children over the same period.
- The combination of the Depression and the SA's ruthless action against the trade unions, the SPD and the Communists, destroyed the power of the labour movement to demand higher wages. Wages were now set at lower levels enabling companies to invest more money in production.

The gold standard

The system by which a currency is valued in terms of the amount of gold for which its units can be exchanged.

In February 1933 Hitler promised to solve the unemployment problem within four years of taking power. For the Nazi regime to survive, unemployment had to fall dramatically, and for that to happen industrial production had to rise. The new government in its own words applied 'a multitude of interrelated measures' to revive the economy and increase employment . Rearmament was traditionally viewed as a means of 'kick-starting' German economic recovery, but it was only one of the factors that produced the rapid revival. Others were:

- Many unemployed young people were removed from the labour market and were employed temporarily by organisations such as the Voluntary Labour Service, which in 1935 employed almost under half a million young men.
- In May 1935 compulsory military service was introduced for all 18-year-old males. The *Luftwaffe* (German air force), which was formed in the spring of 1935, and the navy absorbed hundreds of thousands of recruits, many of whom were unemployed. By the end of 1936 the armed services together with industry had engaged most of the unemployed.
- In the Law for Reduction of Unemployment the government reduced unemployment by squeezing women out of the labour market. This was done by offering young couples who were about to get married an interest-free loan worth up to 1000 *Reichsmarks* for as

long as the wife remained at home and did not re-enter the labour market until it was paid off. To encourage production the loan was not issued in cash but in vouchers that had to be redeemed for goods such as furniture and household equipment.

- A billion *Reichsmarks* was invested in public works' schemes such as road and canal building, and government subsidies were provided for house construction.
- The motor industry was aided by tax concessions, which dramatically improved sales and helped the components industries. From March to June 1933 those employed in the motor industry increased by 40 per cent.
- The length of the working week was shortened so that more people were needed to do the work.

ACTIVITY Enquiries

Study Sources A and B and compare these sources as evidence for Hitler's success in overcoming unemployment in Germany.

Figure 4.1 Ground flattening for a swimming pool, 1933.

Source

(A) Table 4.1 The number of unemployed (in millions), January 1934–39

1934	3.773
1935	2.974
1936	2.520
1937	1.853
1938	1.052
1939	0.302

Adapted from B. Gebhardt (1959). *Handbuch der Deutschen Geschichte*, Vol. 4 (p. 352), edited by K.D. Erdmann. Stuttgart: Union Verlag.

(B) The historian Richard Evans comments on the employment statistics of 1934–35:

The regime was indeed far from averse to cooking its books. Not only men drafted into labour service but also previously unregistered family and other effectively unpaid farm workers, most of whom were women, were now counted as employed. None of these people could be considered as active participants in the labour market; none of them received a regular wage with which they could support themselves, let alone support a family. On this reckoning there were at least one and a half million 'invisible unemployed', and the total number, which Nazi statisticians put at over two million, was in fact nearer four.

Richard J. Evans (2006). *The Third Reich in Power* (pp. 334–35). London: Penguin.

Conclusion

Helped by the upturn in the economic cycle Nazi efforts to revive the economy and create unemployment were successful, although their success was exaggerated. By the summer of 1934 unemployment had fallen to 2.5 million, however it remained fixed at that level until conscription and the acceleration of rearmament resulted in a further dramatic fall in 1936; and by the summer of 1938 there was virtually full employment.

> ***ACTIVITY***
> ***Period Studies***
> To what extent had Hitler transformed the German economy by 1939?

How did Hitler assist the *Mittelstand* and the farmers economically?

Mittelstand

Before coming to power the Nazis had directed much of their electoral propaganda at the German ***Mittelstand.*** Small shopkeepers hated the big department stores (which they contended were owned by the Jews) because they could sell services and goods more cheaply than they were able to. Artisans with small workshops and peasants with small holdings were undermined by larger competitors such as factories and agricultural estates.

> **Mittelstand**
> This was the German lower middle classes: farmers, small businessmen, self-employed craftsmen and white-collar workers.

The department stores more than anything else symbolised big business for the *Mittelstand.* In the spring of 1933, SA stormtroopers attacked and terrorised many of them. In Braunschweig a restaurant in a local department store was literally shot to pieces by a local band of SA men, who shared the *Mittelstand's* hostility towards big business.

The *Mittelstand* was hoping that the Hitler government would support their interests and follow policies that would keep big business in check and in particular close down the department stores. To some extent it did. Under the Law for the Protection of Individual Trade chain stores were forbidden from opening new branches, adding new lines to their products or maintaining self-contained departments such as hairdressers or restaurants. Also the purchase coupons given as marriage loans for furniture and household equipment could not be spent in the department stores.

> **BIOGRAPHY**
> **Hjalmar Schacht (1877–1970)**
> Schacht was a leading banker in the inter-war years. In 1923 he was appointed president of the *Reichsbank*, where he was responsible for halting hyperinflation and introducing the *Rentenmark* currency (see page 23). He resigned in 1930 in protest against the Young Plan. As a German Nationalist he supported a coalition with Hitler and in 1933 was re-appointed to the *Reichsbank*, and then in September 1934 was appointed Economics Minister. As a result of disagreements over the economic consequences of rearmament and his preference for overseas rather than eastern expansion he resigned in 1937 and was dismissed from the *Reichsbank* in 1939. He remained a minister until 1944, when he was incarcerated in a concentration camp on suspicion that he was involved in the 20 July plot to kill Hitler. He was tried at Nuremberg but acquitted.

However, these concessions were cosmetic. Big business was needed to kick-start the economy and accelerate rearmament. The business community therefore was reassured that there would be no 'wild experiments'. **Hjalmar Schacht**, the head of the *Reichsbank*, was responsible for ensuring that job creation schemes did not lead to inflation.

Big business continued to expand at the expense of small-scale enterprises. Between 1933 and 1939, for instance, the number of shoe repair shops declined by 14 per cent and many self-employed craftsmen earned less than workers in the large factories. Department stores were not closed down. On the contrary, they were supported by the government. The Hermann Tietz chain of stores whose profits fell by 41 per cent in 1933, leaving the company on the brink of collapse, was saved by a government loan of 14 million *Reichsmarks*. Such a spectacular bankruptcy would have involved the loss of 14,000 jobs and damaged the businesses of suppliers and the banks, all of which would have undermined the government's 'battle' against unemployment. However, the loan was conditional on the resignation of the company's Jewish owners, the Tietz brothers. The stores were then renamed Hertie to signify that they were no longer owned by Jews.

Farmers

Farmers on the other hand received much more help than the small shopkeepers and self-employed craftsmen. By 1932 German agriculture, which employed about 29 per cent of the population, was in deep economic crisis. Between 1927 and 1932 the number of small farms going bankrupt rose from 2,554 to 6,200. The Nazis seized the opportunity to win support among discontented small farmers in the 1928 electoral campaign and in the next five years continued to blame the Weimar Republic for the farmers' plight.

Agriculture was vitally important to the Nazis for two reasons:

- Food shortages had contributed much to the defeat of Germany in the Great War of 1914–18. So, in preparation for the next war Germany had to be as self-sufficient or **autarkic** as possible in food production. In 1936 as part of the Four Year Plan, a special department was set up with responsibility for this (see page 99).
- The peasantry were the 'life source of the German nation' and needed to be protected no matter how bad the economy was. They safeguarded Germany's racial heritage and raised strong young men who could be recruited to fight for the nation. The Nazis called this their 'blood and soil' policy.

Autarky

A self-sufficient economic system, which attempts to manufacture and grow all it needs.

Moratorium

A temporary suspension of debt repayments.

Tariffs

Taxes placed on imported goods to help the home economy.

To relieve the problems of agriculture, Alfred Hugenberg, who was both Minister for Economics and Minister for Food in Hitler's Cabinet, began by placing a **moratorium** on peasants' debts until the end of October 1933; he also increased **tariffs** on key agricultural imports, and assisted dairy farmers by directing that butter must be added to margarine. He was succeeded in June 1934 by Richard Darré, who believed passionately, to quote the historian Richard Evans, 'that the essential qualities of the German race had been instilled into it by the peasantry …'

To help revive the farming industry Darré set up the Reich Food Estate to take responsibility for all aspects of food production and the future of German farming. Farmers, wholesalers and retailers agreed to fix the prices at which agricultural produce was sold. At first it boosted prices, but the government needed to prevent prices rising too high. So, after the summer of 1935 price controls were imposed on farmers to stop them from benefiting from food shortages. As a result agriculture remained relatively unprofitable and farm labourers continued to desert the countryside for the towns. Nevertheless by 1938–39 productivity was 25 per cent higher than a decade earlier and the country was 83 per cent self-sufficient, although there was a serious shortfall in fats.

Darré's second major reform, the Reich Entailed Farm Law of 29 September 1933, was more controversial and was inspired by Nazi ideology. Its aim was to maintain 'the peasantry as the blood-spring of the German nation' and to make the small farmer more secure by ruling that farms between 7.5 and 125 hectares could not be divided up or sold.

The owners of farms had to be good farmers and 'honourable'. Any farmer who was incompetent could be replaced under a special court ruling in favour of his wife or one of his children. It hindered the development of large-scale farms which were more efficient. It was also unpopular with the peasantry because it prevented farmers from dividing up their land between their children or even using it to raise a loan from the bank to pay for a daughter's wedding.

Another of Darré's plans was to resettle the sons of farmers who did not inherit any land on the estates of bankrupt **Junkers** in east Germany, but this was strongly opposed. The Junkers appealed through Hindenburg to Hitler and exerted their influence on the army in an attempt to keep their estates intact. In support the army argued that big estates were vital for producing food to feed the population in wartime. Hitler was not particularly interested as he believed that the land required would be found in Russia once it was occupied by the Germans. The result was that by 1938 only a few small farms had been created along the Reich's eastern frontier regions.

Junkers

These were the aristocratic landowning families of Prussia and eastern Germany to the east of the river Elbe.

German agriculture in the war

In 1939 when war broke out Germany was much better prepared than in 1914. Ration cards were already available in anticipation of war and were immediately issued; this meant that until 1944 the population was reasonably well fed. Many farm workers were called up for military service, but they were replaced by prisoners of war. Territories that were occupied also became sources of food supply. However, the longer the war went on, the more acute food shortages became. One of the pressures on food supply was the British blockade of German-dominated continental Europe; this prevented feeding stuffs for cattle and pigs and fertilisers from outside Europe reaching Germany. Another was the shortages of farm machinery, in particular the halt in tractor production, because of the need for iron and steel in the manufacturing of military equipment.

Germany's wartime rations

The German population was adequately fed for most of the war, unlike in 1918. A fair ration system had been created and a minimum standard was set below which living standards would not be allowed to fall. Soldiers' families were given special ration cards for food and rent. Up to 1944 average consumers were granted rations which were between 7 and 15 per cent above the minimum calorific standard, but in 1944 these were drastically cut. Workers in heavy industry were guaranteed adequate rations which were often more generous than their peacetime diets. However the German population benefited relatively little from the occupied areas, as the Allied blockade deprived western European agriculture of imported fodder and fertilisers, and the Ukrainian grain harvests were taken over by the army to feed the troops.

Conclusion

The small farmers and the *Mittelstand* did not benefit as much as they expected to from the Nazi regime. Hitler never closed the department stores and never attempted to weaken the influence of big business and industry. Farmers, however, enjoyed certain real benefits, but became frustrated by the bureaucracy of the Reich Food Estate and the government's refusal to allow them to charge what they wanted for their crops.

ACTIVITY

Describe Nazi measures to revive agriculture and assist the *Mittelstand*.

How did Hitler rearm Germany and to what extent did he overcome the economic problems that rapid rearmament caused?

What were the initial stages of rearmament?

While overcoming unemployment was important politically in the short term, Hitler's real priority was rearmament. He told his Cabinet on 8 February 1938 that 'every publicly supported job creation scheme must be judged by the criterion of whether it is necessary from the point of view of rearmament'. The new motorways were to be built with troop movements in mind, while the expansion of the motor industry would contribute to the future motorisation of the German army. Even the expansion of the Labour Service helped 'toughen up' young men and prepare them for army life later.

Rearmament began as soon as Hitler became Chancellor. The question was how it was to be paid for at the same time as setting up huge work creation projects without inflating the currency and risking inflation. This was solved in the summer of 1933 when Schacht devised the 'Mefo bills', which were crucial in raising the necessary funds.

How did Mefo bills work?

Government agencies used 'Mefo bills', or credit notes, to pay manufacturers of military equipment. These were issued by four large private companies and two government ministries under the name of the *Metall-Forschungs AG* (Metal Research Co – abbreviated to Mefo). On receiving Mefo bills the *Reichsbank* paid the holder of the bills cash to ensure that companies were promptly paid. The bills were valid for a five-year period, so the government raised large sums of money by offering them at an interest rate of 4 per cent per annum on the money market and by forcing banks to invest 30 per cent of their deposits in them.

How effective was the New Plan?

German rearmament was threatened by recurring balance of payments crises as the revival of the economy led to a rapid rise in imports. The imports needed for rearmament had to be paid for. To do this, Schacht, who became Economics Minister in 1934, introduced the New Plan, which involved:

- The introduction of strict controls so that the government could limit imports to the essentials required for rearmament.
- Special Supervisory Offices were set up to check up on imports.
- Only when they gave their approval would the *Reichsbank* release foreign exchange to pay for the imports.
- A series of bilateral trade agreements with the Balkan and South American states by which German purchases were paid for in *Reichsmarks*. This money was used by these countries to purchase German goods and to invest in the construction of plants, which would later produce goods required for the German war economy. Schacht targeted states in these areas because they were not part of the British or French empires, which levied duties on exports to Germany.

ACTIVITY

Why was the New Plan necessary and how successful was it?

The New Plan managed to increase imports from South America and South East Europe, but as rearmament accelerated and economic recovery quickened, increasing amounts of imports were needed. The Defence Ministry demanded the doubling of copper imports in December 1934, for example, but there was not enough foreign exchange to pay for this; in such cases it meant that rearmament would have to be paid for by profits made from exports.

How significant was the Four Year Plan in creating a total war economy

Schacht warned about the increasing cost of rearmament and the need to slow down its pace, however Hitler rejected this. He bypassed Schacht and in 1936 appointed Hermann Göring as Commissioner of Raw Materials and Currency. In September a Four Year Plan was announced with Göring as its head. It was, as the historians Noakes and Pridham have observed, 'one of the basic documents of the Third Reich', revealed clearly that Hitler was preparing Germany for war and was a desisive step towards creating a **total war economy**. Hitler stressed that:

- politics was 'a struggle of nations for life'
- Bolshevik Russia, which, he believed, was controlled by the Jews, was seeking world domination
- Germany must by ready for war by 1940 by increasing production and encouraging the use of substitutes for imported raw materials.

Total War Economy

An economy in which all production is dictated by the needs of war.

Figure 4.2 Göring inspects security police at the State Parliament Building. Göring's willingness to give Hitler what he wanted – both 'guns and butter' – quickly saw him bypass Schacht.

The historian Richard Overy argues that the Plan marked 'the point at which the armed forces' conception of recovery of defensive strength gave way to Hitler's plans for large-scale war'. In the winter of 1936–37 Göring took over responsibility for rearmament from the Ministries of Economics and Defence, and Schacht resigned in November 1937.

Göring set up a separate Four Year Plan organisation which consisted of six departments for:

- the production of raw materials
- the distribution of raw materials
- the labour force
- agricultural production
- price supervision
- foreign exchange matters.

By appointing the State Secretaries of the Ministries of Labour and Agriculture to take charge of the labour and agricultural departments he effectively subordinated these departments to the Four Year Plan and ensured they carried out his wishes.

A key aim of the Four Year Plan was to increase production in synthetic rubber, fuel oil and iron ore by relying mainly on private industry. Large plants were built for the production of synthetic rubber and oil and the Hermann Göring Steelworks was constructed to exploit local low-grade ores. In 1938 the Plan's offices took over the major Austrian iron, steel and machinery companies and six months later the Skoda works in the Sudetenland. Huge increases in production were achieved, but targets were not met; consequently imports continued to be a drain on Germany's currency reserves.

Guns and butter

This refers to an economy which can produce both consumer and luxury goods and armaments.

Historical debate on the German war economy: Guns and butter or total mobilisation for war?

Economic historians looking at the German war economy were surprised that it reached its maximum output only in 1944. They concluded, in the words of the American historian Burton H. Klein, that despite the Four Year Plan the 'scale of Germany's economic mobilisation for war was quite modest'. Klein also argued that **consumer goods** output had increased by over 30 per cent between 1936 and 1939. The conclusion that many historians drew from these figures was that Germany managed to produce both '**guns and butter**', and that Hitler was only prepared to wage a brief ***Blitzkrieg*** rather than long wars of attrition. However, more recent research by Richard Overy and Adam Tooze has challenged these assumptions and shown that the Four Year Plan really was, to quote Overy, 'a decisive step towards preparing Germany for total mobilisation'. Overall, according to Overy, 'consumption as a share of national income declined from 71 per cent in 1928 to 58 per cent in 1938', and between 1936 and 1939 armaments and preparations for war absorbed over 60 per cent of all capital investments made. Hitler would have welcomed a brief war, but in May 1939 he warned his generals 'the government must ... also prepare for a war of from ten to fifteen years' duration'.

Had rearmament caused a growing economic crisis by 1939?

Large-scale rearmament created a number of economic problems, such as:

- production bottlenecks
- inter-service rivalry for scarce resources
- labour shortages
- lack of sufficient foreign exchange to pay for imports
- an increasing danger of inflation as the bank note circulation trebled between 1933 and 1939.

Can it be argued that Hitler was forced into war in 1939, in the words of the historian Tim Mason, 'because of domestic pressures and constraints which were economic in origin and also expressed themselves in acute social and political tension'? The German economy faced economic problems as Hitler refused to tolerate any financial restraints on rearmament, and between September 1937 and September 1939 the volume of money in circulation had doubled.

The situation was temporarily eased in March 1939 when Walther Funk, the Economics Minister, introduced the New Finance Plan. This included the condition that the government would pay businesses 40 per cent of the cost of manufacturing armaments in the form of tax certificates which could only be redeemed by paying off future taxes. This enabled the government to hold on to a proportion of the money it would otherwise have had to pay out.

Consumer goods

These are goods, such as clothes and furniture, that are purchased to satisfy the consumer's needs.

Blitzkrieg

A quick or 'lightening war' using bombing followed by swift and surprise attacks on opposing forces.

ACTIVITY

Period Studies

To what extent had Hitler successfully rearmed Germany for war by 1939?

Labour shortages were overcome by recruiting foreign workers from southern and central Europe, the introduction of labour conscription and large-scale industrial retraining programmes.

ACTIVITY ***Enquiries***

Study Sources A and B.

Compare these sources as evidence both for the importance and the success of the Four Year Plan.

Sources

(A) Hitler wrote the following memorandum which Göring presented to the German Cabinet on 4 September 1939:

... Germany will, as always, have to be regarded as the focus of the Western world against the attacks of Bolshevism.

I thus set the following tasks:

I The German armed forces must be operational within four years.

II The German economy must be fit for war within four years.

J. Noakes and G. Pridham (eds) (1984). *Nazism, 1919–45, Vol. 2: State, Economy and Society, 1933–39* (pp. 281–87). Exeter: University of Exeter Press.

(B) Table 4.4 Four Year Plan targets and actual production figures (000 tons), 1936–42

Commodity	1936 output	1938 output	1942 output	Plan target
Mineral oil	1,790	2,340	6,260	13,830
Aluminium	98	166	260	273
Buna rubber	0.7	5	96	120
Nitrogen	770	914	930	1040
Explosives	18	45	300	223
Powder	20	26	150	217
Steel	19,216	22,656	20,480	24,000
Iron ore	2,255	3,360	4,137	5,549
Brown coal	161,382	194,985	145,918	240,500
Hard coal	158,400	186,186	166,059	213,000

D. Petzina (1968). *Autarkiepolitik im Dritten Reich. Der national-sozialistische Vierjahresplan* (p. 182). Stuttgart: Deutsche Verlags-Anstalt.

How effective was the Total War Economy, 1939–45?

Following victory over Poland in September 1939 the German army desperately needed more tanks and ammunition. The seven-month delay before they advanced westwards into France provided the time needed to supply the army with new tanks and ammunition. The resulting spectacular victories over France and Britain the following year changed the balance of power in Europe and presented Germany with the opportunity to create an economic bloc in continental Europe to rival those of the USA and the British Empire.

The German people, however, had little time to bask in their crushing victories. By July 1940 the army was already preparing for war against Soviet Russia.

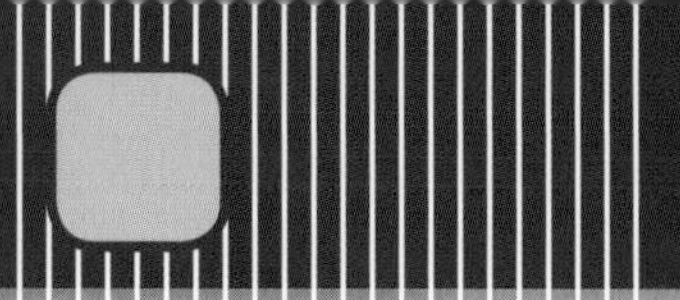

Germany launched on 22 June 1941 the largest single military operation ever recorded. It was called Operation Barbarossa and depended for success on defeating the Russians before the winter set in. It failed when the Russians counter-attacked outside Moscow in December. By the following winter the German war economy was in crisis. The failure to defeat Russia and the massive cost of the continuing war in the east increased the pressure to escalate the manufacture of new and replacement weapons at a time when millions of young men were being withdrawn from the labour market to fight on the eastern front.

Rationalising

This means to use the existing resources in a rational and economic way.

These problems could only be overcome by **rationalising** production. On 3 December 1941 Fritz Todt, the Armaments Minister, set up a series of 'Main Committees', each of which had responsibility for producing a particular class of weapon or equipment. Albert Speer succeeded Todt, who was killed in an air crash in February 1942.

Building on what Todt had achieved, Speer accomplished what the historian Richard Overy calls a 'production miracle'. In April 1942 he successfully persuaded Hitler to create the Central Planning Board. This enabled him to organise the allocation of raw materials to each sector of the economy; he removed the armed forces' right to design their own weapons. Industrialists were also pressurised to rationalise production, maximise their plant capacities and standardise designs.

ACTIVITY

How did the German war economy rise to the challenge of total war,1939–45?

Despite heavy Allied bombing, German armaments production reached its peak in 1943–44.

BIOGRAPHY

Albert Speer (1905–81)

Speer was the son of a well-known architect and was won over to the Nazis when he attended one of Hitler's rallies in 1931. He joined the Nazi Party and in 1934 and became the 'Party architect'; during the next eight years he designed large state buildings for the new Germany. In 1942 he was appointed the Armaments' Minister. In 1946 he was sentenced to 20 years imprisonment at Nuremberg. Later he published his diary and wrote his memoirs, in which he bitterly criticised the Third Reich.

Figure 4.3 Albert Speer's work on the Germany economy was vital to maintaining the faltering German war campaign.

How was the labour crisis solved in the war industries?

Labour shortages constantly threatened to limit production in the German war economy. On 31 May 1939, 24.5 million men were employed in the economy. A year later that had declined to 20.5 million as four million workers had been called up into the armed services. The question was how to fill the gap.

One way was to increase the number of female workers, but in September 1939 they already composed 37.4 per cent of the total German labour force, which was a considerably higher proportion than in Britain. In the spring of 1940 the Reich Labour Ministry attempted to persuade Hitler to introduce comprehensive female conscription, but the unpopularity of this measure both at home and with married soldiers on the front persuaded Hitler to delay its introduction. Instead, Polish and, later, French prisoners of war were employed.

By January 1943 the pressures on German manpower had intensified. On the Eastern Front, German monthly losses amounted to 150,000 men, but only 60–65,000 reinforcements could be raised each month. This led to fresh demands for calling up men in reserved occupations and replacing them with female and foreign workers. At the end of January 1943 all males between 16 and 65 who were not in the armed forces and all females between 17 and 45 were ordered to register for war work. Mothers with young children and wives of the self-employed were exempted, the age level was raised by Hitler for women from 16 to 17 and lowered from 50 to 45; however only about 900,000 women were actually called up. The gap was once more filled by foreign prisoners of war from Poland, France and Russia. By the end of 1944 there were over seven million foreign workers in Germany.

Conclusion

One aim of Nazi economic policy was quickly and substantially to reduce unemployment, however the principal aim was rearmament. As the pace of rearmament accelerated, the economy overheated and sucked in vast quantities of imports which were expensive to pay for. When the New Plan failed, Hitler rejected Schacht's advice to slow down rearmament and instead announced the Four Year Plan. Regardless of cost, he was determined that Germany should be ready for war by 1940, but when war broke out the country was far from ready for a long war. Despite huge investments, the actual production of war material was disappointing, as much of the investment had gone into constructing barracks rather than tanks. Only when the German army became bogged down in Russia in December 1941 did Hitler give Fritz Todt and then Albert Speer the powers to bypass the bureaucracy and increase production.

ACTIVITY

How successfully did the Nazi regime overcome the problems caused by rapid rearmament, 1933–45?

How successful was the *Volksgemeinschaft* in uniting the German people and transforming German society?

The *Volksgemeinschaft*, or 'People's Community', was inspired by the 'spirit of 1914', which had temporarily united Germans at the beginning of the Great War. The bitter divisions that tore the Weimar Republic apart aroused a nostalgia for that previous period of national unity. With that in mind Hitler during the electoral campaigns of 1930–33 (see pages 45–47) promised to create a new united People's Community.

The Nazi People's Community appeared to respond to the yearnings for national unity and stability, however its real aim was to create a united classless racial community of 'Aryan' Germans from which all Jews, 'aliens', '**deviants**', the mentally sick and incurably ill would be excluded. It would be used to forge a new kind of German, who would fight for the Führer and the Fatherland.

Deviants

People who behave in a way that doesn't conform to the social or cultural norms of a society.

ACTIVITY

How successful was the Nazi *Volksgemeinschaft*?

How far did the Nazi regime seek to transform German youth?

The Nazi regime attempted to transform youth on three levels, by:

- ensuring that school syllabuses and teachers lost no opportunity to reflect and reinforce Nazi values
- the creation of new elite Nazi schools
- putting pressure on children to join the Hitler Youth and League of German Girls.

Introducing Nazi values into the education system

Many schoolteachers were Nazis and the majority of university lecturers were sympathetic to the German Nationalist Party. Teachers and lecturers were employed by the state and the Law for the Re-establishment of the Civil Service, passed in April 1933, was used to remove anyone deemed to be politically unreliable. To become head of a school depended on whether you were a member of the Nazi Party. In May 1936 the National Socialist Teachers' League became responsible for the political indoctrination of teachers.

There was no change to the structure of the school and university systems. In appearance the traditional structure of the German educational system remained in place, however what it taught radically changed the educational content. Syllabuses were revised according to Nazi ideology. More time was given to the teaching of History, Biology and German, as these subjects were best suited to exploitation by Nazi propaganda. From 30 July 1933 the teaching of History, for example, was to be built around 'the concept of heroism in Germanic form, linked to leadership'. In practice students would be set essays on Hitler and various Nazi heroes such as Horst Wessel (see page 49).

Nazi propaganda was less successful in the universities. Special courses on Nazi ideology were introduced and the Nazi Students' League insisted that all students should do six months' labour service before beginning their studies. However, the Nazi regime failed to dominate the universities as they did the schools because most university teachers, whatever their politics, were sceptical of Nazi ideology and perceived its irrelevance to their subject. Historians, for instance, were reasonably free to write articles for learned periodicals on anything but the most recent history.

German physics, chemistry and mathematics

The Nazis attempted to 'Nazify' Physics. In May 1933, Dr Johannes Stark was appointed President of the Imperial Institute of Physics and Technology. He was a bitter rival of **Albert Einstein**, whom he hated as a Jew, passivist and supporter of the Weimar Republic. He dismissed Einstein's Theory of Relativity, and contrived to have an obscure Nazi aerodynamics expert, Wilhelm Müller, appointed as Professor of Physics in Munich instead of the world famous scientist Werner Heissenberg.

There were also attempts to develop 'German Maths', which focused on Geometry rather than Algebra, as the former was somehow linked to the ideal Aryan racial type. Unsurprisingly, this was ignored by most university teachers. Similar efforts were made to launch 'German Chemistry', but this too was rejected as absurd.

What new schools did the Nazis create?

The Nazis set up a number of special schools and institutions which were entrusted with the task of educating the future elite of Germany. These consisted of the following:

- The Napolas (National Political Educational Establishments). These were boarding schools which were later taken over by the SS. By December 1938, 21 had been founded and a further 20 were created during the war.
- The Adolf Hitler Schools, the first of which was set up in 1937, were under the control of the Hitler Youth. The original idea was to have one of these schools in every *Gau*, and that no one should be appointed to a key position in the Nazi Party unless they had attended one of these schools. However, only ten were opened by 1945.
- The *Ordensburgen*, which were intended to be the finishing schools for the future Nazi elite. Their aim was to create a disciplined, tightly knit group, comparable to **medieval knightly orders**.

Medieval knightly orders

These were organisations such as the Teutonic Knights, who were a military crusading order which conquered much of the Baltic areas in the 13th and 14th centuries

In reality very few students attended these schools; in particular they failed to attract many pupils from the professional classes, who continued to send their children to the grammar schools and universities.

ACTIVITY ***Period Studies***

1 To what extent did the Nazi regime change the educational system?

2 Assess the view that the Nazis failed to create a specifically Nazi school system but did manage to penetrate the existing system with Nazi values.

The Hitler Youth

Figure 4.4 The Hitler Youth assembles before Hitler in the Nuremberg stadium, September 1938.

The Hitler Youth (HJ) was the most effective means of indoctrinating and transforming Germany's youth. Only 55,000 young people belonged to it at the beginning of 1933. The Nazis were determined to change this and in 1933 dissolved all rival youth groups, with the exception of the Catholic Youth Movement, and imposed massive pressure on young people to join. By 1936 60 per cent of young Germans were part of it. Membership was made compulsory in 1939 and the Catholic Church was forced to dissolve its own youth organisations. The Hitler Youth controlled all sporting activities for young people and was independent of the Reich Ministry of Education. It was a huge organisation that sought to control young males and females from ages 10 to 18. The organisations for males were:

- the *Deutsches Jungvolk* (German Young people) for those 10–14 years old, and
- the *HJ* for those 14–18 years old.

Those for females were:

- the *Jungmädel* (Young Girls League) for those 10–14 years old, and
- the *Bund Deutscher Mädel* (German Girls League) for those 14–18 years old.

Those in the Hitler Youth were indoctrinated in Nazi ideology through teachings about Nazi heroes, the Jewish 'threat' and the greatness of the *Führer*. Boys engaged in sports and war games. Girls were taught traditional female domestic skills, physical fitness and personal hygiene in preparation for motherhood. Older girls learned about military nursing and air-raid protection duties.

With the outbreak of war the demands of the Hitler Youth on both boys and girls intensified. In 1942, for example, 600,000 boys and 1,400,000 girls helped with the harvest. For boys, the Hitler Youth was increasingly used to prepare them for joining the army.

Figure 4.5 German youth groups, such as the *Deutsches Jungvolk*, laid out a full programme of progress for the youth in Nazi Germany.

The Hitler Youth movement had the capacity to inspire many young people through a sense of belonging and adventure. Christa Wolff, who was later one of East Germany's

leading authors, recalled in her memoirs how at first it seemed to offer 'the promise of a loftier life'. However, once joining became compulsory it lost much of its early appeal. By the late 1930s it had become a huge bureaucratic organisation run by middle-aged leaders. Compulsory membership forced many bored and resentful teenagers to join. Most of them ignored the propaganda, but enjoyed the sporting facilities. Unsuccessful attempts were made to boost its prestige by introducing an induction ceremony to rival those of the Christian Confirmation or First Communion ceremonies.

ACTIVITY **Period Studies**

Assess the effectiveness of Nazi policy towards young people.

One reaction among young people disillusioned with the Hitler Youth was to form alternative groups. Two in particular were hostile to the ethos of the Nazi Youth movement:

- The Swing Movement. This was mostly made up of university students who loved jazz, which the Nazis dismissed as *Negermusik* – 'nigger music' – and American dances like the 'jitterbug'. They also cultivated British and American fashions and refused to reject Jews. Such defiance of the social norms of the People's Community provoked Himmler into threatening their ringleaders with imprisonment in the concentration camps.
- The *Edelweiss* Pirate groups. These were made up of young teenage workers, for the most part living in the Ruhr and Rhineland cities. It emerged at the end of the 1930s as a reaction against regimentation in the Hitler Youth and the factories. At first their activities were limited to boycotting Hitler Youth activities, but during the war they attacked Hitler Youth patrols and secretly distributed Communist and Allied propaganda. In Cologne-Ehrenfeld in 1944 hostility turned to opposition when an *Edelweiss* Pirates, gang colluded with an underground group which assisted army deserters, escaped prisoners of war and foreign workers. It also attacked military installations and assassinated the head of the Cologne *Gestapo*, before it was broken up.

ACTIVITY **Enquiries**

1 Study sources B and C (page 108) and compare them as evidence for the popularity of the Nazi Youth movements.

2 Study all the sources and use your own knowledge to assess how far these sources support the view that Nazi educational policy had more to do with teaching military values than a wider cultural and social view of the National Community.

Source

(A) The following maths question is an example of how the Nazis used every subject as a vehicle for their ideology:

'A modern night bomber can carry 1800 incendiaries (fire bombs). How long (in kilometres) is the path along which it can distribute these bombs if it drops a bomb every second at a speed of 250 km per hour?'

J. Noakes and G. Pridham (eds) (1991). *Nazism 1919–45, Vol, 2*: State, Economy and Society (p. 439). Exeter: University of Exeter Press.

(B) Christa Wolf, who later became one of East Germany's most well-known authors, recalls the impact which the League of German Girls made on her as a child:

...What a pleasure it was to enjoy the joviality of the leader, a merry young woman by the name of Marianne, called Micky. 'Just call me Micky, I look like Micky Mouse anyway.' Another kind of pleasure was to crowd around the leader, together with all the others, at the end of the evening, forgetting one's own shyness, to grasp her hand, to enjoy the extraordinary familiarity. And on the ride home, to become familiar with a new word by repeating it to herself: 'comradeship'. It meant the promise of a loftier life.... .

C. Koonz (1987). *Mothers in Fatherland, Women and the Family and Nazi Politics* (p. 193). London: Cape.

(C) The following is an extract from one internal Hitler Youth report on a swing festival in Hamburg in February 1940:

... the jazz music was all English and American. Only swing dancing and jitterbugging took place. At the entrance to the hall stood a notice on which the words 'swing prohibited' had been altered to 'swing requested'. The participants accompanied the dances and songs, without exception, by singing English words. Indeed, throughout the evening they attempted only to speak English; at some tables even French.

The dancers were an appalling sight ... When the band played the rumba, the dancers went into wild ecstasy. They leapt around and joined in the chorus in broken English. The band played wilder and wilder items; none of the players was sitting down any longer, they all 'jitterbugged' on the stage like wild creatures. Several boys could be observed dancing together, always with two cigarettes in the mouth, one in each corner... .

J. Peukert (1989). *Inside Nazi Germany. Conformity, Opposition and Racism in Everyday Life* (pp. 186–87). London: Penguin.

(D) A report in the Hamburg teachers' newspaper of December 1937 on a recent teachers' camp explains how the National Socialist Teachers' League attempted to indoctrinate and create a sense of community amongst teachers:

Uniforms, field exercises, songs, lectures and discussions, sport, marching, eating and sleeping, when they take place in camp, acquire team spirit. Only those who have experienced it, and those who have the experience ahead of them are capable of appreciating the HJ [Hitler Youth], only they can educate towards the educational goal of National Socialism.

J. Noakes and G. Pridham (eds) (1984). *Nazism, 1919–45, Vol. 2: State, Economy and Society, 1933–39* (p. 432). Exeter: University of Exeter Press.

(E) In 1935 at the Nuremberg rally Hitler proclaimed in a speech:

In our eyes the German boy of the future must be slender and supple, swift as greyhounds, tough as leather and hard as Krupp steel. We must bring up a new type of human being, men and girls who are disciplined and healthy to the core. We have undertaken to give to the German people an education that begins already in youth and will end with 'the old fighter'. Nobody will be able to say that he has a time in which he is left entirely alone to himself.

Richard J. Evans (2006). *The Third Reich in Power* (p. 273). London: Penguin.

To what extent did the Nazis transform the lives of women and reshape the family?

There was widespread agreement throughout Germany in 1933 that a woman's place in society was in the home with her family. Also, the fall in the birth rate at this time was a general concern. So the Nazis had little trouble finding support for their policy on women.

For the Nazis the future of the Third Reich depended on children: the nation's future warriors and settlers who would conquer and colonise eastern Europe. Women therefore needed to play their part as wives and mothers. To perform these roles they would have to marry, have children and care for them in the home.

Female children were indoctrinated in the idea of the woman's role in society at school and in the League of German Girls. Two women's organisations were also set up: the National Socialist Womanhood and the German Women's Enterprise; these had a membership of several million. They organised Mother's Schools which ran courses in household management and motherhood skills. A Women's Section was also formed in the German Labour Front in July 1934 under **Gertrud Scholtz-Klinik**, which carried out similar policies. The government also issued a series of laws restricting the number of hours women could work in factories and prohibiting them from undertaking heavy work in certain industries.

The Nazi government launched a massive propaganda campaign aimed at raising the status of mothers and housewives within the People's Community. As part of this the regime decided to award a special medal to mothers, the Mother Cross. Those with eight or more children were given the medal in gold, those with six children received one in silver and those with four received one in bronze. To stress their duty to produce children, women were strongly advised to reject make-up and to give up smoking.

In 1933 financial inducements were offered to persuade married women to give up their jobs (see pages 93–94) and have children, but they were not available 'if one of the partners was suffering from a hereditary or mental or physical illness'. Also, women who helped their husbands on farms or in small businesses were excluded from the scheme as their labour was seen as indispensable to their husband's business.

Professional women suffered most from these measures. Women in the higher ranks of the civil service and in medicine were dismissed and senior positions in the legal profession were barred to women; they were also excluded from playing any part in politics. Young women were discouraged from going to university. In January 1934 the Minister of the Interior ruled that the proportion of girls entering higher education should be 10 per cent of the male graduates. In 1937 the government went further: it abolished grammar school education for girls and banned them from learning Latin, which was a compulsory requirement for university entrance.

The government however did accept that women would continue to make up a significant part of the workforce. In 1937, at a time of growing labour shortages, women were recruited to work in many of the new industrial plants set up under the Four Year Plan (see pages 99–100). The ideology of the Nazi government, to quote the historian Tim Mason, 'found itself in head-on collision with a long-term process of social and economic change', so in November 1937 it relaxed its ruling that only unemployed married women were eligible for the marriage loan. By May 1939, 12.7 million women were in employment and made up 37 per cent of the German workforce. Increasingly the government was prepared to consider encouraging married women with children to work part-time.

BIOGRAPHY

Gertrud Scholtz-Klinik (1902–99)

Scholtz-Klinik was married at the age of eighteen and had six children. She joined the Nazi Party and became leader of the women's section in Berlin. Hitler appointed her Reich Women's Führer and head of the Nazi Woman's League. In one speech, she stressed that 'the mission of woman is to minister in the home and in her profession to the needs of life from the first to last moment of man's existence'. In July 1936, Scholtz-Klinik was made head of the Women's Bureau in the German Labour Front. After the war she went into hiding, but was arrested in1952 and sentenced by a French military court to eighteen months in prison.

As the labour market tightened in the late 1930s, women were permitted to rejoin the professions in increasing numbers. The *Racial Observer* newspaper observed in 1937 that 'today we can no longer do without the woman doctor, lawyer, economist and teacher in our professional life'. The number of women doctors increased from 5 per cent in 1930 to 7.6 per cent in 1939, and in 1937 girls were again encouraged to enter teaching. In 1937, the Ministry of the Interior persuaded Hitler that women could, in exceptional cases, be appointed to senior posts in the civil service, provided it was only in the administration of welfare, which was considered a more appropriate area for women. Later they were allowed to join the departments of education and health.

After 1939 women were increasingly involved in war work. Despite Hitler's opposition to female conscription, by 1942 52% of the German labour force was composed of women. By June that year young women in the Reich Labour Service were conscripted to serve as auxiliaries in the armed forces, and two years later they were replacing men in operating searchlights and anti-aircraft batteries.

ACTIVITY

Period Studies

'The Nazis talked much about protecting the family, but in reality they did much to undermine it'.

How far do you agree with this view of Nazi policy towards the family?

The family

Though the Nazis perceived the family as the 'germ cell' of the nation, they undermined the privacy of family life through imposing racial laws and eugenic policies that intruded on personal choices on marriage and having children. Pressure on young people to join the Hitler Youth also undermined the authority of parents. Nazi policies also made divorce easier. In 1938 a new law set out the grounds for ending a marriage: adultery, refusal to have children, venereal disease, a three-year separation, mental illness, racial incompatibility and eugenic weakness.

The priority of the Nazis was not so much the family as the birth of healthy 'Aryan' children. Hitler specified that 'it must be considered reprehensible conduct to refrain from giving healthy children to the nation'. This led to the banning of abortion, but it improved the status of the unmarried mothers despite the conservatism of the Reich and the Party.

Himmler and the Well of Life maternity homes

The unmarried mother's greatest champion was Himmler, who argued that as a contributor to the birth rate she should be 'raised to her proper place in the community, since she is during and after her pregnancy, not a married or an unmarried woman but a mother'. Provided children born of single mothers were 'racially and hereditarily valuable', he was, where necessary, ready to offer them 'legal guardianship'. He set up in 1936 the *Lebensborn* (Well of Life) homes for pregnant and nursing mothers whose partners were or had been SS men and 'other racially valuable Germans'. In all 8,000 children were born in these homes. They offered good facilities at very cheap rates and, ironically, were used by many married couples.

On the outbreak of war the government made provision to protect married women and their dependents from its impact. Soldiers' families, who suffered considerably in the First World War, were given extra food rations and assistance with paying rent. Even so, the longer the war lasted the more difficult life became. Mothers and children were evacuated to the countryside. The wives of owners of small farms and businesses took over in place of husbands and sons called up to fight. In 1942 a German soldier concluded that 'a peasant wife whose husband is at the front...has not a single quiet minute from 4 in the morning until 9 at night'.

How successful was Nazi policy at increasing the birth rate?

Statistically the number of births increased from 971,174 per annum in 1933 to 1,275,212 in 1937, but it was just as likely to have been the consequences of the end of the Depression as it was a direct result of Nazi policies.

ACTIVITY ***Enquiries***

1 Study Sources B and D.

Compare these sources as evidence for Nazi policy on the role of women in the Third Reich.

2 Study all the sources.

Use your own knowledge to assess how far the sources support the view that Nazi policy was aimed at **mainly** encouraging women to have as many children as possible and to stay at home as wives and mothers.

Source

(A) Table 4.5 Rate of births and marriages, 1933–39

Year	Number of marriages	Live births
1932	516,793	933,126
1933	638,573	971,174
1934	740,165	1,198,350
1935	651,435	1,263,976
1936	609,631	1,277,052
1937	618,971	1,275,212

C. W. Guillebaud (1939). *The Economic Recovery of Germany: From 1933 to the Incorporation of Austria in March, 1938.* London: Macmillan.

(B) In his address to the National Socialist Women's Section on 8 September 1934, Hitler summed up the Nazi view of the woman's position in society:

If one says that man's world is the State, his struggle, his readiness to devote his powers to the service of the community, one might be tempted to say that the world of woman is a smaller world. For her world is her husband, her family, her children and her house. But where would the greater world be if there were no one to care for the small world?...Providence has entrusted to women the cares of that world which is peculiarly her own.... Every child that a woman brings into the world is a battle, a battle waged for the existence of her people....

N. Baynes (1942). *Hitler's Speeches, Vol. 1* (pp. 528). Oxford: Oxford University Press.

(C) The historians J. Noakes and G. Pridham wrote the following on Nazi policy towards women and work:

By 1936–37, however, as the rearmament boom and the reintroduction of compulsory labour service and conscription in 1935 made themselves felt, a labour shortage began to develop, and it became clear that women provided the main untapped source of labour. In this situation the regime was forced to do an about turn: having previously discouraged women from going to work, it now had to encourage them to do so. From now on its anti-feminist ideology and the requirement of the labour market worked at cross purposes.

J. Noakes and G. Pridham (eds) (Date1984). *Nazism, 1919–45, Vol.2: State, Economy and Society, 1933–39* (p. 463). Exeter: University of Exeter Press.

(D) In 1934 the Nazi Advice Centre for the Improvement of Genetic and Racial Health published the 'Ten Commandants for the Choice of a Spouse':

1 *Remember you are a German*

2 *If you are genetically healthy you should not remain unmarried*

3 *Keep your body pure*

4 *You should keep your mind and spirit pure*

5 *As a German choose only a spouse of the same or Nordic blood*

6 *In choosing a spouse ask about his ancestors*

7 *Health is also a precondition for physical beauty*

8 *Marry only for love*

9 *Don't look for a playmate but for a companion for marriage*

10 *You should want to have as many children as possible*

J. Noakes and G. Pridham (eds) (1984). *Nazism, 1919–45, Vol.2: State, Economy and Society, 1933–39* (p. 463). Exeter: University of Exeter Press.

(E) The Security Service of the SS reported in 18 November 1943 on the impact the war was having on the family:

... Many women are also concerned that the stability of their marriages and the mutual understanding of their partners is beginning to suffer from the lengthy war. The separation which, with short breaks, has now been going on for years, the transformation in their circumstances through total war and, in addition, the heavy demands which are nowadays made on every individual are changing people and filling their lives. When on leave, the front-line soldier often no longer shows any understanding for his family's domestic circumstances, which are governed by the war, and remains indifferent to the many daily cares of the home front. This often produces an increasing distance between the married couple. Thus wives often point out that having looked forward to being together again during their husband's leave, the occasion is spoilt by frequent rows caused by mutual tensions. That even happens in marriages which were previously models of harmony... .

J. Noakes and G. Pridham (eds) (1998). *Nazism 1919–45, Vol. 4: The German Home Front in World War II* (pp. 360–62). Exeter: University of Exeter Press.

Were the lives of the workers transformed?

Hitler claimed that in creating the People's Community he had 'broken with a world of prejudices' and created equality between the 'workers of the brain and fist'. Was this in fact a myth? How integrated were the workers into the People's Community? Were they effectively 'in a great convict prison', to quote the former SPD trade union leader Wilhelm Leuschner, or did they benefit from the new regime?

Hitler claimed he had set the workers free from their unpatriotic union and political leaders and had given them a more respected place in society. However, in reality they were forced to join the Labour Front and their bosses, who were now called 'plant leaders', had much more power over them. Elected Councils of Trust were set up in all factories where there were more than twenty workers, but after the 1935 elections they were abruptly ended because the workers were electing representatives whom the Nazis considered to be politically 'unreliable'. In theory a Council of Trust could take an employer to a Court of Social Honour provided it had the support of the local Labour Trustee, an official appointed by the Ministry of Labour, but this seldom happened. Between 1934 and 1936 there were only 616 cases out of a workforce of well over 20 million.

Welfare capitalism

This is the practice of privately owned businesses looking after their workers by providing higher wages and services such as health care and pensions.

Though the Labour Front was primarily an instrument for controlling the workers, it also carried out what Hitler called 'socialism of the deed'. To achieve this aim it set up two sections which owed much to the experiments in **welfare capitalism** in the 1920s:

- The 'Beauty of Work' scheme, headed by Albert Speer (see page 107), attempted to persuade employers to make their factories a more humane environment by, for example, installing swimming baths, showers and canteens. By 1939 nearly 70,000 companies agreed to such improvements.
- The other section, 'Strength Through Joy' (KDF), was a leisure organisation. Its aim was, as its head **Robert Ley** observed, to dispel boredom as from it 'sprang stupid, heretical, yes, in the end criminal ideas ...'. It organised concerts and plays for the workers and arranged subsidised cruises or holidays in the German countryside.

One of the most popular projects of the KDF was the ***Volkswagen*** (VW) car. Work started on it in the summer of 1938. Workers were offered a savings scheme to enable them to purchase the car. However, cars would only be delivered *after* the final payment had been made. By 1940, 300,000 people had signed up, but production was halted by the war and the cars were not produced until after it ended. The workers' money was used to finance the war industries.

In 1933 the Nazis took control of most private charities and the welfare funds of the Communists and the SPD. The National Socialist People's Welfare organisation was set up to promote 'the living, healthy forces of the German people', which meant that asocials or anyone other than 'Aryans' would be excluded! By 1939 it had over 17 million members and had developed an extensive network of nurseries for children, holiday homes for mothers, and it provided food for large families. Along with the KDF it was arguably the most popular party organisation in Nazi Germany. But it was also feared by the poor as it had no compunction in calling in the *Gestapo* to deal with alcoholics and the work shy.

To what extent were workers able to exploit full employment?

Full employment, which one German historian, Franz Neumann, called Hitler's 'sole gift to the masses', gave workers economic power which even in the Third Reich they were able to exploit. In 1936 there was an increase in **go-slows** and absenteeism, and an outbreak of lightning strikes forced the regime to take steps to control the situation. However, workers breaking their contracts with their employers to move on to better paid jobs were liable to have their **work books** confiscated, as without them they could not be legally employed. In June 1938, in an effort to stop employers attracting workers from one another's factories by offering them higher wages, the Trustees of Labour were given the power to fix uniform wage levels in key industries. Labour conscription was also introduced to direct workers towards particular industries. A final deterrence was the terror of the *Gestapo* and 'the camps of education for work', which were almost as brutal as the concentration camps. However, these measures failed to halt rising wages in the armaments industries, where workers managed to exploit the conditions of full employment and win concessions from the employers. These concessions included increased overtime rates or a large Christmas bonus.

The workers and the war, 1939–45

Workers exempted from conscription because they were needed for work in the war industries experienced opportunities and frustrations on the home front. After 1942 they needed to adapt to new mass production work practices introduced by Speer (see page 102) and to being evacuated to factories relocated out of the range of Allied bombers. The threat that they could be ordered to fight on the Eastern Front and their dependence on employers for extra rations instilled a discipline that, unlike in 1918, was maintained despite the

BIOGRAPHY

Robert Ley (1890–1945)

Ley was the leader of the Reich Labour Front. He joined the NSDAP in 1924 and became a Nazi member of the *Reichstag* in 1924. He committed suicide in 1945.

Volkswagen

The people's car.

Goslows

These occur when workers who have a grievance use certain tactics to slow down production or a service.

Work books

A document containing details of a person's work place and employer, etc.

ACTIVITY

To what extent were the workers integrated into the People's Community?

abolition of overtime payments and the extension of the working week to 60 hours in 1944. Opportunities for promotion to supervisor or foreman was also possible given the massive inflow of inexperienced workers and foreign labour.

How did the workers respond to the huge influx of foreign labour? Those working in factories were involved in the surveillance and repression of foreign workers. Many foreign workers were treated brutally, especially after air raids, but there were instances of decent and humane treatment. In general most German workers were preoccupied with their own problems and had little time to worry about the foreign workers. As the historian Ulrich Herbert has written: ' the foreigners were simply there, as much part of wartime life as ration cards or air raid shelters ...Their own privileged position as Germans vis-à-vis these workers was likewise nothing exceptional, certainly no cause for misgiving.'

The peasantry

The peasantry was ambivalent about the People's Community. Though Nazi propaganda portrayed them as the blood stock of the German nation, the labyrinthine bureaucracy of the Reich Food Estate and the often negative impact of the Reich Entailed Farm Law (see page 97) in practice rapidly disillusioned the peasantry. By 1934 peasant farmers were hostile to the Nazis. However, they did little about their grievances. As the historian Richard Evans comments, 'what really mattered to them was that they were making a decent living, better than they had done in the Depression years, and they could live with that'.

Nazism appealed more to the younger rural generation. Their view of the world was broadened through belonging to organisations of the Nazi Party, such as the Hitler Youth, the Labour Service and then the army, and the opportunities for jobs in the cities and towns as a result of rearmament. Village life, however, particularly in south Germany, was not seriously affected by the Third Reich. Loyalty to the village community and to the Catholic Church came before politics.

ACTIVITY

To what extent were the peasantry loyal members of the People's Community?

The *Mittelstand* and professional classes

The *Mittelstand* expected much from the Nazis. But they were disappointed economically (see pages 95–97); by 1935 they were complaining about increased taxation, the burdens of paper work and the shortage of raw materials. However they recognised the improvements under the Nazis since the Depression, and this checked their discontent from turning into a more serious mood.

ACTIVITY

What did the Mittelstand and professional classes gain from the people's community?

White-collar workers and salaried employees resented the abolition of their trade unions and being forced to join the Reich Labour Front, as they saw themselves superior to the workers. In spite of this they were grateful to Hitler for having crushed 'Marxism', and they tended to blame the Nazi Party rather than Hitler for their troubles.

Members of the professions, such as doctors, dentists and lawyers, were aggrieved at a loss of independence as their professional associations were closed down and brought under Nazi control. Certain professions, particularly law and teaching, were downgraded in importance, while others, like the army and medicine, gained in prestige.

ACTIVITY **Enquiries**

Compare Sources A and B.

Compare these sources as evidence for the success of the Nazis in destroying traditional workers' organisations and cultures.

Sources

(A) The following report by the SOPADE, the German Social Democratic Party in Exile, in 1935 comments on how the Nazis managed to destroy the class solidarity of the workers:

The National Socialists are well aware that the sense of solidarity is the source of the working class's strength, and as a result the aim of all their measures, whether directed for or against the workers, is to stifle the sense that solidarity... The National Socialists have now reduced the worker to the point that he often goes to the boss on his own to try to avert a deterioration in wages, especially over piece rates, and gets a concession out of the boss on the condition that he tells his workmates nothing about it. One often has the impression, particularly with young workers, that the idea no longer even occurs to them that their demands might carry more weight if backed by collective action – even if only on the smallest scale.

D. Peukert (1989). *Inside Nazi Germany. Conformity, Opposition and Racism in Everyday Life* (p. 114). London: Penguin.

(B) If the workers became too threatening in their demands, employers could always send for the *Gestapo*, as the following SOPADE report of January 1939 on a factory in Silesia shows:

The company D reduced the piece work rates in the lathe shop, the paint shop, and for the boilermakers without having previously informed the workforce. This produced a storm of protest and work came to a halt as groups of workers met to discuss the issue. The works manager charged furiously through the plant ordering people to resume work. When this had no effect, he shouted to the workers: 'Go and see the Trustee, he ordered the reduction'. He vanished and phoned the Gestapo which came at once. There were informers among those involved in discussions who denounced to the Gestapo those stirring up opposition. Twenty-two workers were arrested and taken to the Brown House in Görlitz. The other workers were threatened with immediate dismissal and transfer to forced labour in the event of repetition. In the meantime 8 out of 22 have been released. They did not, however, return to the factory but had to go to fortification works in the West.

J. Noakes and G. Pridham (eds) (1984). *Nazism, 1919–39, Vol. 2: State, Economy and Society, 1933–39* (pp. 368–39). Exeter: University of Exeter Press.

Conclusion

Theoretically all members of the Community were equal, but the reality was different. Big business and industry prospered and made huge profits, but the workers' wages were strictly controlled. On the other hand they certainly appreciated the security of full employment and used the facilities of the KDF and the National Socialist People's Welfare organisation. Older workers were more resistant to Nazism, but many younger workers for whom the Hitler Youth had provided new opportunities took advantage of retraining and transferred to more skilled jobs. Material benefits like longer holidays and low heating and lighting costs were popular, and many workers admired Hitler's foreign policy successes. It was Hitler's popularity and the initial economic and foreign policy successes, such as the *Anschluss* of Austria in 1938, that consolidated the *Volksgemeinschaft*.

ACTIVITY

Period Studies

'The People's Community was essentially a confidence trick; it was held together by terror.'

How far do you agree with this assessment of the People's Community?

Herrenvolk

The ruling or racially dominant people (volk).

Untermenshen

Racially inferior people.

Euthanasia

This is the practice of putting an end to the life of a human being who is suffering from an incurable illness.

Congenital deformities

A disease or deformities existing from birth.

Genetic factors

These are genetically inherited factors.

ACTIVITY

What groups within Germany, apart from the Jews, were discriminated against by the Nazi regime?

What groups were excluded from the 'People's Community'?

The People's Community was composed of a racially homogeneous 'Aryan' people, **das Herrenvolk**, whose health and racial purity were at all costs to be protected. A series of laws increasingly discriminated against Jews, ethic minorities and those Germans who were judged to be of 'lesser racial value' or **unteremenschen**.

Euthanasia

Given the desire for a racially pure Community, the existing pure 'blood stock' of Germany needed to be protected. In one way this was to be achieved by preventing those with incurable illnesses from having children. This involved invoking a policy of **euthanasia**. From the winter of 1938–39, euthanasia was practised in great secrecy on children with **congenital deformities**, when 5,200 were gassed; a few months later it was extended to adults. When the practice became public knowledge, it was condemned by the Bishop of Munster in August 1941 and was halted. But it was secretly restarted later and was soon extended to foreign workers judged to be suffering from incurable physical illnesses, racially 'inferior' babies of eastern European women working in the Reich, terminally sick prisoners from the prisons, and sometimes even to German soldiers suffering from incurable shell-shock.

The asocials

The Nazis believed that criminal and asocial behaviour such as alcoholism or prostitution, as well as sexual deviancy, were determined by **genetic factors**. So, anyone with these perceived 'disorders' had to be sterilised for the good of society, to prevent these conditions being passed on to future generations. The Law of November 1933 against Dangerous Habitual Criminals, for example, introduced the principle of compulsory castration for certain types of sexual offenders. Increasingly punishments and the treatment of people in prisons and concentration camps were determined by biological, or racial, criteria.

The persecution of homosexuals

Homosexuality flourished in the large cities of the Weimar Republic even though it was technically a criminal offence. To the Nazis homosexuality was degenerate and a threat to the Aryan race as it discouraged the birth of children. The murder of Röhm, a homosexual, on 30 June 1934 triggered a wave of homophobia in the Nazi Party and its organisations.

A special department was created in the *Gestapo* for dealing with homosexuals within the Party and in 1935 a much tougher law against homosexuality was announced. Raids and arrests were coordinated by a new Reich Central Office for the Combating of Homosexuality and Abortion. During the Third Reich a total of 50,000 homosexual men were arrested, two-thirds of whom were imprisoned. When released many were re-arrested and sent to the concentration camps.

The non-Jewish racial minorities

The sterilisation laws were extended in 1937 to apply to the small number of mixed race Afro-German children living in Germany. Some had been fathered by French African soldiers during the Rhineland occupation (see page 14–15); others were the children of German fathers and African women who had returned in 1919 from Germany's former colonies, which had been handed over to the League of Nations.

The Nazis inherited from the Weimar Republic a legacy of hostile policies towards the Sinti and Roma (gypsies). In 1935 an SS-financed research unit in the Ministry of Health came to the conclusion that 90 per cent of the Sinti and Roma were of mixed race and therefore likely to have criminal and asocial tendencies, and should therefore be sterilised. In September 1939 Himmler ordered the deportation of the 30,000 gypsies in the Reich to specially designated sites in occupied Poland. The programme was speeded up from December 1942 so that by 1945 only a few hundred had escaped being sent to Auschwitz.

Given the German minorities in Poland and Czechoslovakia, the Nazi government tolerated the **Sorbs** in Germany because of the possibility of retaliation. However the occupation of Czechoslovakia and of Poland in 1938–39 eliminated this threat, so the leaders of the Sorb and of the Polish communities in Germany were arrested and sent to concentration camps.

Sorbs

A Slavonic race related to the Czechs in south-eastern Germany and the poles.

The Jews

To the Nazis the Jewish 'threat' was in a class by itself. Although there were only 500,000 Jews in Germany in 1933, most of whom were fully integrated into German society and were patriotic Germans, they were seen by the Nazis to be plotting on a worldwide scale the destruction of Germany and the German people, and were the real power behind Bolshevism. Many anti-Semitic Nazis probably had never met a Jewish person in Germany, but in their minds, according to the historians Noakes and Pridham, they 'formed a propaganda stereotype, a collection of negative attributes representing the antithesis [opposite] of the qualities of a true German'. For most Nazis the Jews had attained the status of mythological demons, upon whom they focused their anxieties about the modern world.

To what extent did the German nation at that time as a whole share this view? From the 19th century anti-Semitism had been an issue in Germany. The Jewish businessman and writer Walther Rathenau (see page 22), writing in the 1890s, decribed the Jews 'as an alien secluded race in the middle of German life', which were only saved from the power of the law 'holding in check all natural violence'. While brutality against the Jews shocked most Germans, there was a general feeling that Jewish influence was somehow alien to German traditions and had grown too powerful during the Weimar Republic.

ACTIVITY

Why did the Nazis fear and hate the Jews?

Anti-Semitic policies, 1933–36

When Hitler first came to power he did not issue any policy directives on the Jewish question, but escalating violence by the SA against individual Jews and their property threatened to damage the Nazi government's reputation abroad. To avoid this Hitler attempted to channel the violence into a boycott of Jewish shops on 1 April 1933. This, however, was quickly cancelled when it failed to deter Germans from using Jewish shops and businesses, and met criticism both at home and abroad. Hitler then attempted to appease the Party by expelling the Jews from the civil service, the universities and journalism.

Party activists and the SA, however, continued to demand further action against the Jews. The Night of the Long Knives temporarily discouraged the SA from further measures, but by the summer of 1935 widespread violence against the Jews again broke out. Hitler's concern was that the regime was losing public support and that the attacks on the Jews would again alarm international opinion. His response was to announce to a specially summoned session of parliament at Nuremberg the notorious Law for the Protection of German Blood, forbidding marriage or sexual intercourse between Jews and German gentiles, and the Reich Citizenship Law, which deprived Jews of their German citizenship. A Jewish person was defined as somebody who had at least three out of four Jewish grandparents. Hitler's hope was that both laws would satisfy the Party and end the damaging attacks on Jews but they disappointed many Nazi fanatics who suspected that Hitler had accepted the advice from his civil servants rather than from the Party.

ACTIVITY
Period Studies
To what extent can it be argued that Nazi policy towards the Jews was surprisingly moderate, 1933–37?

The Nuremberg Laws actually ensured that anti-Semitism became more deeply embedded in German society. Jews were increasingly banned from restaurants, libraries, swimming pools and other public places. They were not allowed to employ women under 45 as servants, and sex between Germans and Jews was prosecuted at special courts as cases of 'racial defilement'. By the end of 1935 there was an improvement in the situation for Jews but only because Berlin was due to host the Olympic Games the following summer. The regime needed to project an image of unity and tolerance for the thousands of overseas visitors attending the Games.

Why did pressure increase on the Jews, 1938–39?

The improvement in how Jews were treated was short-lived. By the spring of 1938 Party activists demanded more radical measures against them, and Göring, as Commissioner of the Four Year Plan, wanted to confiscate their assets to help pay for rearmament. The nationalist mood stimulated by the *Anschluss* of Austria and the growing threat of war over Czechoslovakia also fuelled the demand by the Party for further action against the Jews. In the event of war the regime wanted to be rid of the 'enemy in its midst', which is how it perceived the Jews of Germany. To this aim a range of anti-Semitic decrees were promulgated:

- Jews with gentile names were compelled to add Jewish names, such as Israel or Sarah, to their existing names.
- Jewish dentists, doctors, lawyers, chemists and vets lost their right to accept non-Jewish clients, though they still could have Jewish ones.
- Jewish wealth and property had to be registered as a preliminary for expropriation by the state.

The turning point in the treatment of the Jews was the *Reichskristallnacht* (Night of Broken Glass) riots of 9–10 November 1938. After the riots, the Jews had to pay a collective fine of one and a quarter billion marks. They were forced out of their jobs, and in April 1939 what remained of their wealth was seized and they were also banned from using public buildings or places, such as theatres, beaches and parks. Jewish children who were still pupils in state schools were expelled. Reinhard Heydrich, the Chief of the Security Police and the SD, was given the responsibility for organising the future emigration of the 214,000 Jews who were still in Germany.

Reichskristallnacht or Night of the Broken Glass

The cause of this pogrom was the shooting on 7 November 1938 of Ernst von Rath, a junior diplomat in the German Embassy in Paris, by Herschl Grynszpan, a seventeen-year-old student, whose parents together with 17,000 other Jews of Polish descent had recently been expelled from Germany. Von Rath died of his wounds two days after the attack. To Hitler and the Nazi leadership it was the opportunity to drive the Jews out of Germany. 'Spontaneous' attacks on synagogues and Jewish-owned businesses were launched. Millions of marks of damage was inflicted and 30,000 Jews were imprisoned in concentration camps, although most were released a few weeks later. It is referred to as the Night of the Broken Glass because so many shop windows were shattered.

Figure 4.7 *Kristallnacht* marked a turning point in Nazi policy towards the Jews. This photo shows arrested Jews being taken through the streets of Baden-Baden on the day after Kristallnacht.

Apparently, on 12 November 1938 Hitler informed Göring, verbally through his Chief of Staff Martin Bormann and by phone, that 'the Jewish question [should] be now once and for all coordinated and solved one way or another'. However, he never publically associated himself with the anti-Semitic policies that followed the events of *Kristallnacht.* He maintained to foreign diplomats that he was actually preventing a general massacre of the Jews at the hands of the Germans! But on two occasions in January 1939 he made it clear what the fate of the Jews were. He told the Czech Foreign Minister of his intention to 'destroy the Jews', and soon afterwards made his notorious statement in the *Reichstag* that the outbreak of war would lead to the 'annihilation of the Jewish race in Europe'.

How should these remarks be interpreted? To the intentionalists they are evidence of Hitler's ultimate aims, but the structuralists remain unconvinced and argue that Hitler's words should not be taken too literally. Hans Mommsen, for example, argues that Hitler 'considered the "Jewish question" from a visionary political perspective that did not reflect the real situation', and is convinced that Hitler was stirring up a ritual hatred of the Jews, rather than announcing a definite plan for the Holocaust.

On the other hand, by January 1939, Hitler was facing the prospect of war with a fast rearming Britain and France. They were both supplied with equipment and loans from the USA, which he regarded as dominated by the Jews. His threat to annihilate the Jews in Europe, if war broke out, can therefore be seen as an announcement that in the event of war, the Jews would be hostages in a German-dominated Europe, and if necessary murdered.

ACTIVITY
Period Studies

To what extent did *Reichskristallnacht* mark a fresh stage in Nazi anti-Semitic policy?

The Holocaust

With the outbreak of war on 3 September 1939 the nature of the 'Jewish problem' for the Nazis changed dramatically. Up to now there were only a few hundred thousand Jews in Germany, Austria and Bohemia. But with the German conquest of Poland another three million more Jews came under Hitler's power. To deal with the problem the Reich Security

Holocaust

Literally this means 'a sacrifice totally consumed by fire or a burnt offering'. The word is deliberately used to distinguish the massacre of the Jews from all other massacres and to emphasise its horrendous nature.

Head Office (see page 81) planned under Heydrich to create Jewish reservations and ghettos in occupied Poland. There the Jews could be resettled from Germany and the former Polish territories which had been annexed to the Reich. However, the scale of resettling hundreds of thousands of people in wartime forced Göring to halt the programme in March 1940.

Meantime the German government continued to encourage German Jews to emigrate; nearly 80,000 did so. After defeating the French in June 1940 the Nazis planned resettling the European Jewish population in the French colony of Madagascar; however this was impossible given Britain's unwillingness to make peace and the Royal navy's control of the Indian Ocean.

Plans for resettling Jews in Madagascar and Siberia

The planned 'resettlement' of Jews in Madagascar, and later in Siberia, was not an alternative to extermination. The vast majority of Jews would have perished from disease on Madagascar, so, to quote the German historian Hermann Graml, mass murder would be 'given the appearance of a natural process'. Significantly, Philipp Bouhler, who had been in charge of the euthanasia programme in Germany, would have been the Nazi governor of Madagascar.

As an alternative the German authorities returned to the idea of resettling the Jews in camps and ghettos in occupied Poland. This caused serious logistical problems, as it coincided with the military build-up for the invasion of Russia. However Hitler refused to halt the deportation programme and overruled the suggestion that the Jews in Reich territory should work in the local war industries.

The invasion of Soviet Russia in June 1941 was a turning point in Nazi policy towards the Jews; it led to another three million Jews coming under Nazi control. The war now became an ideological war directed at the extermination of 'Jewish Bolshevism'; by the spring of 1942 over a million Russian Jews had been murdered. Undoubtedly these massacres signified an escalation in Nazi policy towards the Jews and prepared the way for the Holocaust.

When did the Nazis decide to drop the plans for resettlement in favour of systematic extermination in the death camps? Structuralists argue that this was inevitable when it became clear that the war in Russia would not be won quickly. With the German army waging a massive war against the Bolsheviks, the main priorities in Poland and western Russia were supplying the army with the equipment and men to fight. Resettling millions of Jews in Poland would only create acute organisational problems as they would have to be housed and fed. For the German historian Martin Broszat the Holocaust 'was a "way out" of a blind alley into which the National Socialists had manoeuvred themselves'.

The intentionalists understandably regard this as downgrading the Holocaust to an unforeseen consequence of the military situation in eastern Europe. By late 1941 so many Nazi plans were being issued for the eventual extermination of the Jews that it is more than likely, to quote the historians J. Noakes and G. Pridham, that 'a green light was coming from the highest level' – that is, Hitler. At the very least, it was clear to senior Nazis and officials that he favoured such policies. Arguably, this was sufficient to guarantee that they would 'work towards the *Führer*' (see page 76) and ensure that the policies would be carried out.

The intentionalist-structuralist debate

The intentionalists, particularly Lucy Dawidowicz, Klaus Hildebrand, Karl Dietrich Bracher and Daniel Goldhagen, argue that Hitler from the beginning *intended* the mass murder of the Jews, even though he could not do it immediately. Structuralist scholars, such as Martin Broszat, Hans Mommsen and Karl Schleunes, do not dispute Hitler's anti-Semitism, but they argue that the Holocaust was a result of the chaotic way in which Nazi Germany was administered. They argue that the bureaucracy and Nazi leaders competed with each another in formulating anti-Semitic policies which led to ever-more radical policies being implemented. Understandably, the intentionalists are highly critical of what they regard as attempts to depersonalise the responsibility for what ultimately led to the Holocaust. Dawidowicz describes this as initiating a new 'cycle of apologetics' in German history.

The historians Burleigh and Wippermann argue that the structuralists focus so much on the 'chaotic details of the regime's administrative details that one loses sight of the motive force and consensual climate' which brought about the Holocaust. This view is forcefully supported by Daniel Goldhagen, who stresses that the majority of the German population was to a greater or lesser extent anti-Semitic and consequently at the very least passively condoned the persecution of the Jews and ultimately the Holocaust.

In January 1942 at the Wannsee Conference in Berlin details were drawn up for the mass conscription of Jews into labour gangs in eastern Europe, where it was assumed that 'a large number will drop out through natural elimination'. The remainder would then be 'dealt with accordingly'. Extermination camps with gas chambers were constructed in 1942 at Belzec, Sobibor and Treblinka, and in 1943 two more death camps were opened at Majdanek and Auschwitz. Estimates place the final death toll at nearly six million.

ACTIVITY

Period Studies

To what extent did the outbreak of war make the Holocaust inevitable?

Conclusion

We have seen that one of the main principles of the People's Community was to create and preserve a racially pure Germany. This strategy was carried out in two ways:

- Mothers and young women were to be instructed in the importance of hygiene and bringing up healthy families.
- All those who threatened the German race were to be excluded from the People's Community.

These threats could come from a distinct racial group like the Sorbs, the gypsies or the African Germans, or from asocials, homosexuals and those with inherited diseases which could be passed on to their children. Protecting the Community involved sterilisation, imprisonment in concentration camps or euthanasia.

In a different category were the half million German Jews who were feared and hated by Hitler and the Nazis as an enemy of Germany. It was Hitler's intention to free Germany and then Europe from the Jews. How this was to be accomplished wasn't clear until German war successes in 1939–42 left most of Europe's Jews at his mercy.

ACTIVITY **Enquiries**

1 Study Sources A and B.

Compare these sources as evidence for Hitler's belief that the Jews were plotting to destroy Germany.

2 Study all the sources.

Use your own knowledge to assess how far the sources support the view that Hitler had always intended to wipe out the European Jewish population.

Sources

(A) In *Mein Kampf* Hitler argued that the Jews would try to use Marxism to destroy Germany:

In the organised mass of Marxism he [the Jew] has found the weapon which lets him dispense with democracy and in its stead allows him to subjugate and govern the peoples with a dictatorial and brutal fist.

Adolf Hitler, *Mein Kampf*, edited by D. C. Watt (1974) (pp. 295–96). London: Hutchinson.

(B) In a speech delivered to the *Reichstag* on 30 January 1939 Hitler warned the Jews of their fate should war break out:

Today I will once more be a prophet: If the international Jewish financiers in and outside Europe should succeed in plunging the nations into a world war, then the result will not be bolshevisation of the earth and thus the victory of Jewry, but the annihilation of the Jewish race in Europe!

N. Baynes (1942). *Hitler's Speeches*, 1922–39, Vol. 1 (p. 741). Oxford: Oxford University Press.

(C) Heydrich issued the following orders to the commanders of the *Einsatzgruppen*, or mobile task forces, which moved into the USSR behind the front line on 23 June 1941:

All of the following are to be executed:

Officials of the Comintern ... top and medium-level officials and radical lower-level officials of the Party, Central Committee**, and district and sub-district committees,*

The people's Commissars

Jews in Party and state employment, and other radical elements (saboteurs, propagandists, snipers, assassins, inciters, etc.)....

M. Burleigh (2000). *The Third Reich* (p. 602). London: Macmillan.

* The Communist International, which organised Communist parties outside the USSR

** One of the key governmental committees of the USSR

(D) Although Göring and the Reich Ministry of Labour were pressing for the employment of eastern European Jews in the German war industries in February 1931, on 22 April 1941 Hitler vetoed the request. An official of the Reich Ministry for Armaments and Munitions issued this statement:

Following a directive from the *Führer*... there should be no attempt to transfer Jews from the east to the Reich for use as labour.

It is thus no longer possible to contemplate using Jews as replacements for labour which has been withdrawn, particularly from the building sector and from textile plants.

J. Noakes and G. Pridham (eds) (Date 2001). *Nazism 1919–45, Vol. 3: Foreign Policy, War and Racial Extermination* (p. 1084). Exeter: University of Exeter Press.

E Heydrich had been given responsibility by Göring in November 1941 to draw up plans 'for the complete solution of the Jewish question in Europe'. On 20 January 1942 key officials met secretly to discuss the matter in Wannsee, Berlin. The following is an extract from the minutes prepared by Eichmann:

In pursuance of the final solution, the Jews will be conscripted for labour in the east under appropriate supervision. Large labour gangs will be formed from those fit for work, with the sexes separated, which will be sent to those areas for road construction and undoubtedly a large number of them will drop out through natural wastage. The remainder who survive – and they will certainly be those who have the greatest powers of endurance – will have to be dealt with accordingly. For if released, they would, as a natural selection of the fittest, form a germ cell from which the Jewish race could regenerate itself. (That is the lesson of history).

In the process of carrying out the final solution, Europe will be combed through and through from west to east...The evacuated Jews will be initially brought in stages to so-called transit ghettos in order to be transported from there further east ... .

J. Noakes and G. Pridham (eds) (Date 2001). *Nazism 1919–45, Vol. 3: Foreign Policy, War and Racial Extermination* (p. 1131). Exeter: University of Exeter Press.

Review questions

1 To what extent did the Nazis create a united People's Community underpinned by a strong economy?

2 Assess the principles according to which the People's Community was formed.

3 To what extent did Germany undergo an economic miracle under the Nazis, 1933–45?

4 'For the German workers the Third Reich was one great prison camp.' How far do you agree with this view?

5 To what extent was rearmament the main aim of Hitler's economic policy?

6 Who benefited from Nazi domestic policy?

Exam**Café**

Relax, refresh, result!

Relax and prepare

Hot tips

Jemail

I found that I couldn't seem to please my teacher, who kept on telling me what I could have written better. I talked to other people not only at my own college but in other schools. They all agreed. I came to realise that there isn't a right answer and that the teacher wasn't actually getting at me, she was just pointing out some different ideas. This was a big breakthrough. Don't expect there to be just one approach – that is why the subject is interesting.

Hailey

At first I found it difficult to link up the sources with the question. I was describing them far too much and not picking out the right parts. It really helped me to use a highlighter to show the key sentences and then I didn't necessarily use them in the same order as they were in the passage but I though about which were the most important.

Refresh your memory

'To what extent did the Nazis transform German society?'

Racial purity and anti-Semitism: 1933–42

▷ Be aware of Nazi racial views and ideas on racial purity and the mission of the Master Race.

▷ You should know how early measures fell short of total segregation of Jews and 'Aryans'.

The Nuremberg Laws

▷ Be aware of the legal definitions of Jews and that Jews were not allowed to be citizens of the Reich.

Kristallnacht

▷ Be aware that by 1938 the regime was becoming more radical and of the importance of the attacks on Jews in November, which led to more measures against those who had not emigrated.

The decision to implement the Final Solution

▷ The war increased the problems of Jews in Germany and gave the Reich control over millions of Jews in eastern Europe. There is a considerable controversy about the so-called 'Final Solution' that led to the mass murder of Jews. Some think that it was not planned from the beginning of Hitler's political life but evolved when alternative 'solutions' (such as the forced emigration of Jews to Madagascar) was clearly not possible; others see a 'War against the Jews' as an aim from at least the end of the First World War.

Period studies

This key issue lends itself to questions that ask 'how successful?' was a particular aspect of Nazi policy; for example: 'How successful was Nazi economic policy?'. Weaker answers will simply describe what the Nazis did, whereas better answers will focus on 'how successful'.

In answering a question such as this, the introduction plays a crucial role. In the introduction it is important to establish the criteria against which success will be judged: this could be the aims or the results. Each paragraph can be related back to them, making a judgement about each issue. The conclusion should then draw together the judgements reached on each issue and reach an overall verdict. If the aims were being considered it would include issues such as: winning support, building up German military might and achieving autarky. Better answers would also suggest that the emphasis changed over time and that therefore the extent of success changed during the period. However, this is not the only approach and candidates could look at the policy from the point of view of different groups within society, for example big business, the *Mittelstand*, workers and farmers.

Consider this introduction which approaches the following question through examining the aims of Nazi policy.

Exam question

How successful were Hitler's economic and social policies, 1933–45?

Get the result!

Sample answers

Examiner says:

This introduction focuses on the question and establishes a clear set of criteria for changing the policies. The answer is therefore less likely to be chronological but more thematic.

Jasmine's answer:

In order to judge the success of Nazi economic policy it is essential to establish their aims so that economic developments can be judged against them. Hitler had come to power largely as a result of the consequences of the Depression and therefore his main aim was to restore Germany to full employment. This would win Hitler much support and help consolidate the Nazi regime. At the same time economic recovery would mean more resources would be available and this would allow Hitler to rebuild German military power, allowing him to pursue his other priority of territorial expansion. In order to achieve this Hitler believed that it was important for Germany to be self sufficient and geared for war; this was seen as essential following the disasters of the blockade during World War One.

Examiner says:

Jasmine hints also at some prioritisation of factors, suggesting a main aim and also establishing links. This makes it easier for Jasmine's essay to reach a conclusion about '**how successful**'. If the main aims have been achieved then the policy can easily be shown to have been a success, whereas if only more minor aims were achieved the essay can conclude that the policy was less successful as the more important aims were not achieved.

Enquiry studies

Don't neglect the instruction 'using your own knowledge' in enquiry study questions and don't rely too much on the sources. The mark scheme refers to 'excellent evaluation of sources by the use of appropriate contextual and independent knowledge'. Really good answers will link the assessment of sources with knowledge and realise that the sources may be interpreted in different ways. Interpretation: this is a key word that was used at GCSE. It means linking what is in the sources to the key issue in the question.

The following question requires careful evaluation of the sources in relation to the key issue, with links needed to your own knowledge. The full question has five sources on the Nazis' decision to implement a 'Final Solution' and these source part (a) of the question and a full model answer to both parts can all be found on your CD-ROM.

Exam question

(b) Study all the sources.

Use your own knowledge to assess the interpretation that the decision to implement the Final Solution arose mainly from a long-standing and widespread hatred of the Jews.

Sources

(A) A Socialist Party agent, working underground, comments on reactions to the Nuremberg Laws of 1935 and anti-Jewish propaganda.

The recent Jewish laws are not taken very seriously as people have other problems on their mind. But many are influenced to see the Jews as starting all bad things. They have become fanatical opponents of the Jews. The vast majority of the population, however, ignore the anti-Jewish propaganda and even show this by preferring to shop in Jewish department stores. Many still regard the Jew as a friend.

(SOPADE *Reports*, 1936)

(B) A member of the girls' section of the Hitler Youth analyses her own reaction to the events of *Kristallnacht* in Berlin (10 November 1938) on the morning after it had happened. Her account was written to a lost childhood Jewish friend after the Second World War.

To my surprise almost all the shop windows were smashed. A policeman explained: 'In this street they're almost all against Jews. I said to myself: 'The Jews are the enemies; they should take the events of last night as a warning.' As the years went by, I grew better at switching off quickly. I totally identified myself with National Socialism.

(Melita Maschmann, *Account Rendered: A Dossier of My Former Self*, 1964)

Think about what these sources are saying about the key issue – the key phrases are **long-standing** and **widespread hatred of the Jews**. Here is the first part of an answer to question (b); the rest of the answer can be found on the CD-ROM.

Jemail's answer:

Source A shows that not all of Germany had a long-standing hatred of the Jews, as it says that the Nuremberg laws were not taken seriously. They were not a priority for people in 1935 and evidence is given of people continuing to shop at Jewish shops. The Boycott of 1933 had been unpopular and this seems to support this view.

Examiner says:
There is some use of knowledge here.

Hatred did not seem to be widespread as the report states that the vast majority of the population did not respond to the propaganda. The source is clearly not taking too optimistic a picture, despite being written by a member of the SPD, as it does say that some people were influenced to see Jews as starting all bad things.

Examiner says:
There is careful linkage of points in the source with the words of the question.

Source B on the other hand shows that people had hatred of the Jews and had broken windows and damaged houses. The policeman tells the young girl that in the street the people were all against the Jews. There may be some doubt about the hatred being long standing.

Examiner says:
The question is referred to helpfully.

The division of Germany after 1945 and the establishment of Communist rule in the GDR up to 1963

Source

Returning prisoners of war were often virtually unrecognisable even to their own families. As one twelve-year-old put it, in a letter to a schoolfriend, describing the return of her father from internment:

You can't believe how miserable Daddy looked! He had disgusting old rags and a rough Russian coat on and a dirty Russian cap... Add to this the skeletal face, the shorn-off hair and – the voice!... [T]he voice repelled me so much, that I simply couldn't say 'Daddy' to him. I can hardly describe to you how strange it was! So nervous, so ill and – and I don't know, just so terribly strange!... Naturally he is totally undernourished, had a double lung inflammation, and barely escaped death... He is terribly nervous. But we thank God that He sent Daddy back to us at home at all!

Brigite Reimann (1995). *Aber wir schaffen es, verlaß dich drauf! Briefe an eine Freundin im Westen. (pp. 16–17)*. Berlin: Elefanten Press. Translated by and quoted in Mary Fulbrook (2005), *The People's State: East German Society from Hitler to Honecker* (p. 27). London: Yale University Press .

Key Question:

This chapter will focus on the post-war occupation and division of Germany in the period 1945–49, and on the establishment of Communist rule in the East German state up to 1963, and answer the following key questions:

- Why and with what consequences was Germany divided after the Second World War?
- To what extent and in what ways did Communism transform the GDR?
- How far and in what ways were the economy and social structures changed?
- Sealing the division? The Berlin Wall, 1961.
- What were the interpretations of the transformations of East Germany under Communist rule, 1945–63?

FRG
The Federal Republic of Germany

GDR
The German Democratic Republic

Stasi
The East German secret security system

The Third Reich, at the height of its power, covered vast areas of central Europe. A mere four years after its defeat, much of this territory had been lost entirely to the Soviet Union and to Poland; and what remained was divided into two quite different, ideologically opposed states: the **FRG** in the West, and the **GDR** in the East. The FRG, enlarged by the absorption of the former GDR in the German reunification of 1990, continues to exist as a highly successful democracy today; and even the GDR, despite its collapse in the revolution of 1989, lasted for forty years, far longer than the Weimar Republic and Third Reich put together. In comparison with the turbulence and instability of the first half of the 20th century, German history in the post-1945 period is quite remarkable in its stability.

How different were the eastern and western zones of post-war Germany already at the time of the formation of two separate states in 1949? And in what ways was East German society in the GDR subsequently transformed under a Communist dictatorship of very different ideological colours from the Nazi dictatorship which had preceded it? Were East Germans forcibly repressed by the secret security service, the **Stasi**, and by the highly fortified

borders which prevented flight to the West, or did some of them actually come to terms with and support the new regime? How were they changed by their experiences of a new dictatorship, so soon after the Nazi dictatorship had collapsed?

Why and with what consequences was Germany divided after the Second World War?

Why was Germany divided in 1949? This did not seem to be on anyone's firm agenda for defeated Germany in 1945. An answer to this question must therefore look both at what happened in the course of Allied occupation, and at the wider international context during the early post-war years.

Germany in 1945

With Hitler's suicide at the end of April 1945, a new German government was briefly formed, signing an unconditional surrender on 8 May; but the new government was rapidly disbanded by the victorious Allies, who took over joint control of occupied Germany.

In May 1945, German cities lay in ruins. As the victorious Allies took control, many leading Nazis committed suicide, fearful of what the future might hold in store. Other Germans were more concerned about everyday life, and only too willing to forget the past as quickly as possible.

The devastations of aerial warfare had left hundreds of thousands homeless. Millions of people were on the move, seeking to return to their homes across Europe from periods as prisoners of war, or as foreign slave labour, or as a result of evacuations. Civilians from German territories east of the Oder river had fled westwards in advance of the Red Army coming ever closer to the capital of the Reich in the closing months of the war; and in the summer of 1945, millions of others followed, forcibly expelled by the new post-war authorities in the now lost eastern territories. Villages and towns where refugees were billeted often found their resources overstretched, with competition for scarce food and housing, overcrowding and ill-health.

ACTIVITY

Compare and contrast the condition of Germany at the ends of the First and Second World Wars.

The wretched physical and psychological condition of exhausted German refugees, or those who were victims of bombing and devastation, paled in comparison with the situation of the few surviving former concentration camp inmates, reduced to skeletal shadows, who now found themselves 'liberated' but barely able to move, walk or eat, and whose agonies were compounded by the loss of so many members of their families and communities in the work camps, ghettoes and gas chambers of Nazi Germany. The effects of this trauma are still palpable across the generations, scattered across the world today.

Hitler's 'Thousand Year Reich' had ended in destruction and suffering on a monumental scale. When the Allies rolled in, they were devastated by what they found.

At first, the Allies had no collective plans for post-war Germany. As far as the Americans were concerned, US Treasury Secretary Henry J. Morgenthau's 1944 proposal to turn Germany back into a largely agrarian state, destroying its industrial capacity to wage any further modern war of destruction, never became official American policy. The American ban on any 'fraternisation' of soldiers with Germans lasted little more than a couple of weeks after the occupation started in May 1945. And western notions of the 'collective guilt' of all Germans were also relatively short-lived. The priorities of occupation soon took precedence.

Soviet soldiers in the early months of occupation engaged in mass rape and robbery, taking highly emotional individual revenge for the suffering previously inflicted on their country by Hitler's barbarous ideologically driven warfare in the east. Around one in three women in Berlin, for example, appears to have been raped by Soviet troops. And the Communists soon sought to take close control of developments in their zone. But the records suggest that Stalin at first kept his options open with respect to the future of Germany.

Figure 5.1 Refugees returning to a devastated Berlin in search of homes, August 1945.

There were many immediate needs: to ensure an adequate supply of food and fuel, to reconstruct the transport system and provide energy and lighting, to rehouse the homeless who had been bombed out or fled from homes elsewhere, to try to ensure a degree of sanitation and public health. But there were also long-term major questions which had to be dealt with:

- How could Germany's political system be rebuilt on a more democratic basis, so that this kind of catastrophe could never happen again?
- How should Nazis and the threat of Nazism be dealt with, to ensure there was no resurgence of aggression?
- How should German militarism be contained, not only immediately but for the foreseeable future, given the repeated experiences of German aggression and the use of military force for political purposes in 1864, 1866, 1870, 1914, and 1939?
- How could the German economy be rebuilt, while at the same time ensuring that reparations were made to the powers which had sacrificed so much to fight the evils of Nazism?

The Potsdam Agreement of August 1945

In the summer of 1945, the American, British and Soviet heads of government, accompanied by their foreign ministers and advisers, met at Potsdam, in the beautiful setting of a small princely estate on the lakeside southwest of Berlin. At this meeting the USA was represented by **Harry Truman**, following Roosevelt's death in April 1945; British war-time Prime Minister Winston Churchill was, following the British general election which took place during the course of the meeting, replaced by the new Labour Prime Minister Clement Attlee and his Foreign Secretary Ernest Bevin; only the USSR's **Josef Stalin** remained as the long-term experienced representative of his state.

The French were not present at this meeting, but it was decided that they too should be given a zone of occupation. Given that the borders of the zones had been drawn up during the war, the French zone was carved out of territory in south-western Germany that had been initially allotted to the Americans and the British.

The Soviet zone – which included territory initially occupied by the American military forces and from which they had to withdraw – remained intact. The eastern boundary of the Soviet zone ran along the River Oder and the western branch of the River Neisse, thus giving a significant area of what had formerly been German territory to the newly reconstituted state of Poland, which had, in turn, lost much of its own eastern territories to the Soviet Union. Berlin, the former capital of the Reich, was also to be under four-power control, with respective sectors of influence.

What did the Allies agree on?

The victorious powers at Potsdam were in agreement on broad principles. Germany would be administered under joint Allied control. It should be demilitarised, denazified, and democratised. The economy should be administered as one unit, but each occupying authority should take reparations from their own zone of occupation. Since the Soviet zone was less well endowed with industrial production and natural resources than the economically more advanced western zones, it was allowed to take additional reparations from these areas.

Demilitarisation

The German armed forces were immediately disbanded following their total surrender in May 1945. Given that the German government was also dissolved, it was not possible for Germany under Allied occupation to have any kind of independent military force. Even after the foundation of two new states in 1949, neither side was initially allowed an army. It was not until 1955-56, and amid much controversy, that new armies were founded in the two new German states – this time with opposing political and ideological profiles, and under the strict control of the respective occupying powers, in the context of NATO and the Warsaw Pact military alliances respectively.

BIOGRAPHIES

Harry Truman (1884–1972)

The 33rd President of the United States (1945–53) who pursued the policy of providing military and economic aid to countries that were susceptible to Communist influence.

Josef Stalin (1879–1953)

The leader of Soviet Russia (1928–53) who participated in the post-war conferences that led to Soviet control over those eastern and central European territories liberated from the Germans. His foreign policies after the war contributed to tensions between the USSR and the West that became known as the Cold War.

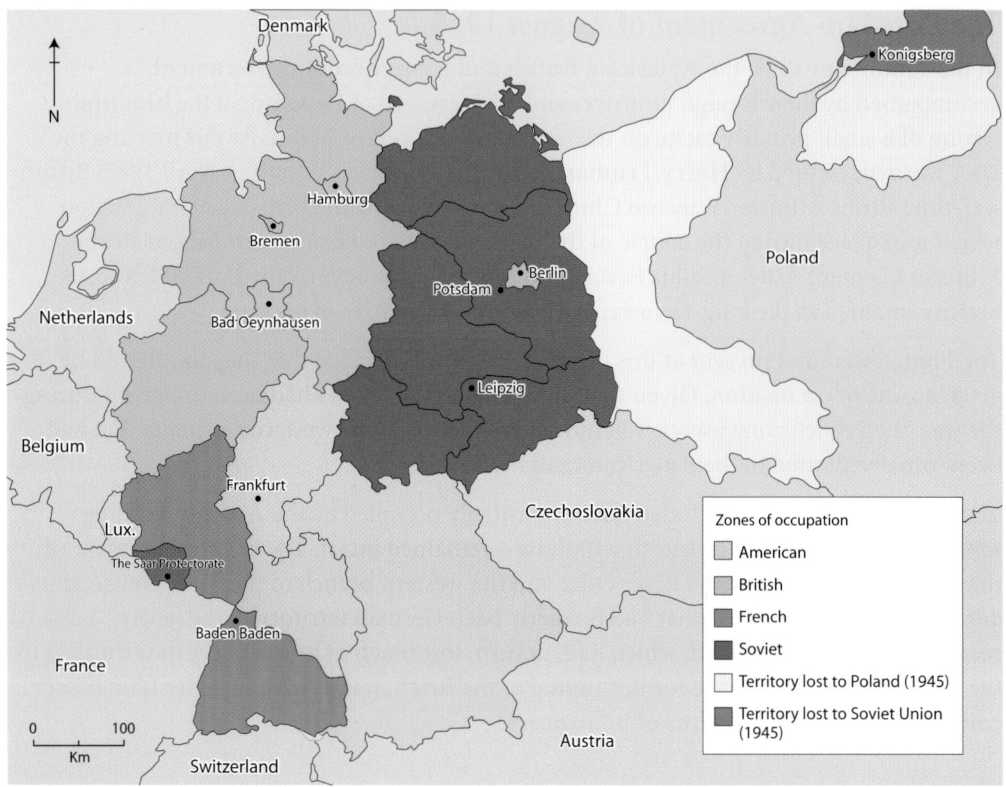

Figure 5.2 Germany divided into the four zones of occupation, summer 1945, with areas handed over to Poland and to the Soviet Union.

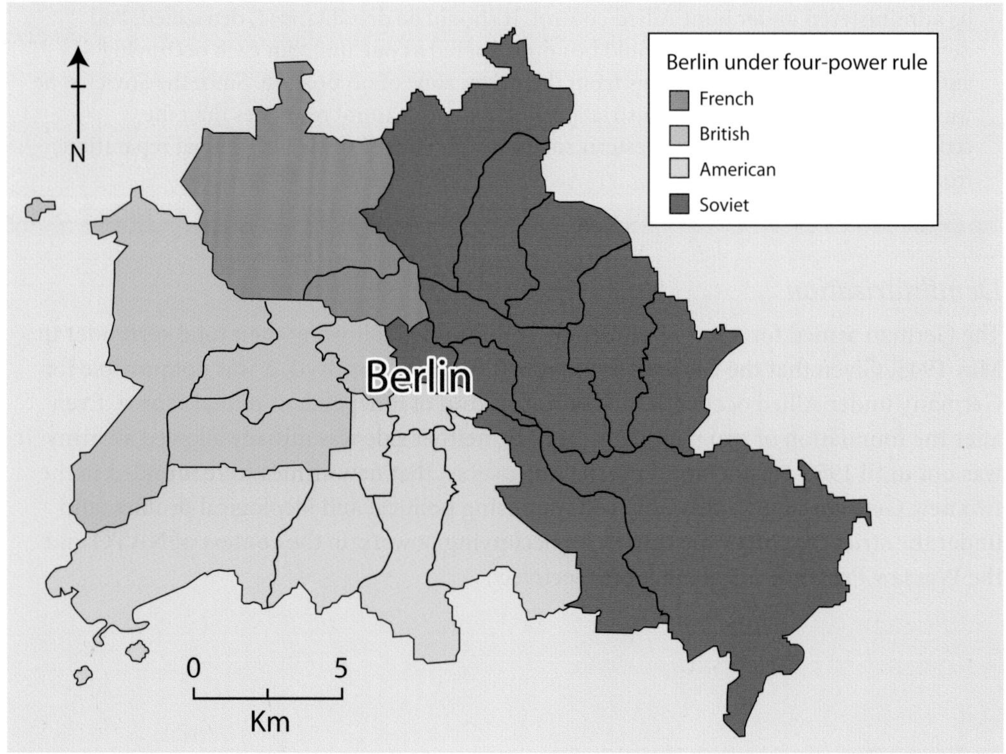

Figure 5.3 Berlin under four-power control.

'Democratisation'?

The Nazi Party (NSDAP) was immediately disbanded – and it had, of course, been the only political party in Nazi Germany. But while the Allies were all very clear on what they were against, they were by no means agreed on what should replace the Nazi system.

Politics in the Soviet zone of occupation

Already at the end of April 1945, a small group of German Communists under the leadership of **Walter Ulbricht**, who had survived the war in exile in Moscow, flew into the ruins of Berlin, seeking to make contacts and take political control on the ground.

One of the members of the 'Ulbricht group', Wolfgang Leonhard, who later defected to the West, described Communist tactics to gain control in Soviet-occupied Berlin in the early summer of 1945 as 'democratic, but we must keep everything under control'.

BIOGRAPHY

Walter Ulbricht (1893–1973)

The Communist leader of the German Democratic Republic (East Germany) from 1949 to 1971. After the war he played a key role in the reconstruction of the German Communist Party along Stalinist lines and as leader of the country he embarked on a programme of restructuring the GDR's economy.

ACTIVITY ***Enquiries***

Study Sources A and C.

Compare these sources as evidence that the Communists never intended to remain democratic in their approach.

Sources

(A) Ulbricht explaining the early role of the Communists in Berlin:

Ulbricht explained that:

'The local government administrations have to be put together correctly, as far as politics is concerned. We can't use Communists as Mayors… In working-class districts the Mayors should be Social Democrats. In the bourgeois areas … we have to put a bourgeois person in at the top, someone who used to belong to the Centre Party, or to the Democratic or the German People's Party. Best of all, if he has the title of Doctor; but at the same time he has to be an anti-fascist and a man with whom we can work well together…

And now as to our own comrades. The first Deputy Mayor, and the person in charge of personnel questions, and the person in charge of education – those must be our people. And then you must also find a totally reliable comrade in every district whom we can use for building up the police force…'

…In his classic Saxony accent he gave us the final, conclusive instruction:

'It's obviously quite clear: It has to appear to be democratic, but we must keep everything under our control.'

Now everything really was clear.

Wolfgang Leonhard (1955). *Die Revolution entläßt ihre Kinder* (pp. 315–17, translation by MF). Munich: Wilhelm Heyne Verlag.,

(B) The KPD's founding declaration:

We are of the opinion that it would be wrong to impose the Soviet system forcibly upon Germany, because this path does not accord with the current conditions of development in Germany.

We are rather of the view that the decisive interests of the German people in the current situation prescribe a different path for Germany, and that is the path of establishing an anti-fascist, democratic regime, a parliamentary-democratic Republic with all the democratic rights and freedoms for the people.

At this historic turning point we Communists call to all working people, to all democratic and progressive forces among the people, to join this great struggle for the democratic renewal of Germany, for the rebirth of our land!

Rolf Steininger (ed.) (1996). *Deutsche Geschichte seit 1945, Vol. 1* (p. 188, translation by MF). Frankfurt am Main: Fischer Taschenbuch Verlag.

(See next page for Source C.)

(C) The characteristics of a Party of a New Type are:

The Marxist-Leninist Party is the conscious avant-garde of the working class....

The Marxist-Leninist Party is based on the principle of democratic centralism. That means firmly upholding the principle of election of the leadership and functionaries and the accountability of the elected to the members. The strong party discipline, which springs from the Socialist consciousness of the members, is based on this internal party democracy.

Party decisions are valid for all party members without exception, and particularly for those party members who are active in parliamentary bodies, in governmental and administrative organs, and in the leadership of the mass organisations.

Democratic centralism means the development of criticism and self-criticism in the Party, and monitoring of the stringent carrying-through of decisions by the leadership groups and members.

Matthias Judt (ed.) (1998). *DDR-Geschichte in Dokumenten* (p. 46, translated by MF). Berlin: Christoph Links Verlag.

The Soviet military administration in Germany (SMAD) was, in its Order No. 2 of 10 June 1945, the first to license the official formation of political parties in its zone, not least to legitimise the already very active KPD. Despite its not entirely democratic tactics, the KPD's founding declaration was surprisingly open in tone and message.

Very soon after the KPD was refounded, the Social Democratic Party (SPD) followed suit. The KPD and the SPD merged in 1946 to form the SED. A number of liberal parties joined together to form the Liberal Democratic Party of Germany (LDPD), while the former Catholic Centre Party and a variety of Protestant conservative parties came together to form the CDU.

However, within three years, the SED (Socialist Unity Party) had given up any pretence of democracy in the western sense, and, in the crucial year 1948–49, openly proclaimed that it was a **Marxist-Leninist** 'Party of a New Type'.

Marxist-Leninist

The view that was inspired by Karl Marx's commitment to the overthrow of capitalism by a proletarian revolution, but which also took from Lenin the notion of the 'leading role of the Party', since the masses could not necessarily be relied on to know what was in their own long-term best interests.

BIOGRAPHIES

Karl Marx (1818–83)

A German philosopher who is regarded as the founder of Communism, which was the idea that a society should be one in which people cooperate rather than compete with one another. This is achieved through the common ownership of the means of production which inevitably leads to the destruction of social classes.

Vladimir Lenin (1870–1924)

Lenin was a Russian Marxist revolutionary who led the Bolshevik Revolution in October 1917 and became the first leader of the Soviet Socialist Republic.

The SED increasingly sought to gain control of the other parties in the Soviet zone, and even set up two entirely new ones, to appeal to those who would never commit themselves to a left-wing working-class party or to the CDU or LDPD. The National Democratic Party of Germany (NDPD) was designed to target and incorporate former Nazis, while the Democratic Peasants Party of Germany (DBD) was oriented, as its name suggested, to the constituency of peasants. All parties were to be brought together in a supposedly united 'anti-fascist bloc' or 'National Front' in the common fight against the remnants of Nazism.

Additionally, a number of so-called 'mass organisations' were formed in the Soviet zone, covering culture, youth, women, the trade unions and so on. All of these, too, were increasingly under Communist control openly.

The political parties in the Soviet zone of occupation (1945–49) and German Democratic Republic (from 1949):

SED Socialist Unity Party: the leading Communist Party, formed in April 1946 out of the union of the **KPD** and the **SPD**

The 'bloc' parties (all increasingly under the control of the SED):

LDPD Liberal Democratic Party of Germany

CDU Christian Democratic Union

NDPD National Democratic Party of Germany

DBD Democratic Peasants Party

Politics in the western zones of occupation

The formation of political parties and organisations in the western zones of occupation took place very much more 'from the ground up'. People who wanted to form a political party had to be based at a local or regional level, and apply to be granted a licence. Only those parties that were committed to democracy were allowed. The British Military Government issued a directive on 15 September 1945 to this effect.

ACTIVITY

What were the problems faced by the Allies in seeking to reintroduce democracy in post-Nazi Germany?

Source

In order to encourage the development of a democratic spirit in Germany and prepare free elections for a date yet to be appointed, the following directives are issued herewith:

Art. 1. Formation of political parties

1 *Political parties can be formed in a district (Kreis) according to the provisions contained herein.*

2 *The military government can allow parties which have been formed according to these directives to unite with one another in larger areas…*

3 *Membership in political parties must be voluntary.*

C. C. Schweitzer et al. (eds) (1984). *Politics and Government in the Federal Republic of Germany: Basic Documents* (p. 11). Leamington Spa: Berg.

As in the Soviet zone, in the western zones the SPD and KPD quickly refounded themselves. The western branches of the SPD however totally opposed any merger with the KPD, and so after its foundation in 1946 the Communist-dominated SED was not able to make any inroads in the western zones.

The various former Christian and conservative parties eventually agreed to come together to form a party known in most areas of West Germany as the CDU (Christian Democratic Union), but in Bavaria the party was called the Christian Social Union (CSU). The CSU retained a separate regional identity throughout the history of the FRG. Somewhat unlike western European conservative parties, the CDU had an openly Christian view of society, informing its later views on the 'social market economy' of West Germany.

ACTIVITY
Period Studies
To what extent did the political systems in the Soviet and western zones of occupation differ even before the foundation of two separate states?

A multitude of liberal parties popped up all over the western zones, eventually coming together as the Free Democratic Party (FDP), something of a chameleon party combining certain liberal principles with some very right-wing views and business interests.

There were also a number of smaller parties representing, for example, refugee organisations (such as the League of Expellees and Refugees, the BHE), and far right-wing groups. These stayed, for the most part, within the democratic framework laid down first by the Allies and subsequently by the West German 'Basic Law' or constitution of 1949, although the right-wing Socialist Reich Party (SRP) and the Communist Party of Germany (KPD) were eventually banned. One of the small parties which later disappeared, the German Party (DP), helped to form the first CDU-led coalition government along with the CSU and FDP.

Denazification
The attempt, by all the occupation zones, to root out or convert former Nazis.

'Denazification'?

One of the most significant questions was what to do with the millions who had actively supported Hitler's murderous regime.

Major war criminals were brought to some form of justice in the Nuremberg war crimes trials, which lasted from November 1945 to October 1946. But those tried, including Göring, Hess and Speer, were only a handful of the hundreds of thousands who had made the Nazi system function. The question of how to deal with them was far less clear.

The first reaction, in both the Soviet and western zones, was mass internment of people who had held significant political responsibility in the Third Reich, or leadership positions in organisations such as the SS. The US Directive JCS 1067, which set out US occupation policy right at the start, sought to remove former Nazis from all positions in society.

Source

The US Directive JCS 1067:

All members of the Nazi Party who have been more than nominal participants in its activities, all active supporters of Nazism or militarism and all other persons hostile to Allied purposes will be removed and excluded from public office and from positions of importance in quasi-public and private enterprises...Persons are to be treated as more than nominal participants in Party activities and as active supporters of Nazism or militarism when they have (1) held office or otherwise been active at any level from local to national in the Party and its subordinate organisations or in organisations which further militaristic doctrines, (2) authorised or participated affirmatively in any Nazi crimes, racial persecutions or discriminations, (3) been avowed believers in Nazism or racial and militaristic creeds, or (4) voluntarily given substantial moral or material support or political assistance of any kind to the Nazi Party or Nazi officials and leaders. No such persons shall be retained in any of the categories of employment listed above because of administrative necessity, convenience or expediency.

Beat Ruhm von Oppen (ed.) (1955). *Documents on Germany under Occupation 1945–55* (p. 17). London: Royal Institute of International Affairs.

ACTIVITY
In what ways was the early US directive JCS 1067 undermined and why?

But very soon this policy appeared to be impracticable. Denazification turned into a policy, not so much of cleansing Germany of Nazis, but of cleansing individuals of the taint of Nazism.

In the western zones, by the spring of 1946 the policy had become one of seeking individual motives and dealing with denazification on a case-by-case basis, through use of a detailed questionnaire or *Fragebogen*. Since the penalties in terms of imprisonment or fines could be severe, it was in people's interests to downplay their Nazi pasts, and to present what became popularly known as 'persil certificates' or affidavits from colleagues and friends assuring the

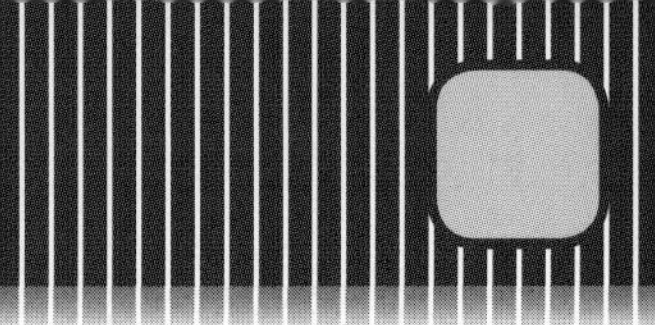

authorities of their clean consciences and good characters, exchanging (often quite literally as well as metaphorically) their old Nazi brown shirts for new white ones. This was hardly the way to achieve any kind of genuine confrontation with the past. Once the task was handed over to the German authorities, many former Nazis managed to escape entirely without penalty or needing to account for their acts. Some indeed were assisted in their escape by virtue of their usefulness to the western authorities in the new anti-Communist crusade.

In the Soviet zone, there were at first mass internments, with many deaths caused by appalling conditions in the re-used former Nazi concentration camps of Buchenwald and Sachsenhausen as well as elsewhere. Real or imagined political enemies of all colours, as well as outright former Nazis, might be subject to sudden arrest and internment. But a distinction was, as in the western zones, soon made between 'active' and purely 'nominal' Nazis. The latter, insofar as they were willing to commit themselves to the new Communist system, were from 1947 welcomed back into political life. Because of the growing emphasis on being the 'anti-fascist state', which had been 'liberated' by the Red Army, East Germany was relatively easily able to downplay issues of Nazism and guilt, at least in official proclamations.

The Marxist view of history suggested that not only a change in personnel, but also major structural changes were required to ensure that Nazism could never arise again. Denazification in the Soviet zone was thus very closely related to economic restructuring.

Economic restructuring or a form of 'denazification' in the Soviet zone

The Communists used denazification partially as a pretext for major socioeconomic changes. The theory was that Nazism had arisen as a form of fascism, which was allegedly the last gasp of **monopoly capitalism** in crisis. To deal with the roots of Nazism thus meant abolishing capitalism as a system in its entirety.

Monopoly capitalism
A Marxist term for the supposedly final stage of capitalism.

In September 1945, larger landed estates (over 100 hectares in size, around 247 acres, or somewhat over one-third of a square mile) and property belonging to former Nazis were confiscated and redistributed among landless agricultural labourers, refugees, and others (including some state ownership). In the course of 1945–46 banks and factories were taken over too. Some were taken into Soviet ownership as Soviet stock companies (SAGs), which later became part of the GDR state system. Some equipment was simply dismantled and taken straight back to the Soviet Union for reparations. The Soviets even went so far as to kidnap experts and scientists who were needed in the Soviet Union to reconstruct technical equipment which had been taken from German soil with little know-how on the Soviet side concerning how to put it together again!

Diverging approaches

There was no such radical restructuring in the western zones. Indeed, some German initiatives for partial nationalisation were rebuffed. Although there were gestures towards the kind of decentralisation of the economy that had been urged at Potsdam, these did not go very far.

The first three years after the war were years of immense economic deprivation and hardship. Indeed, in order to feed the population in its zone of occupation, the British even had to reintroduce rationing at home. The harsh winter of 1946–47 saw famine on a massive scale in Germany. As people hoarded fuel and food, money became almost worthless, and cigarettes, stockings and chocolate, as well as personal favours and formerly

prized possessions, became widespread currency. Those who lived on the land, or who were unemployed and hence able to go out scavenging, were often better off than those with wages, working in towns.

Bizonia

A British–American merging of zones for ease of administration in 1947.

Trizonia

When the French joined Bizonia in 1949 it became known as Trizonia.

The difficulties of achieving economic recovery led to pressures to relax inter-zonal boundaries. In 1947 the British and Americans merged to form **Bizonia**, an economic unit which could be administered in common. The French at first resisted, but eventually came to join what now became **Trizonia** with effect from the beginning of 1949. The capitalist economy of West Germany was effectively resuscitated with little change in either structure or personnel, quite unlike the situation in the East.

Growing divergence between the economies of the western and the Soviet zones, as well as disputes over Soviet reparations from the western zones, led to greater tensions between the western powers and their former Soviet Allies.

Figure 5.4 Soviet soldiers overseeing the taking of reparations, in the rather unusual form of cows, through the ruined streets of Berlin.

Why was Germany divided in 1949?

It was clear already in the early months after the end of the war that there was fundamental distrust building up between the Allies – distrust which had, perhaps only tactically, been kept under control while the principal goal was to defeat the common enemy of Nazism.

Among western historians, the traditional view was that Stalin had evil designs to spread Communism in a bid for eventual world domination. Revisionist historians argued that the Cold War was stirred up more by US fear of Communism than by any realistic analysis of the Soviet threat at the time: following the devastating experiences of German invasion and destruction, the Soviet Union was in no economic shape to seek any kind of expansion or commit military resources to new conflicts. Furthermore, the US stood to gain both economically and politically by its new interventionist role in Europe and the wider world. Current thinking suggests at least that Stalin was keeping his options open at the time.

The Cold War, the Truman Doctrine and the Marshall Plan

By the spring of 1946, the Western Allies claimed that the Soviets were seeking to expand their sphere of influence. Former British Prime Minister Winston Churchill famously articulated this concern in his 'Iron Curtain' speech, delivered in Missouri on 5 March 1946 (see Source A).

ACTIVITY — ***Period Studies***

1. 'At the present moment in world history nearly every nation must choose between alternative ways of life.' How far do you agree with this view?
2. To what extent was the Truman Doctrine the **main** reason for the stablilisation of West Germany?

Sources

(A) Winston Churchill outlines his views on the emerging Communist influence:

From Stettin in the Baltic to Trieste in the Adriatic, an iron curtain has descended across the continent. Behind that line lie all the capitals of the ancient states of central and eastern Europe... and all are subject, in one form or another, not only to Soviet influence but to a very high and increasing measure of control from Moscow... [I]n a great number of countries, far from the Russian frontiers and throughout the world, Communist fifth columns are established and work in complete unity and absolute obedience to the directions they receive from the Communist centre... .

Reprinted in Martin McCauley (ed.), (1983).*The Origins of the Cold War* (pp. 114–15). Harlow: Longman.

(B) US President Truman's speech to Congress, 12 March 1947:

At the present moment in world history nearly every nation must choose between alternative ways of life. The choice is too often not a free one.

One way of life is based upon the will of the majority, and is distinguished by free institutions, representative government, free elections, guarantees of individual liberty, freedom of speech and religion, and freedom from political oppression.

The second way of life is based upon the will of a minority forcibly imposed upon the majority. It relies upon terror and oppression, a controlled press and radio, fixed elections, and the suppression of personal freedoms.

I believe that it must be the policy of the United States to support free peoples who are resisting attempted subjugation by armed minorities or by outside pressures.

I believe that we must assist free peoples to work out their own destinies in their own way...

The seeds of totalitarian regimes are nurtured by misery and want, They spread and grow in the evil soil of poverty and strife. They reach their full growth when the hope of a people for a better life has died.

We must keep that hope alive.

The free peoples of the world look to us for support in maintaining their freedoms...

Great responsibilities have been placed upon us... .

Reprinted in Martin McCauley (ed.) (1983). *The Origins of the Cold War* (pp. 121–22). Harlow: Longman.

Fear of Communist expansion in south-eastern Europe led directly to the Truman Doctrine in which it became a major US foreign policy goal to prop up governments fighting for 'freedom' against Communist influence.

ACTIVITY

How important was the Marshall Plan to the transformation of West German politics as well as to the country's economy?

A further strand in US anti-Communist 'containment' policy was that of ensuring a basic level of material well-being in countries which were potentially exposed to Communist takeover through the ballot box. The Americans assumed that discontented people were more likely to succumb to the attractions of Communist political propaganda than were well-fed and satisfied workers. Thus they were prepared to put material resources into the reconstruction of the post-war European economy in the **Marshall Plan.**

On 5 June, 1947, US Secretary of State George C. Marshall delivered a speech at Harvard University announcing very generous financial aid for war-torn Europe – but only on certain terms. The Soviet Union, as expected, refused to agree to these terms.

The Marshall Plan

The Marshall Plan involved a very generous package of economic aid to those European countries which were prepared to meet certain conditions with respect to convertible currencies, market economies, and mutual economic cooperation. West Germany was a principal beneficiary of Marshall Aid, which included not only monetary benefits but also a wider impact in terms of training programmes and the 'Americanisation' of industrial management styles. This assistance played a key role in defusing social discontent and turning potential 'class warfare' into reformist trade unionism in West Germany. The USA benefited from the reduction in the threat of Communism as well as profiting economically from involvement in the Western European economic recovery.

Currency reform and the Berlin blockade

The black market was so prevalent that in June 1948 a currency reform introducing the new Deutschmark (DM) had to be introduced in the western zones before American aid could be effectively introduced. Again, the Soviets refused to effect the currency reform in the Soviet zone of occupation. Instead, within days of the introduction of the western Deutschmark into West Berlin, a new currency, the East German mark, was introduced into East Berlin and the SBZ.

The Soviet Union now also sought to cut off West Berlin – which formed a little island under the control of the three western Allies within the larger surrounding zone which was the SBZ – from the western zones of occupation. The Soviet authorities blocked all transport links by air, road, rail or waterway from the western zones to West Berlin, hoping to starve out the West Berliners and force the incorporation of this part of Berlin into the Soviet sphere of influence.

The Allies responded with what became known as the Berlin Airlift, repeatedly flying provisions in from the West. Parcels of flour, milk, medicine, other foodstuffs, fuel – and at Christmas, small parcels and presents for children – were dropped in rapid succession at Berlin's Tempelhof airport, and a new airport was rapidly built in the Tegel area of French Berlin to allow even more planes (popularly known as 'raisin bombers') to land. The airlift was maintained for very nearly a year, from late June 1948 until the Berlin blockade was called off by the Soviets in May 1949. During this time, the western attitude to Berliners ceased to be one of hostility and suspicion, as Berlin was symbolically transformed into the last outpost of western democracy in a sea of Communism.

The Berlin blockade proved to be a key turning point in relations between the former war-time Allies. From now on, the key issue for the USA and Britain was the defence of western democracy against the communist threat; the protection of West Berlin, without provoking a third World War, became a central symbol of the Cold War. In retrospect, this was the moment when the division of Germany was effectively sealed. From the summer of 1948 onwards, western discussions were focussed not on how to deal with Nazism, nor on whether there would or should be political division, but rather on pragmatically developing a constitution for a new West German state.

Bizonia, Trizonia and the formation of two German states

Whatever view one takes of the origins of the Cold War on the wider stage, a major question must be that of why the 'Iron Curtain' should end up running through the middle of Germany, dividing post-war Germany into two hostile states. Rather than a united neutral Germany – as was the case with Austria, where four-power occupation ceased in 1955 – two separate states were formed, each integrated increasingly closely into the respective Cold War spheres of influence.

By the time the Berlin blockade was finally called off, the fate of German division had been sealed. It was increasingly clear that ever-closer economic cooperation in the western zones required greater political control and direction. By the spring of 1949 France had joined the British and American economic sphere, Bizonia, to become part of an economic unity, Trizonia, in distinction to the Soviet zone.

From the summer of 1948, as relations with the Soviet Union deteriorated, a meeting of western representatives in a 'Parliamentary Council' had sought to devise a constitution for a new democratic capitalist state. In May 1949, four years after the defeat of Hitler's 'Thousand Year Reich', the Federal Republic of Germany came into existence.

In October 1949, in direct response to developments in the West, the German Democratic Republic was formed in what had been the Soviet zone of occupation.

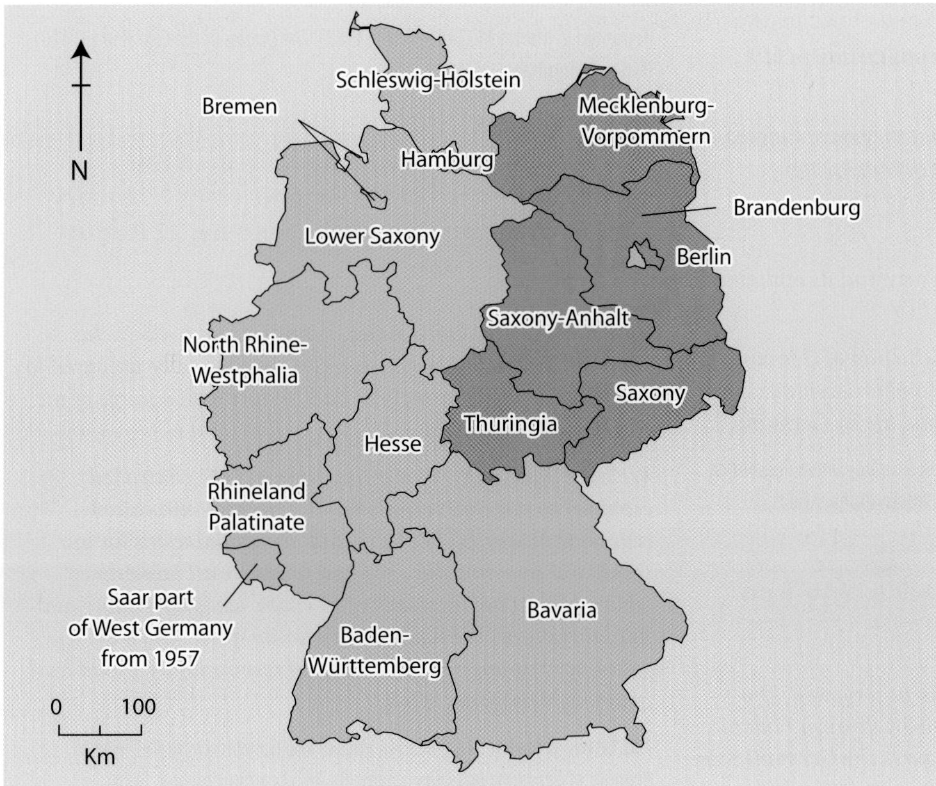

Figure 5.5 The two German states in 1949, with the *Länder*.

ACTIVITY **Period Studies/Enquiries**

Study the sources on aspects of the Cold War and then answer the following:

(a) How far do you agree with the view that it was the Cold War that led to the division of Germany in 1949?

(b) Study sources B and E

Compare the sources as evidence for reasons why the establishments of Communist GDR may have been inevitable.

Sources

A An extract from the Potsdam Agreement, 1945:

Agreement has been reached at this Conference on the political and economic principles of a coordinated Allied policy toward defeated Germany during the period of Allied control.... German militarism and Nazism will be extirpated and the Allies will take in agreement together, now and in the future, the other measures necessary to assure that Germany will never again threaten her neighbours of the peace of the world...

The purposes of the occupation of Germany by which the Control Council shall be guided are:

i The complete disarmament and demilitarisation of Germany...

ii To convince the German people that they have suffered a total military defeat and that they cannot escape responsibility for what they have brought upon themselves...

iii To destroy the National Socialist Party and its affiliated and supervised organisations...

iv To prepare for the eventual reconstruction of German political life on a democratic basis and for eventual peaceful cooperation in international life by Germany.

Beat Ruhm von Oppen (ed.) (1955). *Documents on Germany under Occupation 1945–55* (pp.42–43). London: Royal Institute of International Affairs.

B Stalin's response to Churchill's 1946 'Iron Curtain' speech:

The following circumstances should not be forgotten. The Germans made their invasion of the USSR through Finland, Poland, Rumania, Bulgaria and Hungary. The Germans were able to make their invasion through these countries because, at the time, governments hostile to the Soviet Union existed in those countries. As a result of the German invasion... the Soviet Union's loss of life has been several times greater than that of Britain and the United States of America put together. Possibly in some quarters an inclination is felt to forget about these colossal sacrifices of the Soviet people which secured the liberation of Europe from the Hitlerite yoke. But the Soviet Union cannot forget about them. And so what can there be surprising about the fact that the Soviet Union, anxious for its future safety, is trying to see to it that governments loyal in their attitude to the Soviet Union should exist in these countries? How can anyone, who has not taken leave of his senses, describe these peaceful aspirations of the Soviet Union as expansionist tendencies on the part of our state?

Reprinted in Martin McCauley (ed.) (1983). *The Origins of the Cold War* (p. 116). Harlow: Longman.

C Ludwig Erhard, who had directed the Economic Council of the Bizonia since 1 January 1947, on the social market economy, 22 August 1948:

It isn't as if we had any choice, What we had to do in this situation was to loosen the shackles. We had to be prepared to restore basic moral principles and to start with a purge of the economy of our society.

We have done more, by turning from a State-controlled economy to a market economy, than merely introduced economic measures. We have laid new foundations for our social and economic life. We had to abjure all intolerance which, from a spiritual lack of freedom, leads to tyranny and totalitarianism. We had to strive for an order which by voluntary regrouping and a sense of responsibility would lead to a sensible organic whole.

C. C. Schweitzer et al. (eds) (1984). *Politics and Government in the Federal Republic of Germany: Basic Documents* (p. 14). Leamington Spa: Berg,.

 **A historian's view in 1995:**

[W]hat sealed the divergence of the Soviet from the western zones of occupation was the most heavily contested item in the Potsdam negotiations: reparations... Different reparations policies meant incompatible economic policies; incompatible economic policies led to different political structures. Slowly but inexorably each zone of occupation became a separate political unit.

Peter Pulzer (1995). *German Politics 1945–95* (p. 27). Oxford: Oxford University Press.

 **A historian's view in 2006:**

Although few details have transpired about Soviet plans for the post-war world, there can be little doubt that in the spring of 1945 the Kremlin had no appetite for exporting Bolshevism. After a monumental struggle that had cost it more than 20 million lives and nearly one-third of its national wealth, the Soviet Union desperately needed peace as a basis for its domestic reconstruction... New research has strengthened the view that the Kremlin's policy towards the defeated enemy was not based on a fixed scheme but designed to offer Stalin maximum flexibility... [Policy] was bound to be guided by two overriding goals: reparations; and lasting security against a new German threat.

Dirk Spilker (2006). *The East German Leadership and the Division of Germany* (pp. 19–21). Oxford: Oxford University Press.

To what extent and in what ways did Communism transform the GDR?

The GDR's constitution and political system

The GDR's constitution in 1949 was at first glance compatible with that of the FRG, on the assumption – at least at face value – that it was a temporary, provisional state, pending German reunification. While the constitution was revised in 1968, the pose of awaiting and working for reunification was at least formally maintained (with greater or lesser degrees of conviction) until international recognition of the GDR in the early 1970s, following which the constitution was revised again in 1974.

In the constitution of 1949, the GDR had a parliament, the *Volkskammer*, which claimed to be representative of the people, and an Upper House, the *Länderkammer*, which represented the five regions or *Länder*. There was initially a President, Wilhelm Pieck, who was the formal head of state, and a Prime Minister, Otto Grotewohl, as head of government. The role of President was replaced after the death of Wilhelm Pieck in 1960 by the collective Council of State (*Staatsrat*). The Prime Minister took less and less of a political role in comparison with the SED General Secretary.

The real political force remained the ruling Communist Party, the SED, with its General Secretary, Walter Ulbricht. The SED's political hierarchy ran from the General Secretary and the Politburo at the top, through the Central Committee (ZK), via the various regional and local levels through to the basic organisational units of the Party in the workplace or residential area.

The representatives of the people who served as members of the *Volkskammer* were not democratically elected in the western sense, for two reasons. First, the numbers of seats for each political party had been pre-allotted in advance of the elections, so the outcome in terms of representation of different parties was a certainty. Secondly, all the 'bloc' parties were increasingly under the control of the ruling SED, although it took some time for this to be effected, particularly in the provinces. But the SED's role as the 'leading party' was only officially enshrined in a new constitution in 1968; until then, and even afterwards, there was a formal pretence at a multi-party system.

ACTIVITY

How 'democratic' was 'democratic centralism' in the GDR?

'Democratic centralism'

The Marxist-Leninist principle that decisions taken at the centre should be passed down and implemented below; and that views and opinions at the grass roots should be influenced as far as possible by the Communist Party and should be closely monitored for evidence of the 'lack of clarity' or the 'influence of the Class Enemy'. Views at the grass roots should also be conveyed up to the central decision-makers to be taken into account.

'False consciousness'

The view that, under capitalism, people were influenced by bourgeois ideology in such a way that they did not fully understand their own class interests. The Communist Party was there to lead and to change people's views.

Given the relatively great power of the regions in the traditionally rather decentralised state of Germany (although Hitler had done a good deal to centralise government already in 1933–4), the *Länder* of the GDR were abolished in 1952 and replaced by somewhat more numerous and smaller local units, the *Bezirke*. These were easier to control by both party and state. The Upper House was abolished in 1958, several years after the abolition of the regions which it had pretended to represent.

A shadow 'state within a state' was that of the State Security Service (*Staatssicherheitsdienst*, often popularly known as the *Stasi*), founded in February 1950 to act as the 'sword and shield of the Party'. This was backed up by more visible armed forces: the 'People's Police in Barracks', which in 1956 became the National People's Army (NVA); the regular police forces and border guards; and, of course, the very visible presence (and threat) of Soviet tanks.

Even from the very beginning, '**democratic centralism**' in the GDR was very different from parliamentary democracy in the West. Yet many at the time saw the GDR as potentially the 'better Germany', run by people who were heroes of the 'anti-fascist resistance' to Hitler. There was little trust among Marxists for the silent majority of Germans who had supported Hitler, and great faith in the view that politics, art and literature should be put at the service of actively changing people's views. Marxists thought that people living in a capitalist system were suffering from '**false consciousness**' and needed re-educating by the Vanguard Party.

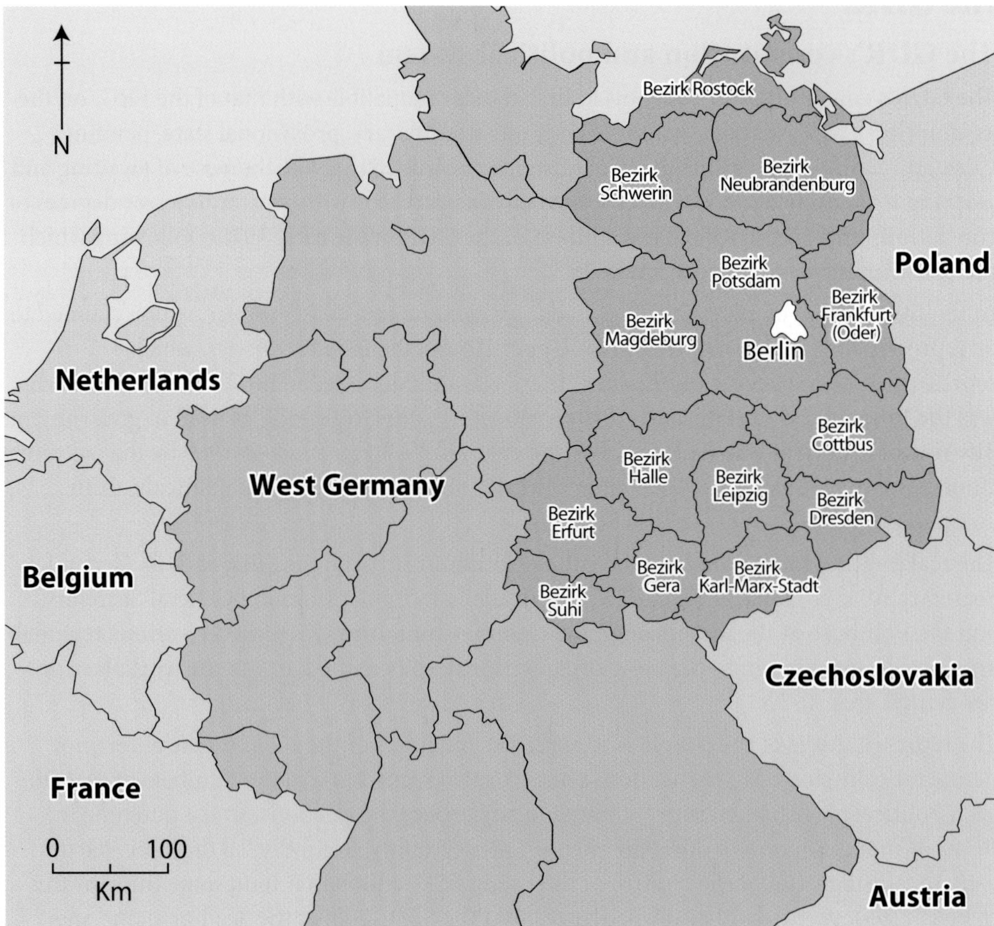

Figure 5.6 The GDR after 1952, with *Bezirke* (after the abolition of the *Länder* and their replacement with *Bezirke*).

Source

The writer Christa Wolf, who was born in 1929, reflecting on her experiences in the post-war years:

When we were fifteen, sixteen years old, and under the shattering influence of the whole truth about German fascism, we had to turn away from those who, in our opinion, had in these twelve years become guilty by virtue of their presence, their going along with it, their keeping silent. We had to discover those who had been victims, those who had actively resisted. We also had to learn how to identify with them. But of course we could not really identify with them either, we had no right to. That meant, when we were sixteen, we could identify with no-one. That is a major starting point for my generation… Then an attractive offer was made to us: You can, they said, get rid of or work off your not yet fully realised participation in this national guilt by actively taking part in the building up of the new society, which is the precise opposite, the only radical alternative to the criminal system of National Socialism… In addition to this, particularly for me but not only for me, came the close relationships with Communists, anti-fascists, who I met through my work in the Writer's Guild after 1953… .

Matthias Judt (ed.) (1998). *DDR-Geschichte in Dokumenten* (pp. 59–60, translated by MF). Berlin: Christoph Links Verlag.

Famous intellectuals, such as the writers Anna Seghers, Hermann Kant, and Bertolt Brecht, chose to live in the GDR rather than the West. And many younger people, socialised in the Hitler Youth organisations, barely knew where to turn. With a sense that their elders, who had been responsible for Nazism, were no longer to be trusted, many turned instead to supporting the new regime, aware that political constraints were only too necessary in the aftermath of the Third Reich.

But while some were genuinely convinced of the potential for the new state to transform the German people, many others were critical of the continued low standard of living and constraints in political freedoms in comparison with developments in the West.

Abandonment by the West

In the early 1950s, it was – despite the formal foundation of two separate states – still not entirely clear how long the 'temporary' division of Germany would last.

In 1952 Stalin, who was increasingly worried by West German Chancellor Konrad Adenauer's moves towards rapid integration in the western military and economic alliances, made a last-ditch effort to prevent the inclusion of the industrially powerful West German state in the American-dominated NATO camp. In a series of notes which many contemporaries as well as historians have seen as written more for public effect than as a genuine offer, Stalin proposed to give up the GDR in favour of a united, neutral Germany. Konrad Adenauer and the western powers chose to rebuff this advance as mere propaganda, and the chance for reunification was lost.

At the same time, within the GDR rapid social and economic changes were stirring up widespread unrest, and the need for increased protection and fortification of the inner-German boundary became ever more apparent to the SED leadership. In May 1952, a five-kilometre exclusion zone along the border between East and West Germany was created, with the forcible removal of 'unreliable' people from their homes and villages, and the erection of a firmer border fence and no-man's land.

ACTIVITY

What do you think were the most important features of the East German political system in the 1950s?

The uprising of 17 June 1953

Unrest was growing, with the tightening of the borders, the enforced collectivisation of agriculture, and the emphasis on enhanced productivity and more rapid change embodied in the 'Building of Socialism' which was announced in 1952. But following the death of Stalin in March 1953, ideas for a 'New Course' were circulating in Moscow; and the new leadership in the USSR was not happy with developments in the GDR.

At the beginning of June 1953, Ulbricht and other members of the SED Politburo were summoned to Moscow and asked to make changes. On returning to the GDR, quite contradictory announcements were made by the Politburo. While the middle classes were reassured, it appeared that the condition of workers would become worse: they were to produce 10% more ('raised work norms') while their wages would remain the same.

ACTIVITY

Why was widespread early opposition to the regime not successful?

The reversal of policy was announced quite suddenly, without the usual preparation of the party organs in the press and the provinces, and quite different opinions therefore – quite unusually – came to the fore. Different messages came out in the Communist Party newspaper, *Neues Deutschland* (edited by Rudolf Herrnstadt), and the official trade union newspaper, *Tribüne*, which followed the Ulbricht line.

On 16 June 1953, workers on Berlin's prestige building project, the construction of the Stalinallee in the centre of the capital city, downed tools and marched in protest to the House of Ministries, demanding a retraction of the raised work norms.

Amidst the mixed messages and confusion of the demonstration, one worker seized a loudspeaker and announced a general strike for the following day (look back at the general strikes in the early Weimar period, see Chapter 1). Echoed by the West Berlin radio station RIAS, the news spread throughout the GDR, inaugurating the first mass uprising against Communist rule in the history of the Soviet bloc. (This was later followed by the better-known uprisings of 1956 in Hungary and Poland, and of 1968 in Czechoslovakia. This together with the repeated unrest in Poland in the Solidarity movement of the 1980s, presaged the eventual collapse of Communism in 1989–91.)

Figure 5.7 Soviet tanks suppressing unrest in Berlin, 17 June 1953.

On 17 June 1953, hundreds of thousands of workers protested against the social and economic policies of the Ulbricht regime, and eventually called for the downfall of Ulbricht and reunification with the West. By the afternoon, however, Ulbricht had called on the help of the Soviet Union, and the uprising was crushed by Soviet tanks. The West German government under Konrad Adenauer looked on but did not intervene, for fear of precipitating a major international conflict.

There were several, partially contradictory, consequences. Despite the forceful repression of the uprising, and the violence and mass arrests which accompanied it, the workers won concessions and the policy on increased work norms was reversed. But the brutal suppression of the demonstrations and the failure of the West to intervene meant that East Germans felt abandoned and resigned to their plight.

Moreover, the inadequacy of the secret security service, the Stasi, in noticing signs of unrest in the months before the uprising now led to a massive growth in its size and powers to intervene – a growth which continued exponentially right into the 1980s. And the SED leader Walter Ulbricht, who had been coming under criticism within the Party, paradoxically had his position strengthened, since anything else would have appeared to have been capitulating to the demonstrators. So in the end, the situation only served to polarise the political camps, with the SED ever more paranoid about the views of the people, and determined to crush any sign of unrest at the earliest opportunity.

In the course of the following years, they were bound ever more tightly into the Soviet bloc, with integration into the regional economic group or **COMECON**, and the military alliance of the **Warsaw Pact**. In response to West Germany's remilitarisation and foundation of an army, the *Bundeswehr*, the 'People's Police in Barracks' of East Germany were formally transformed into the National People's Army (NVA), in 1956.

In the view of some historians, the 1953 uprising led to a 'latent civil war' that was to last until the downfall of the regime in 1989. In the view of others, however, there was a degree of stabilisation after the building of the Berlin Wall. Popular unrest only set in again on a massive scale with the growing economic problems of the later 1970s and 1980s.

How far and in what ways were the economy and social structure changed?

Life on the land

Large landed estates had already been expropriated and handed over as small peasant plots in 1945. Very rapidly, the new owners found it impossible to farm these new small plots profitably, without adequate resources by way of livestock, seed-corn, fertiliser, machinery and other equipment. The 'solution', in the SED's view, was collectivisation; the formation of 'land production cooperatives' (*Landesproduktionsgenossenschaften*, or **LPGs**).

A first wave of collectivisation took place in 1952, coinciding with the 'building of socialism'. This was sufficiently unpopular that many farmers preferred simply to abandon their farms and flee west, while there was still the opportunity. Resulting problems with food supply to the towns contributed to the widespread social unrest which was the background to the 1953 June uprising. A second great wave of collectivisation in 1960–61 also precipitated mass flight, playing a major role in the decision to build the Berlin Wall, closing off the last escape route to the West in August 1961.

COMECON

COMECON stood for the Council for Mutual Economic Assistance, a grouping of Eastern European (and later also other) communist states under the leadership of the Soviet Union. United largely by common political ideologies under the official doctrine of Marxism-Leninism, the participating states were supposed to derive economic benefits from enhanced cooperation, although given different levels of economic development across Eastern Europe this was not always easy.

Warsaw Pact

The Warsaw Treaty of Friendship, Cooperation and Mutual Assistance, signed in May 1955, was a military alliance of Eastern European States under the leadership of the Soviet Union. It was intended as a counterbalance to NATO (the North Atlantic Treaty Organisation), which, with the inclusion in 1955 of the Federal Republic of Germany, appeared to pose an ever-growing military threat to the security of the Communist bloc.

LPG

A collective farm, often made up of several previously independent farms which were now joined together. There were three main types of collective, ranging from those that shared only machinery to those that held all of the farmland, livestock and property in common.

ACTIVITY

Compare the conditions of farmers in 1945–63 with the conditions in the 1920s and 30s. What were the similarities/differences and why?

But over a longer period of time, East German agriculture became increasingly efficient. By the 1970s, East German farmers were increasingly well-trained, becoming agricultural specialists in crop or livestock production, and treating the collective farms in much the same way as industrial workers treated large factories, as a place of work rather than an inherited property. The 'peasantry' in eastern Germany had changed out of all recognition.

Industry

Changes on a similarly massive scale took place in the area of industrial production. Many large enterprises were taken into Soviet control or state ownership in the occupation period. In the course of the 1950s, remaining private enterprises were increasingly squeezed out; by the mid-1960s, the private sector was a tiny percentage of the total industrial economy. People increasingly worked in what were called 'People's Own Factories' (*Volkseigene Betriebe*, **VEBs**).

VEB

A 'People's Own Factory', effectively owned and managed by the state 'on behalf of the people', in which the Party played a large role in setting production targets and keeping an eye on the workforce, work discipline, and related social activities.

In the course of the 1950s, the emphasis was on heavy industry, with a focus on production targets. Quantity, not quality, was the key measure of performance. Targets were determined centrally, with little regard for consumer demand. Unrealistic five-year plans were constantly being introduced, revised, and replaced by new plans.

As a result of the SED economic priorities of the 1950s, although living standards slowly improved, there was nothing in the GDR to match the 'economic miracle' of the increasingly affluent West Germany in the 1950s (see Chapter 6). Rationing continued until 1958. Despite the extraordinary strides made by the Soviet Union in space travel in the late 1950s, Ulbricht's claim that the GDR would 'overtake the West without having to catch up' increasingly appeared laughable. The stream of refugees to the more affluent West continued until the erection of the Berlin Wall.

The Wall, however horrendous on a personal level, served to stabilise the labour force. With this, it was possible to experiment with a less centralised economy. In 1963, the 'New Economic System for Planning and Direction' (NÖSPL) was introduced, allowing more flexibility and input at intermediate levels, and reintroducing the profit motive. Emphasis was now on profitability, and quality rather than quantity could be a measure of productivity. As with many of Ulbricht's experiments of the 1960s, this was terminated by his successor **Erich Honecker**, whose influence grew in the later 1960s even before he formally took over the reins of power as SED leader in 1971.

BIOGRAPHY

Erich Honecker (1912–1994)

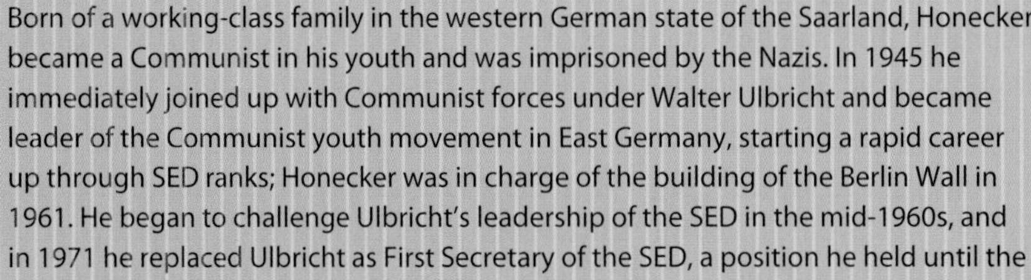

Born of a working-class family in the western German state of the Saarland, Honecker became a Communist in his youth and was imprisoned by the Nazis. In 1945 he immediately joined up with Communist forces under Walter Ulbricht and became leader of the Communist youth movement in East Germany, starting a rapid career up through SED ranks; Honecker was in charge of the building of the Berlin Wall in 1961. He began to challenge Ulbricht's leadership of the SED in the mid-1960s, and in 1971 he replaced Ulbricht as First Secretary of the SED, a position he held until the revolution of autumn 1989.

Despite a continued emphasis on subsidising the necessary basics of everyday life, available in the state-run 'HO' shops, consumerism became more of a priority after the June uprising.

This continued in the course of the 1960s and 1970s in special shops, such as the Delikat and Intershops, where special goods could be bought at higher prices or in western currency.

Everywhere, housing and health were and remained major priorities. And in some areas, such as the new town of Stalinstadt (later renamed Eisenhüttenstadt) on the Oder river at the border with Poland, a kind of frontier mentality helped to build up a new spirit of starting afresh and building a new life after the devastations of Nazism.

How far and in what ways did East German society change?

In the first two decades after the war, the demographic structure of East Germany was very lopsided. There had been a massive loss of young males in warfare. Although the population was briefly greatly swollen by the millions of refugees from lost eastern territories, many of these fled further into the more affluent and politically welcoming West Germany. In the period up to the building of the Wall, a further three million or so fled to the West. As a result of the socioeconomic policies – expropriation of landed estates, nationalisation and state ownership of industry, squeezing out of the middle classes – the social structure of East Germany began to change.

Upward social mobility

There was an unprecedented opportunity for upward social mobility on the part of those who were prepared to be politically committed to the system. The major beneficiaries were those from working class or peasant backgrounds who were politically on the left; and women.

Over time, party loyalists from poor working class or peasant backgrounds acquired educational credentials and specialist degrees. Managers of factories were no longer private capitalists in their own right, but were increasingly Party apparatchiks installed to oversee production in the new 'People's Own Factories' (VEBs). The old middle classes began to give way to a new '**Socialist intelligentsia**', committed to the system; for example, while the majority of medical doctors after the war were male and influenced by or committed to racist Nazi views, by the mid-1960s the medical profession was increasingly made up of newly trained young doctors, many of whom were women.

Socialist intelligentsia

The term used to denote the professional classes under Socialism, displacing the old propertied and educated middle classes of capitalist society. A wide term, this could include critical intellectuals, writers and artists, journalists, engineers, scientists, doctors, architects and other professional groups.

Women were given greatly increased support, in order to ensure their full participation in the workforce as well as being wives and mothers. Maternity care, work-based crèches and after-school childcare facilities, were all expanded to ensure that women could play a full role in both production and reproduction. The entry of women into the workforce in increased numbers, particularly at lower levels or in part-time positions, also meant enhanced upward mobility for males.

So for those who were willing to make the necessary political compromises, there was a rising generation who had a genuine stake in a system which appeared to be giving them significant opportunities.

Mass organisations

Mass organisations were extremely important in the GDR political and social system. The state-controlled Free German Trade Union League (FDGB), of which virtually every working adult was a member, was run by the state, and controlled by SED policies. But it was experienced by many workers as an enabling organisation which often did represent workers' interests on particular issues, and which was the main institution organising workers' holidays in trade-union-owned hotels, hostels and campsites across the GDR.

Other mass organisations catered for and sought to appeal to special interest groups, such as the Democratic Women's League of Germany (DFD) for women, or the League of Culture (KB) for a wide range of cultural, creative and artistic pursuits. Many intellectuals also still believed in the possibility of a new anti-fascist state, devoting their creative energies, for example, to the 'Bitterfeld Way' seeking to develop links between the experiences of workers and writers. The Society for Sport and Technology (GST) and the German Gymnastics and Sports League (DTSB) offered a variety of sporting opportunities, geared not merely to individual health and enjoyment but also to physical preparedness for military action. The German-Soviet Friendship Society (DSF) attempted to foster good relations between Germans and their former arch-enemies, who they now had to believe had 'liberated' rather than 'defeated' them.

There were also, of course, the state-run youth organisations of the Free German Youth (FDJ).

ACTIVITY

How important do you think mass organisations were in the GDR, in drawing people into state-controlled organisations and participating in organised leisure activities?

The following are significant mass organisations in the Soviet zone of occupation/GDR:

FDGB	League of Free German Trade Unions
FDJ	Free German Youth
DFD	Democratic German Women's League
KB	League of Culture
DSF	German-Soviet Friendship Society
GST	Society for Sport and Technology

Religion and the Churches

For those who were not prepared to come to terms with Communism, the situation was of course very different. This was particularly the case for those committed to a quite different moral and religious worldview. Christian beliefs were, however, in principle compatible with political positions across the spectrum; and while the majority of Protestants had come to terms with or even supported Hitler, and the Catholic Church had made its peace with the regime, individual Christians had stood out in principled opposition to Nazism. The situation with respect to the Churches in the GDR was thus from the outset complex.

East German society after the war was still highly religious. Of the 17 million people living in the GDR, just under 15 million were Protestant and around one million were Catholic. In the Marxist view of history, however, religion was but 'the opium of the people', the 'sign of an oppressed creature' and was doomed to 'wither away' under the new Communist society. And despite good relations between individual Communists and those few pastors and priests who had actively opposed Nazism, the SED was there to help this 'withering away' along.

The Churches at first appeared to be exempted from the radical changes introduced by the new Communist authorities in the later 1940s. Church-owned land was not expropriated in the land reform of 1945, and ministers of religion were not subjected to denazification measures or removal from office: the Churches were left to deal with their own internal affairs. But religious belief very soon came under strenuous attack.

Religious instruction was removed from the school curriculum by the 'Law for the Democratisation of German Schools' of 1946, making it far harder to give religious education to young people.

In the early 1950s, there were bitter confrontations between the state and the Churches. In 1952–53 the SED waged a campaign against members of the '*Junge Gemeinde*', the loosely organised youth group of the Protestant Churches, making it increasingly difficult for young Christians to remain at school and take the ***Abitur*** or to go on to study at university. Although this campaign against young Christians was called off in June 1953, a new tack was adopted.

The '***Jugendweihe***' (youth dedication service), was resuscitated in 1954 and imposed on young East Germans. Since the Church considered this commitment to the atheist worldview of the Marxist-Leninist state to be incompatible with confirmation and commitment to God, it created immense conflicts for teenagers and their families. Those who refused the *Jugendweihe* would be discriminated against in school and prevented from going on to post-compulsory education or having any kind of professional career outside the Church.

The pressure to conform was enormous, even though the Churches threatened the more long-lasting punishment of eternal damnation for those who left the Christian fold. By the end of the 1950s, the Churches had effectively capitulated, now conceding that the *Jugendweihe* was compatible with confirmation after all. In the course of the 1960s and 1970s, in the course of a somewhat forced 'Christian-Marxist dialogue' in which Stasi spies infiltrated and sought to influence the Church, the Church was increasingly pressurised into finding some form of agreement, a 'modus vivendi' with the atheist state.

Abitur

The German higher school leaving examination (the equivalent of A levels).

Jugendweihe

A secular coming-of-age ceremony which was equivalent to confirmation in church among Christians, or the Bar-Mitzvah among Jews.

ACTIVITY

Using the source on the *Jugendweihe* oath and your own knowledge, assess why the *Jugendweihe* might be seen as being in conflict with religious world views and confirmation in Church.

Source

The *Jugendweihe* oath, 1959 version:

Dear young friends!

Are you prepared, as sons and daughters of our workers' and peasants' state, to work and to struggle for a happy life for the whole German people, then answer me:

Yes, we promise!

Are you prepared, together with us, to put all your power towards the great and honourable cause of socialism, then answer me:

Yes, we promise!

Are you prepared actively to support friendship among peoples and, together with the Soviet people and all peace-loving people in the world to ensure and to defend peace, then answer me:

Yes, we promise!

We have heard your oath, you have set yourselves a high and honourable goal. You have entered into the fold of the millions of people who work and struggle for peace and socialism.

We festively take you into the community of all the workers in our German Democratic Republic and promise you support, protection and help. With forces united – forwards!

Christoph Kleßmann (1997). *Zwei Staaten, eine Nation. Deutsche Geschichte 1955–70*, 2nd edn (p. 573, translation by MF). Bonn: Bundeszentrale für politische Bildung.

ACTIVITY

Compare the FDJ and the JP with the Hitler Youth. (See also pages 105–108.) What are the similarities and differences and why?

BIOGRAPHY

Ernst Thälmann (1886–1944)

A former communist leader, who stood in the 1932 presidential elections against Hindenburg and Hitler. During the Third Reich, Thälmann was imprisoned by the Nazis and was put to death in Buchenwald concentration camp in August 1944 (see page 49). In the GDR Thälmann became, posthumously, a national hero and symbolic leader of the 'anti-fascist resistance'. His name was widely adopted for renaming public spaces such as streets and squares, as well as by the Pioneer youth organisations for children aged 6 to 14.

Youth and education

Young people were highly important to the SED: they represented the face of the future. As well as opposing alternative influences, particularly on the part of the Churches, the SED sought actively to win over the hearts and minds of young people to the Communist cause.

The education system was redesigned to turn nearly all schools into comprehensive 'polytechnic' schools with close links to industry (a very few special schools, for example for those gifted in sport, remained). 'Twinning' arrangements between schools and factories meant that young people gained practical work experience on a regular basis while still at school, and were encouraged to identify with the working class.

A variety of educational routes, including the possibility of returning to study as an adult, and generous scholarships for those from disadvantaged backgrounds, meant that the numbers of those from 'non-traditional' backgrounds who went on to university studies rapidly increased. Meanwhile, children of the traditionally privileged professional classes, and the few remaining members of the East German aristocracy, tended to be discriminated against; many from these better-off backgrounds who now found themselves barred from pursuing their chosen careers took the opportunity to leave the GDR before 1961 to study and work in West Germany.

Outside school, further and higher education, and the workplace, but closely linked to these, were the SED-controlled youth organisations. The Free German Youth organisation (FDJ) catered to young people from the ages of 14 to 25, while for younger children there were the **Ernst Thälmann** Young Pioneers (JP, for ages 6 to 10) and the Ernst Thälmann Pioneers (for ages 10 to 14). These organised both regular school-based activities and more adventurous outings and camps, which many young people enjoyed.

A standard outing for nearly all young people was a form of 'pilgrimage' to the former Nazi concentration camp of Buchenwald, where the Communist leader Ernst Thälmann had been murdered by the Nazis. Young people in East Germany seem to have largely internalised the tales of heroic resistance, and not developed the complex of national shame which became so characteristic of West German political culture.

Alternative youth cultures

Despite all the opportunities the SED sought to offer, most young people in the GDR of the 1950s were not entirely convinced by the old-fashioned, anti-American stance of the SED. Global youth culture – in the form of the cults of Elvis Presley, and Rock 'n' Roll music in the 1950s, and the emergent Beatles and popular culture of the 1960s – increasingly captured a sizable following among East German youth. The responses of the SED authorities wavered from outright clampdowns – going to such lengths as enforcing haircuts for would-be Beatles look-alikes in the mid-1960s – to moments of relative liberalisation and attempts at 'understanding' and more gentle persuasion, with encouragement of GDR-style rock bands.

Again, the Wall appeared to make a difference to SED policies in the early 1960s. Despite Ulbricht's own highly prudish emphases in the 1950s, he supported the 'Youth Communiqué' of 1963, with a title promising to give young people 'trust and responsibility', which argued for a dialogue with and respect for the views of young people. On the occasion of a gigantic international youth festival which was held in Berlin in 1964, the 'Germany meeting' (*Deutschlandtreffen*), a new radio station, DT64, was set up to play popular music, with a ratio of 40 per cent of western popular music allowed.

These efforts to meet young people on their own terms were relatively short-lived, repressed in 1965 at the 11th Plenum by Ulbricht's younger political rival and later successor, Erich Honecker. The same Plenum saw the banning of a number of critical films which had engaged with the problems of building Socialism in the GDR.

Sealing the division? The Berlin Wall 1961

In 1958, the then Soviet leader, **Nikita Krushchev**, sought to deal with the thorny question of Berlin, which was still under four-power control. The western sectors (run by the Americans, British and French), represented an irritating island of the West surrounded by the sea of East Germany. Krushchev presented an ultimatum to the western powers, demanding that West Berlin should be reintegrated with the East and become an integral part of the GDR within six months.

The Allies chose to ignore this ultimatum, and the deadline passed without confrontation. But the Berlin crisis did not go away. When in the summer of 1961 the numbers of East Germans using this last remaining exit route to the West were swollen by the renewed drive to agricultural collectivisation, rapid action was taken. Despite Ulbricht's disavowals ('no-one has any intention of erecting a Wall'), preparations were made in secret. On the morning of 13 August 1961 Berliners woke up to find that, overnight, access between the two sides of the city had been closed off.

The western powers chose not to intervene when the border around their sectors of Berlin was closed. The Berlin crisis of 1961 proved, again, to be a major symbolic turning point in the history of Germany in Cold War context. It became clear that neither side was willing to risk unleashing a major military conflict in the centre of Europe; and, in the following years, the attention of the superpowers was deflected to other flashpoints around the world (notably Cuba and Vietnam). The 'German question' appeared to be no longer on the agenda, leaving each part of divided Germany to develop in distinctive ways.

Figure 5.8 The Berlin Wall going up at Potsdamer Platz, Berlin, 1961.

BIOGRAPHY

Nikita Khrushchev (1894–1971)

Nikita Khrushchev was First Secretary of the Communist Party of the Soviet Union from 1953 to 1964 and Prime Minister from 1958 to 1964, having emerged as leader in the wake of the power struggle which followed the death of Stalin and eventually uniting in his person the leadership of both Party and state. Although he denounced the cult of Stalinism in 1956, and inaugurated some reforms in the USSR, Krushchev pursued hard-line policies both at home and abroad, including approval of the building of the Berlin Wall in 1961. He was ousted from power by Leonid Brezhnev in 1964, following difficulties on the international stage, including the Cuban missile crisis of 1962.

In human terms, the Wall was and remained horrendous. In terms of the history of the GDR, the erection of the Wall achieved the intended effects. The labour supply was stabilised; it was possible to introduce limited experiments in liberalisation and decentralisation; and economic performance improved. People increasingly realised they would have to make their lives as best they could, and many came to terms with life behind the Wall.

Figure 5.9 A divided people: families and friends, once neighbours, wave across to each other over the Berlin Wall, August 1961.

In the course of the 1960s and early 1970s, people even began to hope for improvements, with an increasing emphasis on consumerism and rising living standards, despite lack of freedom to travel, or freedom of speech and of democratic association. Younger generations were born who knew nothing else and took East German conditions for granted. A new form of society began to develop, such that when the Wall finally was brought down by a revolution in November 1989, East Germans and West Germans registered with some shock just how far apart they had grown in the decades of division.

Source

Table 5.1 Numbers of refugees from East Germany who were registered in the West

Year	Refugees	Year	Refugees
1949 (from September)	129,245	1955	252,870
1950	197,788	1956	279,189
1951	165,648	1957	261,622
1952	182,393	1958	204,092
1953	331,390	1959	143,917
1954	184,198	1960	199,188
		1961 (up to 15 August)	159,730
		Total	**2,691,270**

Christoph Kleßmann (1997). *Zwei Staaten, eine Nation. Deutsche Geschichte 1955–70*, 2nd edn (p. 558). Bonn: Bundeszentrale für politische Bildung.

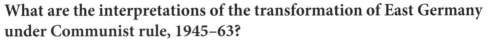

What are the interpretations of the transformation of East Germany under Communist rule, 1945–63?

Historians differ over their interpretations of the character and development of the GDR. Some see it as a repressive 'totalitarian' dictatorship throughout, in which the SED made use of the Wall, the Stasi, and the presence of Soviet tanks to keep people under permanent surveillance and control. Others, particularly social historians, point out that there were different phases of development. While the beginning and the end were particularly characterised by the use of force and violence, the 1960s and 1970s were marked by widespread compromises and acquiescent if often grumbling conformity.

As far as Ulbricht's period in office is concerned, the building of the Wall marked a real break. While he has generally been regarded as a hard-line Stalinist – unwilling even to register the de-Stalinisation announced by the Communist Party of the Soviet Union in 1956 – this appears to have been less obviously the case in the 1960s than in the 1950s. Many of Ulbricht's attempts after 1961 to engage in (always controlled) dialogues and to seek new ways of developing a more dynamic form of Communism were however jettisoned by his successor, Erich Honecker, whose emphasis on the 'unity of economic and social policy' inaugurated the economic decline and eventual political demise of the GDR. Even in the 1950s, despite the use of force, Ulbricht's attempts to bring about a more just society were revolutionary, whereas in the 1970s and 1980s Marxist notions of a social revolution were more or less forgotten, merely part of an empty Party rhetoric; East German society began to stagnate and opportunities were closed off, as the GDR headed towards its ultimate political and economic bankruptcy.

ACTIVITY

Bearing in mind that the figures in Table 5.1 do not completely reflect total numbers fleeing to the West, what conclusions do you think can be drawn about the numbers leaving the GDR each year?

ACTIVITY — Enquiries

Study all the sources (see pages 156–7 also). Use your own knowledge to assess how far the sources support the view that most GDR citizens accepted their state and its aims by 1963.

Sources

(A) From the western weekly magazine Die Weltwoche (The World this Week), 31. 10. 1952:

Merxleben... used to be a village like thousands of others. Even today it is no different, no bigger, no more beautiful than it used to be, and one has got accustomed to the slogans and posters everywhere in the Soviet zone:

'The Party helps working peasants', 'Early fulfilment of the grain production targets – a strike against the warmongers!' 'Be wary of saboteurs and agents of monopoly capital!' are proclaimed from the community centre and the school. On trucks and tractors there are slogans daubed in chalk or oil paints: 'The first corn for the state!' 'Thank you to the Soviet Union!' or simply 'Socialism!'

This sort of thing, to repeat, one finds everywhere nowadays. And yet, if you only stay for half an hour in Merxleben, you already know: here there is a quite distinctive atmosphere.

The People's Police is more numerous here than elsewhere. With watchful eyes they follow every stranger ... Woe betide anyone who cannot show any papers apart from his personal identity card for the Soviet zone... Out of a German peasant village has grown a beleaguered fortress filled with suspicion. And why? Because here the first agricultural production cooperative... on German soil has been founded.

'Germany has its eyes on Merxleben!' 'Celebrations and excitement in Merxleben!' the SED press cries out.

And now for the reality. If a visitor today asks 'How's it going then, with your cooperative farm?' the house door is flung shut in his face. Everywhere. Or at most they say, with a vague hand gesture, 'Well ask that lot over there!' The gesture points to the cars parked on the village street, bringing SED Delegations, Instructors, Agitators, Propagandists, in a never-ending succession to Merxleben.

Die Weltwoche, 31. 10. 1952, reprinted in Christoph Kleßmann and Georg Wagner (eds) (1993). *Das gespaltene Land. Leben in Deutschland 1945 bis 1990. Texte und Dokumente* (pp. 365–66, translated by MF). Munich: C. H. Beck.

(B) From Guideline No. 1/58 of 1958 of the Ministry for State Security Service (Stasi):

The Ministry of State Security is entrusted with the task of preventing or throttling at the earliest stages – using whatever means and methods may be necessary – all attempts to delay or to hinder the victory of socialism.

Karl Wilhelm Fricke (1991). *MfS Intern* (p. 13). Cologne: Verlag Wissenschaft und Politik. Translated by and quoted in Mary Fulbrook (1995), *Anatomy of a Dictatorship: Inside the GDR, 1949–89* (p. 47). Oxford: Oxford University Press.

(C) From Victor Klemperer's diaries, April 1958, comparing East and West Germany:

Personally, I find the people in Bonn hateful; but the pig-headed hostility to culture, the lack of education and the tyranny of the Party here [in the GDR] daily get on my nerves... [I hate] the blatant battle for culture, the blatant education policy, the blatant arse-licking of the LDP, the CDU and NPD... [It's just that] Bonn is even more hateful to me than 'Pankow' [the GDR]...

Everywhere 'flight from the Republic', particularly among doctors, university professors, the intelligentsia. The battle for culture, the passport law, the tyranny, the pressures on conscience, the way children are torn apart – it's Nazism through and through. And in the Bonn state an open Hitler regime, ministers and generals from the Hitler state – but in general the individual lives in somewhat greater freedom... [and] can express opposing opinions in the newspapers, whereas here the press etc. are closed off to individuals – but over there Hitler supporters can openly pursue their hate campaigns etc. etc. Vile, and always the same and every day even more vile.

Victor Klemperer (1999). *So sitze ich zwischen allen Stühlen, Vol. 2, Tagebücher 1950–59* (pp. 680–82). Berlin: Aufbau Verlag. Translated by and quoted in Mary Fulbrook (2005), *The People's State: East German Society from Hitler to Honecker* (p. 252). London: Yale University Press.

The author was a Jewish professor who remained in Germany during the Nazi period and later worked in the East German education system in Dresden.

(D) A West German journalist's report on the Socialist new town Stalinstadt (later renamed Eisenhüttenstadt), in June 1961:

However uncomfortable the name sounds for the western visitor, the experience of Stalinstadt is highly impressive. How many people in West Germany even know that there is a town of this name?

And yet, for years now Stalinstadt has been a living, noisy, smoky and yet friendly and welcoming reality. It is proud of being the 'first Socialist town in Germany' and it really is, in the sense that here there is virtually no private property in land and also no private shops or factories. Everything belongs to the state and is looked after by the state...

...[T]he town itself was shown to me by the Deputy Mayor... [who] was weathered by eleven years of imprisonment under the Nazis... He beams with pride about his home town, and one cannot blame him. It is a model of a well-planned and well-built development, with currently around 24,000 inhabitants, whose hygienic dwellings, schools, and community centres are really ideal.

The town consists in several 'living complexes', each for around 4000 to 6000 people, built in various different periods and showing certain distinctions in their architectural styles, but which nevertheless form a harmonious whole with the green spaces and the community buildings.

Stalinstadt is not only the youngest town in the Republic, it is also a town of youth. Precisely one-third of the population is made up of children under the age of 15... The cheerful hordes of children that one meets skipping and hopping about wherever one goes are, incidentally, like everywhere else in this country, very cheerful in appearance, well nourished, and nicely dressed. There are at their disposal six kindergartens, four after-school care centres, four general Comprehensive Upper Schools with ten classes, one Extended Upper School, as well as a series of technical apprenticeship schools and institutes of further education.

Article in the leading West German weekly newspaper *Die Zeit*, 30.6.1961. Reprinted in Christoph Kleßmann and Georg Wagner (eds) (1993). *Das gespaltene Land. Leben in Deutschland 1945 bis 1990. Texte und Dokumente* (pp. 362–64, translated by MF). Munich: C. H. Beck.

(E) The views of two East German historians in the early 1990s:

Listening to conversations between former citizens of the GDR, one sometimes gets the impression that the people speaking to each other had been living in different countries. Some of them remember the repression, subordination, surveillance, the inadequacies of the economy and the poor provisions, the countless restrictions on freedom, the stupid and dishonest SED propaganda and an education system which, from kindergarten to university, is designed to elicit the obedience of corpses. The others think back to job security, clear professional prospects, individual welfare, crèche places guaranteed by the state, low rents and the bread roll costing five pennies.

Armin Mitter and Stefan Wolle (1993). *Untergang auf Raten* (p. 3). Munich: C. Bertelsmann Verlag. Translated by and quoted in Mary Fulbrook (1995), *Anatomy of a Dictatorship: Inside the GDR, 1949–89* (p. 21). Oxford: Oxford University Press.

Review questions

1 How different were the eastern and western zones of postwar Germany in 1949?

2 In what way was East German society in the GDR transformed under a Communist dictatorship?

3 To what extent did East Germans accept or reject the new regime in the GDR?

Exam**Café**

Relax, refresh, result!

Relax and prepare

Hot tips

Anna

I really didn't know how to get the most out of the books I read at the start of the AS course because I tried to copy everything out instead of making proper notes. When I came to revise, I had piles of notes and then I started to make notes on my notes. I wasn't sure what was relevant. I started to look at the key points a lot more and made sure I had notes which linked with them which helped me out of the comfort zone of just having a huge file.

David

I expected that I would be spoon-fed. We had a lot of help at GCSE with model answers and notes from our teacher. When I went to sixth form college I was expected to do a lot more for myself. I found this difficult when we got on to topics which weren't familiar but I realised that what I needed was to be able to handle sources and to think for myself a lot more. Now at A2 I'm used to doing that.

Getting started...

When comparing sources in (a) questions keep a balance between what the sources say and their nature as evidence. In (b) keep a balance between using the sources and using your own knowledge to give value to the sources and assess the relative weight you give to their judgements.

Refresh your memory

'Why and with what consequences was Germany divided after the Second World War?'

▷ Be able to assess the impact of the Second World War on Germany: the economic consequences, political problems and social issues that needed to be resolved. How serious was each problem?

▷ Be able to explain why Germany was divided by 1949 when at the end of the war the USA, Britain and the USSR were all agreed that Germany should remain a single unit. How far was this due to the actions of the USSR, or was it due to the actions of the USA and Britain?

▷ Explain how and why the Communists were able to gain control in eastern Germany and how they were able to consolidate their power.

▷ Why did Ulbricht emerge as leader of the Communist Party and how successful was he?

▷ Be able to explain the issue of reparations and how this contradicted the idea of economic unity.

▷ Explain the importance of Berlin to both the western powers and the USSR: how it led to the Berlin blockade and the aims of the USSR. Was the blockade seen as a success or failure?

▷ You should be able to explain how the Berlin Airlift crisis led directly to the formation of West Germany.

▷ Be clear what the term denazification means, and what it meant in practice.

▷ Ensure you can explain the causes of the 1953 crisis in the GDR and assess its seriousness.

▷ What economic problems did the GDR government face, what policies were introduced in agriculture and industry and how successful were they in increasing production?

▷ What were the aims and impact of the government's social policies on the Church, trade unions, education and the youth? Did they achieve their aims?

▷ Ensure you can explain why the Berlin Wall was erected and assess its success for the Soviet bloc.

'To what extent and in what ways did Communism transform the GDR?'

▷ Berlin was divided in the Yalta and Potsdam Conferences. It was situated in the Soviet occupation zone. The capital could not just be given to the Russians so it was divided into four zones.

▷ In 1948 Stalin blockaded the city in protest at the closer links between the western zones of occupation. Berlin became a symbol of the West's desire to defend all existing 'free' territory when they flew in supplies.

▷ Ulbricht's Communist regime reproduced many of the repressive aspects of the Nazis. While western aid had rebuilt the West, the Soviets punished the East.

▷ Strains caused an uprising on 17 June 1953, which was suppressed. The East German secret police became larger than the *Gestapo*.

▷ Soviet-style agricultural and industrial policies in the East produced relatively low productivity. This, and high levels of social control, led to refugees flowing into the West, attracted by a better life style.

▷ In 1961 the frontiers were closed and Berlin divided by a wall. The wall became a symbol of the Cold War justified by the East as protection from a hostile capitalist world.

▷ By the end of the period in 1963 there seemed little prospect of a united Germany.

Get the result!

Period studies

You will be aware that at end of the war the USA, Britain and the USSR were agreed that Germany should remain a single unit. However, there were a variety of reasons why, by 1949, two states had come into existence. The following question requires an examination of those reasons, which would include the inability of the victors to agree on aspects of the German problem and the political, economic and strategic importance of Germany. The answer will examine these issues and assess how far each side was to blame.

Exam question

To what extent was the USSR to blame for the division of Germany in 1949?

Here is a paragraph from Katya's essay that examines events in Germany in the period 1946–

Sample answers

Katya's answer:

At the end of the Second World War, Germany had been divided into four zones of military occupation and was run by a joint Allied Control Commission. Despite this apparent agreement there were divisions. The Western allies wanted the German economy to recover so that the people of Germany would be able to feed themselves and not be reliant upon Western aid. In 1946, in order to achieve this, the British and Americans announced on December 2nd they had combined their zones to create Bizonia. This worried the USSR, which thought that the Western powers were trying to recreate a united Germany which, with Western help, would be strong enough to launch an attack. Then in 1948 the Western powers introduced a new currency that was designed to further the economic revival. However, once again the USSR had not been consulted. As a consequence the USSR stopped rail and road traffic between Berlin and the Western zone, establishing the Berlin blockade in June and resulting in the Berlin Airlift.

Examiner says:

The paragraph contains a lot of information about events in Germany in the period after the war. It is factually accurate and reasonably detailed with precise dates for the establishment of Bizonia and the Berlin blockade. However, this knowledge is not directly linked to the demands of the question. The answer largely describes what the western powers did and implies that they were to blame, but this idea is not fully developed. It would take only a few sentences, which are clearly focused on the issue of who was to blame, to turn a descriptive paragraph into one that directly addresses the issue of blame.

Katya's improved answer:

Western actions in their zone during the period 1946 to 1948 were largely responsible for the Berlin blockade and subsequent Airlift, which increased tension between the two sides and led directly to the division of Germany in 1949. The long-term causes were mostly due to Britain and the USA failing to consult the USSR over the union of their two zones and the establishment of a new currency in the non-Soviet zone. Both of these actions created suspicion in the USSR, which saw it as a further example that the Western powers wanted to rebuild the German economy. The USSR was also concerned because they believed that these acts were a clear indication that the Western powers were recreating a united Germany which, after a period of economic recovery and Western support, would be strong enough to attack the USSR. It was the Western powers who had gone against the post-war agreements that Germany should remain a single unit. Therefore, in light of these actions, the establishment of the Berlin blockade by the USSR can be seen as purely a defensive move based on security considerations, despite the West's portrayal of Soviet action as both aggressive and expansionist.

Examiner says

Katya's improved paragraph is focused on the question of blame and clearly puts forward a case that the western powers were to blame for the division of Germany. This is made very clear in the opening sentence of the paragraph and is subsequently developed and supported in the remainder of the paragraph. It is worth comparing the focus of this opening sentence with that of the original answer.

Examiner says

The answer also addresses the issue of 'to what extent?' by suggesting that in the long term it was the actions of the western powers that were to blame. This allows Katya to argue that in other areas the USSR may have been to blame and therefore she can reach a balanced conclusion. The answer does not go into detail about the union of the two zones or the creation of the *Deutschmark* but focuses on how these issues caused concerns in the Soviet Union, which ultimately led to the division. This part of the answer is very similar to the original answer but because of the structure of this paragraph it creates a strong argument, which is not seen in the original answer.

Examiner says

The final sentence also supports Katya's overall argument and establishes a link with the Berlin blockade and Airlift that can be built on in the next paragraph. This helps to give the essay 'flow', or coherence. It also enables Katya to argue that an act, the Berlin blockade, that is usually seen as Russian aggression is actually defensive and only a response to Western actions: therefore that even in this event the West is to blame. In the previous answer this is only hinted at as Katya simply states that the blockade was a consequence of Western actions, but does not develop the point to show how the West could be blamed.

Enquiries

You will be aware that at end of the war the USA, Britain and the USSR were agreed that Germany should remain a single unit. However, there were a variety of reasons why, by 1949, two states had come into existence. The question requires an examination of those reasons, which would include the inability of the victors to agree on aspects of the German problem and the political, economic and strategic importance of Germany. The answer will examine these issues and assess how far each side was to blame. The full question here has five sources about the building of the Berlin Wall in 1961. These sources, the part (b) question and an answer to part (b) are all on your CD-ROM.

Study Sources A and B

Compare these sources as evidence for the building of the Berlin Wall in 1961.

Source

(A) The East Germans defend the closing of the Berlin frontier:

To stop hostile activities by those who want revenge and to conquer us and also by militaristic forces in West Germany and West Berlin, a border control will be introduced at the borders to the GDR, including the border with western sectors of Greater Berlin, as is common on the borders of sovereign states. Borders to West Berlin will be sufficiently guarded and effectively controlled in order to prevent subversive activities from the West.

(An extract from the *Resolution of the GDR Council of Ministers*, 12 August 1961.)

(B) The West German Chancellor is critical of the closing of the Frontier:

Let me finally say a few words to the inhabitants of the Eastern sector of Berlin and the Soviet zone of Germany. Your sorrow and suffering are our sorrow and suffering. In your particularly difficult situation you were able at least to derive some comfort from the thought that, if your lot should become quite unbearable, you could mend it by fleeing. Now it looks as if you had been deprived of this comfort, too, for reasons which have justification in reality. I request you with all my heart: do not abandon all hope of a better future for yourselves and your children

(Adenauer's message to the East Germans after the closing of the frontier in Berlin, delivered in a specially convened meeting of the Bundestag, *18 August 1961.)*

Anna's answer to a):

Sources A and B give a very different picture of the closing of the frontier and the building of the Berlin Wall. A sees it as defensive, to prevent 'hostile activities', while B sees no justification in reality for the decision.

Examiner says:

This starts directly and crisply - there is no superfluous description.

There is no mention in A of the effects of the closing of the frontier in increasing the human suffering such as B expresses. For B the action will deprive East Germans of comfort, but in A they will be protected from subversive activities. A sees little that is abnormal – border controls are usual between sovereign states, but Adenauer has called a special session of the Bundestag so clearly does regard the situation as abnormal.

Examiner says:

This is a good use of the information given about the source which is used directly to make inferences about the difference.

A does not see any element of human tragedy in dividing German from German – it is seen in terms of defending from a hostile, militaristic West; B is an emotional reaction – far from being two separate sovereign states, the two Germanies are linked: 'your sorrow and suffering are our sorrow and suffering'.

Examiner says:

This shows thought - to get to this point, Anna would have had to take time to think about the implications of the passage.

Both sources are written with distinct political intentions and come from the top levels of government.

Examiner says:

This begins to look at provenance.

The GDR ministers are justifying an action which had very adverse publicity in the West and was unpopular in their own country. The wording is overtly propagandistic and reflects the condemned Soviet-style language of the Cold War with the West being as militaristic. Adenauer's speech includes no such condemnation of the East, but its intention is to arouse feelings and is equally part of the Cold War. Both are written shortly after the events and are reliable for showing the emotions of the time.

Examiner says:

Good - there is contextual understanding and the answer starts to make judgement: this also touches on usefulness.

Examiner says:

In terms of key criteria - for an answer which is analytical, structured, some contextual knowledge, compares directly and has some sense of judgement. This is a good answer. Can it be even better?

6 Adenauer's Chancellorship 1949–63: How far did western democratic structures (political, democratic, social) succeed in the Federal Republic of Germany (FRG)?

Source

In 1949 the author Alfred Döblin, a social democrat of German Jewish origins, returned to Germany from exile in France and the USA. He was very struck by the changes he observed:

The people are the same as the ones I left in 1933. But all sorts of things have happened to them. I notice it everyday in my interactions with them... I have the impression, and this remained throughout my visit, that I had just entered a house full of smoke – but the inhabitants simply did not notice it... Leaflets intended to re-educate them have hardly any impact, and are read with a degree of rejection and outrage, as though there was still a dictatorship. And this is why one can get nowhere in discussions about the problem of guilt. This is also why they close themselves off against political discussions with people of different views from theirs... The reports and facts about the concentration camps and other atrocities that are now coming out should in principle help to re-educate. But people are simply not inclined to believe them, since it is generally foreigners reporting. Similarly, the sight of the ruined cities and towns should be having an impact. But then there is the fact of occupation. The occupation has fallen like a gift into the lap of the supporters of the old regime, of whom there are of course masses. The fact of occupation can be used to hinder any kind of re-education and to develop a new 'stab in the back' legend, just like the way people used the revolutionary events in 1918... If one thinks of the situation after the First World War, then those troubled times seem of almost fresco-like clarity compared to the picture today.

Alfred Döblin (1949). *Schicksalsreise*, taken from the extract reprinted in Christoph Kleßmann and Georg Wagner (eds) (1993), *Das gespaltene Land. Leben in Deutschland 1945 bis 1990. Texte und Dokumente* (pp. 67–68, translation by MF). Munich: C. H. Beck.

Key Questions:

In circumstances such as those described above, how was it possible to establish a successful democratic political system in post-war West Germany?

A number of factors are important in trying to explain the successful establishment of a stable democracy in the Federal Republic of Germany (FRG). This chapter focuses on the following key questions:

- What were the key features of the constitution (Basic Law), and what was their significance for democracy?
- The development of the party system: From multi-party coalitions to a 'vanishing opposition'?
- Western integration and anti-Communism in the Cold War: Was stabilisation of the West bought at the expense of abandoning the East?
- How far was the success of West German democracy due to the reintegration of former Nazis and an inadequate 'coming to terms with the past'?
- To what extent was the success of democracy a result of the 'economic miracle'?
- What were the generational and social changes in the post-war context?

The starting point: West Germany in 1949

By 1949, the Cold War between the western powers and the Soviet Union was becoming more important than the question of how to deal with defeated Nazi Germany. In the American, British and French zones of occupation, the introduction of Marshall Aid and the currency reform of 1948 were already beginning to help the economy to pick up, and the black market was coming under control. The political split between the three western zones, which by 1949 were economically merged into 'Trizonia', and the communist-controlled Soviet zone now appeared too great to bridge. But joint economic administration also required coordinated political leadership. Over several months, from the summer of 1948 to the spring of 1949, a new constitution or 'Basic Law' was devised for a democratically elected government to take power in a newly constituted West German state, the Federal Republic of Germany (FRG).

In May 1949, the new constitution was officially adopted and the Federal Republic of Germany came into being. In August 1949, following the first free elections for seventeen years, a new, democratically elected German government under the leadership of conservative Chancellor **Konrad Adenauer** took power. Adenauer was to stamp his mark on the character and development of the FRG for the next fourteen years – longer than Hitler's rule in the Third Reich.

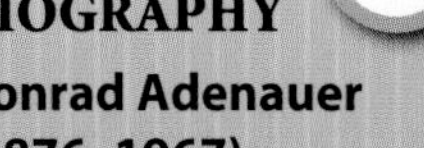

BIOGRAPHY

Konrad Adenauer (1876–1967)

A Catholic and member of the Centre Party in the Weimar Republic, Konrad Adenauer was Mayor of Cologne from 1917 until the Nazis came to power in 1933. He emerged from retirement after the Second World War to take on an active role in the newly formed CDU, and became the first Chancellor of the Federal Republic of Germany from 1949 to 1963.

But in 1949 the future was by no means clear. A mere four years after the defeat of Hitler, and in the light of the disastrous experience of Weimar democracy, how could the stability of the new democratic system be ensured in the long run? The circumstances of its birth were hardly promising.

In 1918, Germans had themselves brought about the defeat of the monarchy and established a democracy; in 1949, the new democratic political system was at least in part imposed by the occupying powers. The provisions of the Versailles Treaty of 1919 had been harsh (see pages 14–16); but the experiences after 1945 of total defeat, continued occupation and massive losses of territory were far harsher. The physical, social and psychological consequences of war losses, bereavement, hunger, and problems of post-war reintegration into civilian society had all been great after the First World War; but arguably these were all far greater in the wake of Hitler's aggressive war of expansion and genocide, with massive brutalisation of young men in the slaughter at the front, widespread casualties and suffering among the civilian population at home, and traumatic experiences of expulsion or flight for millions from former German homelands in the lost eastern territories. The defeat of 1945 was far more total than that of 1918.

In 1949, the majority of Germans were not committed democrats. The experience of the Weimar 'party system' was still very much alive in people's minds. The introduction of parliamentary democracy in Germany after the First World War had been associated with revolutionary unrest, inflation, continued political instability, economic depression and ultimately descent into dictatorship. Although the NSDAP had never won an absolute majority of votes in 1932–33, and although the 'Hitler myth' had begun to wane after German defeat at Stalingrad in 1943, twelve years of Nazi propaganda and brutal practice had made a serious impact on the attitudes of Germans.

ACTIVITY

With reference also to material discussed in Chapter 5, what do you consider to be the key aspects of the situation in West Germany in 1949? Using the list below, discuss the relative importance of each aspect for the establishment of a democratic state.

1 Role of occupation forces (USA, UK, France)

2 Territorial issues and relations with USSR

3 German political attitudes and culture

4 Economy: Reparations and reconstruction

5 Post-war society.

What were the key features of the constitution (Basic Law), and what was their significance for democracy?

Although Germans played a major role in devising the new constitution, they were closely supervised and guided by considerations on the part of the Allies. Freedom of expression, assembly, association and movement were all guaranteed by the constitution. But the new political system was to be more of a 'representative' rather than 'participatory' democracy, in order to ensure that democratically elected political elites would effectively retain control, and demagogic leaders such as Hitler could not come to power. There were also many other safeguards built in to prevent a repeat of the experiences of Germany's first failed attempt at democracy in the Weimar Republic.

West Germany was a federal state, in which the *Länder* (federal states) retained considerable power over regional affairs. They were represented at national level in the upper chamber, the ***Bundesrat***. Members of the lower chamber of parliament, the ***Bundestag***, were to be elected by a complex voting system. This combined the principle of **proportional representation** for parties according to the percentage of votes cast with a **'first past the post'** constituency representative element. A later amendment introduced the '5% hurdle' to ensure that very small parties could not gain representation and build strength without at least a significant share of the votes or one constituency representative elected outright.

The constitution of the Federal Republic of Germany was called a 'Basic Law' (*Grundgesetz*). This was to signal that it was merely temporary or 'provisional', pending a proper constitution for a united Germany once a peace treaty had been signed and the western and eastern zones of occupation reunited. The FRG was committed by the Basic Law to work towards reunification, and to recognise all people of German descent who were living in formerly German territories now under Soviet or Polish rule as entitled to citizenship in the Federal Republic. This meant that anyone fleeing the GDR was automatically able to settle and work in the FRG; over three million Germans fled the GDR in the period up to the building of the Berlin Wall in 1961.

Bundesrat

The upper chamber of parliament, representing the federal states.

Bundestag

The lower chamber of the parliament, elected by the people in the constituencies.

Proportional representation

A voting system in which parties gain seats according to the percentage of total votes cast for them.

'First past the post'

A voting system where the candidate who wins the most votes is elected, and the votes cast for candidates from other parties are disregarded entirely.

In order to ensure that democracy could not be undermined by constitutional means (as had happened in 1932–33), no political party was allowed that was not committed to upholding democracy. Political parties of the far Right or far Left that were not committed to the system of parliamentary democracy would be banned. This would prevent the possibility of a 'wrecking majority' of anti-democratic parties, as had happened in the Weimar Republic.

The President was not to be directly elected by all the people, but by a representative convention. This meant that no demagogic leader or anti-democratic leader could come to power; and the powers of the President were also far more limited than they had been in the Weimar Republic. The powers of the President were largely formal and symbolic, ensuring that there could be no autocratic presidential rule by emergency decree.

Chancellors were still to be appointed by the President, but only with the support and approval of parliament. To ensure the stability of government, a Chancellor could not be dismissed without a new one being voted in, under the so-called 'constructive vote of no confidence'. This meant that the President could not simply appoint and dismiss Chancellors at will. If a proposed Chancellor did not have the support of parliament, new elections would have to be called.

ACTIVITY ***Enquiries***

Use your own knowledge of previous German history to assess why Articles 21 and 54 were included in the Basic Law of the FRG.

Source

Article 21: Political parties

(1) Political parties shall participate in the formation of the political will of the people. They may be freely established. Their internal organisation must conform to democratic principles...

(2) Parties that, by reason of their aims or the behaviour of their adherents, seek to undermine or abolish the free democratic basic order or to endanger the existence of the Federal Republic of Germany shall be unconstitutional.

The Federal President

Article 54 [Election]

(1) The Federal President shall be elected by the Federal Convention...

(3) The Federal Convention shall consist of the Members of the Bundestag and an equal number of members elected by the parliaments of the Länder on the basis of proportional representation.

Article 67 [Constructive vote of no confidence]

(1) The Bundestag may express its lack of confidence in the Federal Chancellor only by electing a successor by the vote of a majority of its Members and requesting the Federal President to dismiss the Federal Chancellor. The Federal President must comply with the request and appoint the person elected.

Basic Law for the Federal Republic of Germany; Official English translation, December 2000.

The development of the party system: from multi-party coalitions to a 'vanishing opposition'?

The major political parties

Two major political parties were to dominate the politics of the Federal Republic of Germany for the rest of the 20th century. On the conservative side was the Christian Democratic Union (CDU), along with its Bavarian counterpart the Christian Social Union (CSU). On the left was the Social Democratic Party (SPD). The third party, which was never very large, but which for most of the following forty years effectively held the balance of power in West German politics, was the Free Democratic Party (FDP).

The CDU/CSU was made up conservative Christians, most of whom had previously belonged to the Centre Party (Catholics) or to one of the various Protestant and other conservative nationalist parties in the Weimar Republic, and many of whom had also readily joined the Nazi Party fold. Now, in the new post-war circumstances, the CDU/CSU sought to project its image as that of supporting capitalism with a human face. While basically in favour of as much competition as possible, there was also recognition of the need for safeguards to protect the weakest members of society, and the importance of a welfare state. Its initial party programme, known as the Ahlen Programme, explicitly appealed to what it proclaimed were traditional Christian values and a social conscience, as well as extolling the virtues of free market capitalism. But by 1957 this programme was formally renounced, and the Christian socialist elements were demoted in favour of a middle-of-the-road conservatism which conformed better with the 'economic miracle' that was well underway.

The significant political parties in the Federal Republic of Germany in the 1950s:

Major political parties:

CDU/CSU Christian Democratic Union (FRG except Bavaria) and Christian Social Union (in Bavaria) – conservative

SPD Social Democratic Party – democratic Socialist.

Smaller political parties:

FDP Free Democratic Party – liberal

DP German Party – right-wing

BHE League of Refugees and Expellees –revisionist, nationalist, special interest group

KPD Communist Party of Germany – banned in 1956

SRP Socialist Reich Party – a neo-Nazi party, banned in 1952.

The Social Democratic Party (SPD) was based on the traditions of the late 19th and early 20th centuries. It had originally been formed out of very different currents – Marxist visions of Socialism on the one hand, and reformist working-class movements on the other. Although the left-wing had split off to form the Communist Party already after the First World War, the SPD had never renounced the Marxist rhetoric that was still embodied in the programme of a party which had, at least since Bismarck's day, actually been remarkably reformist and moderate in practice.

Source

The Bad Godesberg programme of the SPD

Fundamental values of Socialism

Socialists aim to establish a society in which every individual can develop his personality and as a responsible member of the community, take part in the political, economic and cultural life of mankind...

Democratic Socialism... in Europe is rooted in Christian ethics, humanism and classical philosophy...

The Social Democratic Party is the party of freedom of thought...

We are fighting for democracy. Democracy must become the universal form of state organisation and way of life...

We resist dictatorship, every form of totalitarian or authoritarian rule....

The economy

... Free choice of consumer goods and services, free choice of working place, freedom for employers to exercise their initiative as well as free competition are essential conditions of a Social Democratic economic policy.... Totalitarian control of the economy destroys freedom... As much competition as possible – as much planning as necessary...

... Wherever large-scale enterprises predominate, free competition is eliminated... The key task of an economy concerned with freedom is therefore to contain the power of big business. State and society must not be allowed to become the prey of powerful sectional groups.

Private ownership of production can claim protection by society as long as it does not hinder the establishment of social justice...

Cultural life

... Education must give an opportunity to all freely to develop their abilities and capacities. It must strengthen the will to resist the conformist tendencies of our time...

The International Community

The greatest and most urgent task is to preserve peace and protect freedom.

C. C. Schweitzer et al. (eds) (1984). *Politics and Government in the Federal Republic of Germany: Basic Documents* (pp. 215–18). Leamington Spa: Berg,.

But in the course of the 1950s, and in the light of the electoral successes of the CDU/CSU, the SPD realised that if it clung to past traditions, it would never be a party of government. At a historic conference in the Bonn suburb of Bad Godesberg in 1959, the SPD developed a new programme which articulated more clearly its vision for combining social justice with individual freedom in a state-regulated capitalist democracy. What became known as the Bad Godesberg programme of the SPD renounced the inherited Marxist rhetoric and explicitly underlined the SPD's espousal of individual freedoms in a democratic Socialism which was to be sharply distinguished from the kind of Communism practised in the GDR.

The Free Democratic Party (FDP) was to have a historical significance out of all proportion to its size. It was only formed in December 1948, out of an amalgamation of a variety of liberal parties which had been formed in different areas in the western zones of occupation. A small chameleon party, championing both the rights of big business interests and liberal individual freedoms, it was to hold the balance of power between the two major political parties for the best part of half a century, and often had a significant voice in West German foreign policy.

There were at first also many other small parties. These included not only the German Communist Party (KPD), but also the neo-Nazi Socialist Reich Party (SRP), and a variety of regionally based or special interest parties, such as the League of Refugees and Expellees (BHE), representing those who had fled from their homelands in the lost eastern territories taken under Communist control after the war.

How did West German politics develop from a multi-party system to one of a 'vanishing opposition'?

At first, it seemed perfectly possible that West German democracy would be plagued by the problems of the party system in the Weimar Republic: no single party, in this multi-party system, might gain overall control, and there might be ever-changing unstable governmental coalitions. Why was this not, in the end, the case in the FRG?

Part of the answer has to do with features of the constitution and the ways in which these were put into effect.

ACTIVITY

What were the main reasons that West German politics went from a multi-party system to one of a 'vanishing opposition'?

The constitutional emphasis on commitment to the 'free democratic basic order', and the determination never again to allow democracy to be destroyed by democratic means (as the NSDAP had done in the late Weimar years) led to the banning of the two parties of the far Right and far Left. The SRP was outlawed in 1952, and the KPD in 1956.

The electoral system already had a safeguard built in, the system of two votes – first-past-the-post and proportional representation – to ensure that 'too much' democracy would not allow small extremist parties to gain a foothold in parliament and use this to increase support.

This feature was further strengthened by the adoption in 1953 of the '5% hurdle' at federal level (rather than only *Land* level) which meant that any party which did not gain either 5% of the national vote, or a direct mandate through a constituency election, would not gain any representation in the *Bundestag*.

The Bavarian Party, based entirely, as its name suggests, in Bavaria, was a victim of this change, while the CSU, also based entirely in Bavaria, was deemed to be an extension of the CDU. In 1957, the number of constituencies which had to be won outright, if the 5% condition was not met, was raised from one to three, making it even more difficult for very small or entirely regionally-based parties to gain national representation.

At the same time, Adenauer's policy of inclusiveness, and splits within some of the smaller parties, led to the absorption of many right-wing parties into the CDU. While never entirely a 'people's party' (*Volkspartei*), the CDU did encourage a range of profiles among its supporters.

The answer cannot however be sought only in the way the constitution and party system functioned. The ways in which the economy developed, the ways in which Adenauer handled the wider international situation, and the relations between social changes and electoral politics were of major importance.

The elections of 1949, 1953, 1957 and 1961

In the election of 1949, Adenauer's CDU, with less than a third of the overall vote, was only able to take the Chancellorship after weeks of discussion about coalition formation. His coalition government included members of the FDP and the DP in leading ministerial positions. By 1953, following a series of successes with respect to foreign affairs, and having himself taken on the post of Minister for Foreign Affairs when the Allies gave permission for this post to be revived, Adenauer and the CDU scored a greatly increased vote. Yet Adenauer still chose to run a coalition government, including, controversially, Theodor Oberländer of the BHE as Minister for Refugees and Expellees – a topic on which Oberländer was uniquely well qualified, having, as an active Nazi before 1945, played a significant role in Hitler's racist policies in the now lost territories of eastern Europe (he was eventually forced to resign in 1960 following East German accusations of war crimes).

Extraordinarily, after further successes both on the foreign policy front and with clear evidence of rapid economic growth, the CDU/CSU scored over 50 per cent of the vote in the 1957 election – the first and only time a party has scored this level of electoral success in the FRG. Adenauer had by this time achieved an extraordinary profile as a wily politician who could apparently always find a way of seizing opportunities to achieve his goals. His election slogan was 'No Experiments!' and significant numbers of voters were inclined to believe that caution was the best policy.

In 1961 the CDU/CSU vote declined only slightly, nevertheless presaging the beginning of an entirely new political era. By this time, Adenauer – now aged 85 – was clearly beginning to lose his grip.

By the early 1960s, there were only two significant large parties left on the national stage: the CDU/CSU on the right, and the SPD on the left, with the FDP still just clinging on, able to hold the balance of power by its decisions on whether to go into a coalition with one or the other. As the political scientist Otto Kirchheimer observed, this situation could be described in terms of a 'vanishing opposition': there was at this time ever less to choose between the two major parties; both were competing on the middle ground, and claimed to be committed to some variant of capitalism with a human face. Indeed, in 1966 the CDU/CSU and SPD entered into a 'Grand Coalition' with one another.

ACTIVITY

Describe and account for the election results of 1949 to 1961.

It was only from 1969, when there was a coalition government of the SPD and FDP, led by the SPD with **Willy Brandt** as Chancellor, that clear blue water between the two major parties became apparent, particularly over the question of relations with the GDR (known as *Ostpolitik*). But for the first twenty years of the FRG's history, from 1949 to 1969 – virtually half of its history as a separate West German state, prior to the fall of the Wall in 1989 and reunification with the GDR with 1990 – the FRG had a CDU Chancellor. And between 1966 and 1969 the two major political camps formed the government together, in the 'Grand Coalition', leaving many to feel that the only possibility for real political opposition was on the streets, in what became known as 'Extra-Parliamentary Opposition'.

Discussion of constitutional safeguards, while important, clearly do not even begin to explain this pattern of development. It is important then to set the electoral results in the wider context of developments beyond purely party political and constitutional considerations.

BIOGRAPHY

Willy Brandt (1913–1992)

Willy Brandt (born Herbert Ernst Karl Frahm) was leader of the SPD from 1964 to 1987, and Chancellor of the FRG from 1969 to 1974. Vilified by conservative nationalists both for his illegitimate birth and his activities in the resistance against Hitler, Brandt blazed a new trail in West German politics. As Mayor of West Berlin from 1957 to 1966, Brandt stood up for the people of Berlin at the time of the Berlin crises and erection of the Wall. As Chancellor of Germany from 1969 Brandt was the principal architect and leader of *Ostpolitik*, forging new relations with East Germany and Eastern Europe (remembered particularly for his symbolic genuflection at the site of the Warsaw Ghetto), and ensuring that human contacts between the people in the two German states could be maintained. Brandt resigned from the Chancellorship in 1974 when it was revealed that one of his principal aides, Günter Guillaume, was an East German spy, but remained active in German, European and indeed world affairs until his death.

Western integration and anti-Communism in the Cold War: Was stabilisation of the West bought at the expense of abandoning the East?

A major key to Adenauer's success – and a major point of criticism – was the stance he adopted towards rejecting the East and integrating with the West.

Already in the period immediately after the formation of the FRG in 1949, Adenauer sought to make West Germany indispensable to the western powers. International organisations which had, at least partially, originated as a means of tying in the potentially powerful West German economy and ensuring that the FRG would never be in an independent position to wage war again were rapidly transformed into movements for western European economic integration, in which West Germany was accepted as an important partner. The same was true on the military front.

In October 1949, the FRG became a member of the Organisation for European Economic Cooperation (OEEC), and in April 1951 it entered the European Coal and Steel Community (ECSC), both precursors to what, in the Treaty of Rome in 1957, became the European Economic Community (EEC) – which, by the end of the 20th century, had become the European Union or EU. In the early 1950s there were also active discussions on the possibility of founding a European Defence Force (which in the event was not ratified by France) and on West Germany's inclusion in the North Atlantic Treaty Organisation (NATO, founded in 1949), which the FRG did in fact join in 1955.

ACTIVITY

Period Studies

Assess the reasons why Adenauer adopted a stance of rejection of the East whilst integrating or identifying with the West.

Unsettled by this evidence of the rapid acceptance and practical western integration of the FRG, and the consequent strengthening of his Cold War opponents, Stalin sent a series of notes in 1952 to the western powers suggesting the possibility of the Soviets giving up the GDR in favour of a united neutral Germany. At least in the first note, Stalin quite possibly meant this offer genuinely, although historians differ on the extent to which Stalin balanced the advantages of retaining the GDR in the Soviet bloc against the attractions of neutralising the potentially very powerful West. For neutrality was a precondition for Stalin: no all-German government could choose, after democratic elections, to join the western camp.

Source

Stalin's second note to the western powers, 9 April 1952:

The Soviet Union again suggests to the USA, together with the governments of Great Britain and France, to take up the question of a Peace Treaty with Germany and to discuss the question of the unification of Germany and the formation of an all-German government. The Soviet Union sees no reason to delay the solution to this question. It is precisely now that the question is posed of whether Germany can be reconstituted as a state which is united, independent, peace-loving, and belonging to the family of peace-loving peoples of Europe, or whether the division of Germany remains, and with that the related danger of a European war.

Christoph Kleßmann (1982). *Die doppelte Staatsgründung: Deutsche Geschichte 1945–55* (pp. 465–66, translated by MF). Göttingen: Vandenhoeck und Ruprecht.

It is unlikely that the western powers would ever have taken Stalin seriously at this point; but what is quite clear is that Adenauer quite proactively chose to snub Stalin and reject the notes out of hand, without taking any trouble to explore the possibility of reunification further.

In much the same vein, Adenauer's response to the uprising of June 1953 in the GDR (see Chapter 5) was more or less to ignore it, abandoning his fellow countrymen to their fate without risking any western intervention.

Adenauer strenuously refused to recognise the GDR as a separate state, or to have diplomatic relations with any powers that did recognise it, in what was known as the **'Hallstein doctrine'**. West Germans continued to call East Germany 'the Zone' until this doctrine was officially abandoned in the early 1970s.

In 1955 Adenauer scored another major domestic triumph when, against advice from his own colleagues, he effectively ignored the Hallstein doctrine and went to Moscow to negotiate the return of the remaining tens of thousands of German prisoners of war who were still being held by the Soviets. He also oversaw the plebiscite which allowed the Saar to be reincorporated in the FRG in 1957.

Hallstein doctrine

This doctrine, named after its proponent Walter Hallstein, held that the FRG should not legitimise the existence of the GDR by formally recognising it or by having diplomatic relations with other states which recognised the GDR, with the exception of the Soviet Union. The doctrine was abandoned by the SPD government which came to power in 1969.

Although Adenauer's reaction to the Berlin crises and to the building of the Berlin Wall in 1961 were both belated and off target, there is no doubt that his achievements during the 1950s in ensuring that the FRG was recognised as a more or less equal partner among the western powers and an acceptable member of the community of nations were widely recognised. Some achievements, such as the return of the POWs from Soviet captivity, were enormously popular among Germans, and played a significant role in Adenauer's electoral success in 1957. Other developments, such as the remilitarisation of German society and the recreation in 1955 of a German army – the *Bundeswehr* presented as an army of 'citizens in uniform' under the control of parliament – were far more contentious among people who were terrified of the possibility of another war.

In the sphere of remilitarisation and western-oriented foreign policy, Adenauer benefited from a weak political opposition on the part of the SPD. The SPD for much of the 1950s was led by the relatively colourless Erich Ollenhauer, following the premature death in 1952 of the former SPD leader Kurt Schumacher (whose health had suffered greatly from the consequences of imprisonment under the Nazis).

How far was the success of West German democracy due to the reintegration of former Nazis and an inadequate 'coming to terms with the past'?

Wiedergutmachung
The policy of 'making good again' towards survivors of Nazi brutality.

Adenauer performed an extraordinary juggling act with respect to the Nazi past. On the one hand, Adenauer was highly conscious of the impact of the Nazi past on the views of Germany among the international community, but also of the financial and practical needs of the West German populace. For Adenauer, the appallingly misnamed policy of ***Wiedergutmachung***, of restitutions and 'reparations' to the survivors of Nazi brutality, was always closely linked to the reputation of Germany in the eyes of the international community. Adenauer made a famous speech to the *Bundestag* in 1951, which was a masterpiece:

Source

Adenauer's speech to the Bundestag in 1951:

In recent times international opinion has periodically concerned itself with the attitude of the Federal Republic towards the Jews. Here and there doubts have been raised as to whether the new state is led in this weighty question by principles which do justice to the frightful crimes of a previous epoch, and which place the relationship of the Jews to the German people on a new and healthy basis...

The government and with it the great majority of the German people are aware of the immeasurable suffering that was brought upon the Jews in Germany and in the occupied territories during the time of National Socialism. The vast majority of the German people rejected the crimes that were perpetrated against the Jews and did not participate in them... However, unspeakable crimes were committed in the name of the German people,which makes it our duty to make moral and material compensation...

In the light of the extent of compensation – which is a significant problem, in view of the horrendous destruction of Jewish valuables by Nazism – we have to bear in mind the limits to German capacity to deliver that are set by the bitter necessity of looking after the innumerable [German] victims of war and the need to care for [German] refugees and expellees.

'Aussöhnung mit dem Staate Israel und den Juden in aller Welt' [Reconciliation with the state of Israel and with Jews all over the world], Adenauer's speech to the *Bundestag*, 27 September 1951, translated by MF.

In this speech, Adenauer hit the moral high ground by taking responsibility for compensation, while not yielding an inch on the question of real guilt. The 'vast majority' of the 'German people' were simply exonerated; crimes 'were committed', but not apparently by anyone; and Germans retained the right to balance their own need to care for the war victims and refugees, who had suffered as a result of the war unleashed by Germany, against responsibilities to the survivors among their millions of victims. Moreover, when in 1953 the extent of German compensation to be paid to the state of Israel was announced, it was widely held – particularly by right-wing critics of Adenauer – to be extremely generous.

At precisely the same time – or rather, even earlier and even faster – very active efforts were made to reintegrate former Nazis into the new West German state. By the late 1940s denazification measures had become almost meaningless. An article of the constitution was brought into effect as Law 131 in 1951, giving former Nazi civil servants the right to reinstatement in their former jobs or equivalent jobs, if they had lost their positions through denazification, and also gave them full pension entitlement for the period of service to the Nazi state. Adenauer integrated former Nazis at high levels in his governments, including, for example, Hans Globke as his own personal adviser – who had drafted the official commentary for Hitler on the Nuremberg race laws of 1935.

As West German historian Norbert Frei has shown, the Nazi past was not in fact swept away or 'forgotten about' in some form of 'collective amnesia' during the Adenauer period; rather, it was actively addressed in the sense of ensuring that few former Nazis would need to feel any shame or fear of retribution in relation to their misdeeds in the recent past.

There was a vast continuity in personnel between the judiciary, the university elites, and the civil service who had served Hitler, and those who served Adenauer. It was only in 1958 that a small office was opened in Ludwigsburg to investigate possible war crimes. This situation of ignoring the criminality of Nazism was only radically challenged in the very different atmosphere of the 1960s, when the Eichmann and Auschwitz trials forced the facts of genocide back into the public spotlight.

In the view of some historians, this integration of former Nazis, while morally reprehensible, was central to the stabilisation of West German democracy.

ACTIVITY

To what extent, if at all, was the reintegration of former Nazis central to the establishment of German democracy?

To what extent was the success of democracy a result of the 'economic miracle'?

The former Economic Director of Bizonia, Dr Ludwig Erhard, and mastermind behind the currency reform of 1948 which had played such a crucial role in setting the post-war West German economy on the path to recovery, became the brains behind the development of West Germany's 'social market economy'. Influenced by neo-liberal economic theory, as Adenauer's Economics Minister Ludwig Erhard focused on a capitalist economy which would produce ever-growing 'prosperity for all' – as he termed his well-known book of 1957.

The conditions for economic recovery in the West were ripe. War-time damage in the western zones had not affected industrial production to the extent that had at first been feared, and the western zones were not further stripped of industrial plant through reparations in the same way as the Soviet zone was. West Germany benefited massively from Marshall Aid.

The economy also profited greatly from the Korean War of 1950–53, which stimulated demand for precisely the kinds of products it was equipped to provide. The flood of refugees from the lost eastern territories, and from the Soviet zone and GDR, provided a huge supply of cheap and mobile labour: people were prepared to move virtually anywhere in search of work, and were prepared to work for low wages.

As the economy grew, so wages grew. Industrial relations were less and less a matter of workers against employers (the old notion of class warfare), and increasingly revolved around cooperation and the more pleasant task of discussing how to divide an ever-larger cake. Annual growth rates in GNP averaged around 8 per cent, and there was a correspondingly unprecedented growth in average incomes.

ACTIVITY **Enquiries**

Study sources A–C (see next page)

Use your own knowledge to assess the view that rising prosperity following the devastation of 1945 was the single most important factor in the stabilisation of democracy over the years of the Adenauer era?

Source

(A) The Allensbach Institute for Demoscopy was the largest organisation carrying out mass surveys of public opinion throughout the history of the Federal Republic of Germany. Answers to the question:

'Everything that was built up in the period from 1933 to 1939, and a lot more besides, was destroyed by the war. Would you agree that if it had not been for the war, Hitler would have been one of the greatest German statesmen ever?'

Answers given in May 1955	Total (%)	Men (%)	Women (%)
Yes, he would have been	48	51	45
No, he would not have been	36	38	35
Don't know	14	9	18
Other answers	2	2	2

E. Noelle and E.P. Neumann (eds) (1956). *Jahrbuch der öffentlichen Meinung* (p. 277). Allensbach: Verlag für Demoskopie.

(B) Answers to the question:

'In your opinion, at which period in this century did things go best for Germany?'

Period held to be 'best for Germany'	Answers in October 1951 (%)	Answers in June 1959 (%)	Answers in December 1963 (%)
The present, today	2	42	62
During the Second World War	0	0	1
1933–39	42	18	10
1920–33	7	4	5
Before 1914	45	28	16
Don't know	4	8	6

E. Noelle and E.P. Neumann (eds) (1958–64). *Jahrbuch der öffentlichen Meinung*, Vol. 3 (p. 230). Allensbach: Verlag für Demoskopie.

(C) The social market economy and the 'economic miracle'.

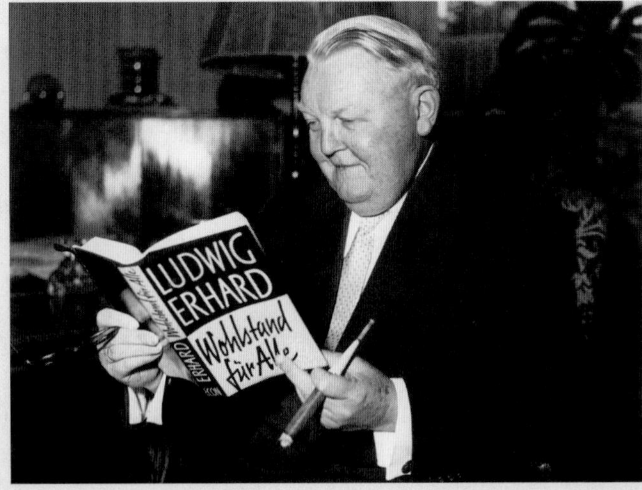

Figure 6.1 Ludwig Erhard, Minister of Economics and architect of the 'economic miracle'. The title of his book, partly obscured by his hand, holding a characteristic cigar, is 'Affluence for all' (*Wohlstand für Alle*).

What were the generational and social changes in the post-war context?

By 1963, somewhere in the region of 12 to 13 million refugees from the eastern territories and from the GDR had been integrated into West German society – around one-fifth of the population. Approximately a quarter of young people in West Germany had grown up in fatherless families. Women, despite their heroic role as 'rubble women' (*Trümmerfrauen*) in clearing the ruined cities in 1945, and exercising positions of responsibility and authority in the family, were increasingly squeezed out of the workplace and back into the home as cheap labour flooded in from the East. Even before this dried up with the erection of the Wall in 1961, the West German government was seeking to attract cheap foreign labour, in the form of the so-called 'guest workers' (*Gastarbeiter*), to take on the lowest paid, least qualified positions in the economy.

Figure. 6.2 Christmas shopping in Frankfurt, the 1950s.

West Germany was an increasingly affluent society, where average incomes had risen by 400 per cent since the foundation of the FRG, and the image of the fat German 'petty bourgeois' (*Spiessbürger*) with cigar in hand, sitting among the symbols of domestic bliss in a newly built home or strolling through a rebuilt city centre street full of sleek cars and consumer goods, was not far off the mark for many. The 'economic miracle' had served to stabilise West German democracy, despite the apparent lack of real choice between the major political parties, and the CDU's seemingly unshakable grip on power. But social changes and underlying, unresolved tensions were bringing with them political changes, in a period where economic growth was beginning to level off and there was even a momentary threat of economic depression. In the mid-1960s, a right-wing party, the NPD, again began to score electoral successes at regional level. There was also growing unrest on the Left.

Youth culture, as everywhere in the western world, was developing rapidly in the new era of mass communications, with radio ownership spreading rapidly and popular music no

longer only taking its lead from the USA but also especially from Britain. But youth culture in West Germany at this time had a particular edge.

In the early 1960s, the renewed prominence of the Nazi past, with the high-profile war crimes trials, and from 1966 the lack of an effective parliamentary opposition, fed into the student movement and development of more left-wing politics in an increasingly polarised society (epitomised by the death of a student as a result of police brutality at a demonstration in 1967). Generational conflict in 1960s West Germany was thus not merely a reflection of wider youth culture in the western world, but also accompanied the beginning of a new and more direct confrontation with Germany's appalling past.

The 'Spiegel affair' – a final straw

Konrad Adenauer's grip on West German politics had already begun to wane before the final blows were dealt by what became known as the 'Spiegel affair'.

In 1959 there were elections to the West German presidency, when the very successful first West German president, Theodor Heuss, was constitutionally bound to step down after ten years in office. Fearing a successful bid by the SPD and concerned to secure his own continued political influence in an era when he would no longer be Chancellor, Adenauer briefly toyed with the idea of standing for the Presidency himself. He was also taken by the idea of expanding the real political power of this largely ceremonial figurehead office. But on further consideration Adenauer withdrew his candidature, harming his reputation as an infallible politician.

Weakened by the affair of the presidential election, Adenauer's loss of political grip was further demonstrated by his behaviour at the time of the erection of the Berlin Wall. When the Wall went up, incarcerating the inhabitants of East Berlin on 13 August 1961, the then SPD Mayor of West Berlin and former resistance fighter against Nazism, Willy Brandt, put up a sterling appeal on behalf of freedom and democracy. The western powers stepped back, unwilling to precipitate a major international conflagration by intervening in this flashpoint of the Cold War. Konrad Adenauer not only failed to intervene; he almost ostentatiously ignored the crisis situation by failing even to make a symbolic demonstration of sympathy, postponing a visit to West Berlin for two days while he fulfilled routine engagements in the West; when he did finally turn up, he was greeted with jeers.

Adenauer's rapprochement with the West was marked by a famous meeting with De Gaulle in Paris in 1963; but even this could not, in retrospect, make up for the damage to his reputation in the declining years of his lengthy chancellorship.

The final straw came with the high-handed way in which Adenauer treated the press in late 1962. The weekly news magazine *Der Spiegel* had published an article which was critical of the readiness of the West German defence forces. The then West German Defence Minister, the colourful Bavarian CSU leader **Franz Josef Strauß** (pronounced Strauss), clearly misled the *Bundestag* in his replies to questions on this matter. The deception was compounded when an attempt was made to silence the *Spiegel* magazine by raiding its editorial offices and arresting some of the journalists involved, including one whose holiday was rudely truncated. There was a public outcry, not so much about the issues to do with defence policy which had precipitated the row, but rather about the way in which Adenauer's government appeared to be trying to muzzle the press in a manner reminiscent of authoritarian dictatorships.

BIOGRAPHY

Franz Josef Strauß (1915–88)

One of the founding members of the Bavarian CSU, Franz Josef Strauß was a rising star in the politics of the 1950s. In 1956 he was appointed Minister of Defence under Adenauer, a position from which he was ultimately forced to resign following the Spiegel scandal of late 1962 in which Strauß lied to parliament and acted outside the law in having journalists arrested and restricting freedom of the press. Strauß nevertheless rapidly made a political comeback, playing a leading role in conservative politics both nationally and in his political base, Bavaria, until his death in 1988.

Figure 6.3 President Charles de Gaulle (left) with former German Chancellor Konrad Adenauer at a meeting at the Elysee Palace, Paris 1963.

In 1963, somewhat ignominiously, Konrad Adenauer finally resigned, after fourteen years as Chancellor. During the course of his chancellorship, the pattern for the development of the FRG as an affluent democracy firmly tied in to western military and economic alliances had been set.

West Germany at a turning point?

By 1963, democracy in West Germany was sufficiently securely established that the political system weathered the Spiegel Affair, even if the Chancellor whose autocratic leadership style had precipitated it did not. With a secure economy, an increasingly affluent society, and an apparently stable democracy, the FRG appeared to have emerged from the turmoil of the early post-war years with remarkable success.

Yet within the course of the 1960s, underlying tensions rose to the surface. The Eichmann trial in Jerusalem, and the Auschwitz trials in Frankfurt, brought Nazi crimes back into the limelight. Renewed attention to the Holocaust and the question of collusion with Nazism added fuel to the fires of a wider generational revolt in the 1960s – a revolt that in Germany, as elsewhere in Europe and north America, concerned not only politics but also challenged the attitudes of an older generation on sex, clothing and hairstyles, and popular music. For those on the Left, American involvement in Vietnam revealed weaknesses in the self-proclaimed guardian of democracy; while economic setbacks brought some voters on the Right to support the neo-Nazi NPD in Land elections. The 'Grand Coalition' between SPD and CDU from 1966 to 1969 seemed to leave little space for any kind of meaningful parliamentary opposition; radicals developed instead the notion of an 'extra-parliamentary opposition', taking to the streets to demonstrate against government policies. West Germany was woken from the comfortable slumbers of the post-war affluent society as the ghosts of the past were summonsed to challenge what appeared to be an all-too-complacent present.

Perhaps the real turning point in West German history came, not with the end of the Adenauer era but with the election of Willy Brandt as SPD Chancellor in 1969. This was the first time the Chancellorship had been held by the SPD since the Weimar Republic; and both in his policies of rapprochement with East Germany and his personal attributes as a former opponent of Nazism, Brandt marked a genuine break with the past. In the longer term, West German democracy proved sufficient flexible to deal with the new terrorist threats and economic troubles of the 1970s and 1980s. By the time of the collapse of the Berlin Wall in 1989, and unification with East Germany in 1990, many West Germans had developed what has been termed a new 'post-national' pride, or 'constitutional patriotism', with real commitment to the democratic political system that had been introduced in such difficult circumstances in 1949.

ACTIVITY ***Enquiries***

Study the sources.

With reference to Sources A to E, that follow, and your own knowledge, what do you consider to be the key factors in the stabilisation of parliamentary democracy in the Federal Republic of Germany during the Adenauer era?

Source

A Table 6.1 Federal election results: Elections to the Bundestag, 1949–61

	CDU/CSU	CDU/	CSU	SPD	SPD	FDP	FDP	KPD	KPD	Others*
Year	**%**	**Seats**	**%**	**Seats**	**%**	**Seats**	**%**	**Seats**	**%**	**Seats**
1949	31.0	139	29.2	131	11.9	52	5.7	15	22.2	65
1953	45.2	243	28.8	151	9.5	48	2.2	0	14.3	45
1957	50.2	270	31.8	169	7.7	41	-	-	10.3	17
1961	45.3	242	36.2	190	12.8	67	-	-	5.7	0

* 'Others':

1949: German Party (DP) 17, German Reich Party 5, Centre Party 10, Bavarian Party 17, Economic Reconstruction Union 12, others 4

1953: German Party (DP) 15, League of Expellees 27, Centre Party 3

1957: German Party (DP) 17

Pól O'Dochartaigh (2004). *Germany since 1945* (p. 205). Basingstoke: Palgrave Macmillan.

B Table 6.2 The composition of governmental coalitions, 1949–63

	Governing parties	Chancellor
1949–53	CDU/CSU, FDP, DP	Adenauer
1953–57	CDU/CSU, FDP, DP	Adenauer
1957–61	CDU/CSU, DP	Adenauer
1961–63	CDU/CSU	Adenauer

(C) Konrad Adenauer's leadership style is suggested in this CDU poster from the 1957 election campaign, with the slogan 'No experiments!'.

Figure 6.4

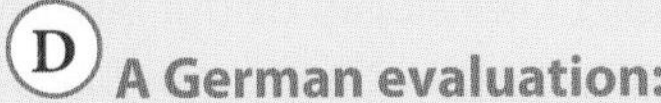

(D) A German evaluation:

In those days, 1957, I was eleven, Elvis Presley's 'Tutti Frutti' suddenly burst out from the radio, and at one stroke the very first bars banished from my youthful heart my previous favourite songs…

He gave us something very special, against our parents, to whom everything otherwise belonged. Up to now we had always only heard: 'You are still too young for that'. With Elvis in our ears we could yell back, 'But you are already too old for this'.

Where did this dynamite come from? Where could we get more of it? Through Elvis I also got to know about Bill Haley, who had already been there, and soon I had a collection of records with 'American howling' and 'Nigger music', and my grandma passed out in a dead faint.

Udo Lindenberger, reprinted in Christoph Kleßmann and Georg Wagner (eds) (1993). *Das gespaltene Land. Leben in Deutschland 1945 bis 1990. Texte und Dokumente* (pp. 294–95, translated by MF). Munich: C. H. Beck.

(E) A British historian's evaluation:

Critics of Adenauer's role talked of the evolution of 'Chancellor democracy' (Kanzlerdemokratie). They saw the democratic process reduced to a series of plebiscites in favour of the governmental incumbent, something far removed from popular self-government. It is undeniable that Adenauer, whose personality had been formed before the First World War, was not the most conciliatory of statesmen and that he frequently behaved in a paternalistic or authoritarian way. Yet as part of the political learning process Chancellor democracy had its points. Under the Weimar Republic and the Empire, polling day had been an opportunity to affirm an ideological allegiance. Under Chancellor democracy it became a way of choosing a responsible government.

Peter Pulzer (1995). *German Politics 1945–1995* (p. 66). Oxford: Oxford University Press.

Review questions

1 Explain why West Germany was created in 1949.
2 What constitutional safeguards were there to prevent the re-emergence of dictatorship?
3 How far was the West German 'economic miracle' due to Western Aid?
4 Why was Adenauer the dominant figure in West German politics for so long?
5. What were the strengths and weaknesses of West Germany in 1963?

Exam**Café**

Relax, refresh, result!

Relax and prepare

Hot tips

Glyn

By the end of the lower sixth I could see some links between my subjects. A lot of the writing skills are the same for the essay subjects and it really helped me to be doing economics when it came to some of my topics in history. It was hard at first because I seemed to be doing so many different things, but when I came to think of it at the end of the course, I realised that it would have been easier if I'd made connections earlier.

Omar

My dad's in business, so I enjoyed the economics, but I found it hard to link them up to history ideas. I could see what they were saying, but not how to link them to anything else that was happening. As I am a maths genius (no, seriously), I felt stupid about this. My advice is: don't expect everything to be too easy. Now I've got there, bring on the stats!

Refresh your memory

'How successful was Adenauer as Chancellor from 1949 to 1963?

▷ Understand the main problems facing the Allies in the Western zone of Germany at the end of the war.

▷ Explain why West Germany was created in 1949.

▷ Know who the main political parties were (CDU, CSU and SPD) and their political beliefs.

▷ What constitutional safeguards were there to prevent the re-emergence of a dictatorship? You should understand the reduced role of the President, the banning of anti-democratic parties and the combination of proportional representation with constituency representatives.

▷ What were the economic problems facing Adenauer on his election? These should include unemployment, refugees and mistrust. Why was Adenauer the dominant figure in West German politics for so long?

▷ The 'economic miracle' is a key feature of West Germany's development in this period. You should be able to explain why this happened and assess its significance. How far was the recovery due to Western aid or other factors?

▷ How and why was West Germany integrated into western Europe? Why was there a rapprochement with France? Why was German rearmament a major issue?

▷ You need to know the election results of 1953, 1957 and 1961 and be able to explain why the CDU were the dominant party.

▷ Why did Adenauer's prestige decline? Although he was an old man by 1961, you should be aware of how his reputation was damaged by his response to the Berlin Wall and his handling of the *Der Spiegel* crisis as well as the recovery of the SPD.

▷ What social developments had taken place in West Germany and how far was social stability achieved?

▷ Be able to assess the strengths and weaknesses of West Germany in 1963.

Historians disagree on whether Adenauer's Germany was simply a continuation of the old Germany or whether he did bring about a new Germany. You should be able to discuss this and be able to reach a balanced and well-supported conclusion. Any essay on this topic would require you to consider issues such as continuity within the civil service and teachers.
On the other hand there was a general feeling within Europe that by the 1960s Germany was ready to be integrated into Europe and German feelings about NATO and rearmament also suggest that her militarism was in the past.

'How far did Western democratic structures (political, economic and social) succeed in the Federal Republic?'

▷ Germany and Berlin were divided into zones of occupation 1945–49

▷ Under the eyes of the Allies, political life restarted. In the West the main parties were the CSU, a recreation of the Centre Party but committed to democracy in a conservative way, and the old SPD.

▷ As a result of pressure from the USSR, the West hastened the creation of a new West Germany with a federal constitution. Adenauer, the first Chancellor, was the CSU leader and firmly committed to the West. He abandoned any hope of unity.

▷ Backed by Western aid and by careful government support, the economy recovered from inflation in 1948 and wartime destruction.

▷ The 'economic miracle' seemed to indicate a better alternative to Communism and West Germany became integrated into key organisations of Europe – NATO and the EEC.

▷ Though there was prosperity, Adenauer was quite an authoritarian figure and the problem of a divided nation remained. Social change was less than in other Western countries.

Get the result!

Period Studies

Although there is no requirement to write a plan for an essay or an introduction it will become more vital as you move on to study for A2 and tackle the themes paper. However, it will also help you focus on the demands of the question and can help you avoid either a narrative or list approach, which will achieve only the lower mark bands.

Consider this title and then look at Marek's plan for it that follows.

Exam question

How successful was Adenauer as Chancellor of West Germany in the period from 1949 to 1963?

Sample answers

Examiner says:

The introduction reflects the plan. It shows that the candidate knows the key events and has a sound factual knowledge, but it does not give any clear indication of the line of argument that will be pursued. There are some implied hints that Adenauer was successful with the comments about election victories, economic growth, social stability and European integration, and possibly a hint of failure with the mention of the Wall and *Der Spiegel*, but certainly no clear indication of Marek's overall view.

Marek's plan:

1. Introduction, who was Adenauer and how he came to power.
2. Economic policies.
3. Election victories of 1953, 1957 and 1961.
4. Foreign policy: France, EEC, NATO.
5. Social stability.
6. Decline of Adenauer, Der Spiegel Crisis.

Marek's introduction:

Adenauer was Chancellor of West Germany from 1949 until 1963. He had been the founder and President of the Christian Democrat Party in 1945 and before that a member of the Catholic Centre Party, but had been forced from office by the Nazis. He dominated German politics during this period. Adenauer won three elections in 1953, 1957 and 1961. During this period the German economy grew and economic and social stability were achieved following the horrors of the Second World War. West Germany also became fully integrated into the European community and joined NATO. In 1961 the Berlin Wall was built and it led to the Der Spiegel Crisis.

Examiner says:

It is obvious from his plan that Marek knows what material needs to be covered. All the essential issues are in the plan, but it is a simple 'shopping list' of the topics: there is no sense of judgement about each. It is therefore likely that Marek will just describe each of the areas listed and therefore probably only imply if the policy was a success or failure. This is made more likely by the introduction which does not address the key issue of success or failure, but instead describes Adenauer's background and rise to power. If the essay does not take this approach it is likely Marek will simply explain whether each issue was a success or failure and therefore produce a list essay, with no sense of judgement. He does not need to completely abandon this plan, but it could be improved by a clear comment about each issue suggesting how far Adenauer succeeded.

How could the plan and introduction be improved?

- The introduction could state the line of argument the essay is going to take.
- The plan could state what line of argument, regarding success, will be taken for each issue. These could then become the opening sentence for each paragraph and make very clear to the examiner the direction of the argument.

Marek's improved plan:

1. Introduction: view, largely successful. Particularly domestically in the 1950s where he brought about economic, political and social stability. In foreign affairs much success. However, decline from 1961.
2. The economic policies of Adenauer were very successful and resulted in rapid economic growth.
3. Social stability was largely achieved as economic prosperity and the provision of housing ensured that West German workers would not respond to communist propaganda.
4. The achievement of three successive election victories is a clear indication that most of the electorate believed that Adenauer was pursuing successful policies.
5. Although Adenauer was successful in reintegrating Germany into Western Europe, there was still some suspicion in France over rearmament and he was also unable to appease the USSR.
6. The last years of his Chancellorship were less successful and created concerns about a revival in authoritarianism.

Examiner says:

This is a vastly improved plan. Each point in the plan relates directly to the question asked and addresses the issue of success and, in most instances, reaches a judgement as to 'how successful'. With this type of plan it is more likely that the answer will follow a similar approach and therefore avoid a description of the policies or a simple list. Each of the points in the plan would make an ideal opening sentence for each paragraph. An examiner would be able to read the opening sentences and have a clear indication of the direction of the answer.

Marek's improved introduction:

Adenauer was largely successful as Chancellor, although this view is somewhat discredited by his last years: his weak response to the building of the Berlin Wall and his attempts to prevent the publication of sensitive material in 'Der Spiegel'. However, against this Adenauer presided over the 'German economic miracle' and was able to use the gains from this to achieve both political and social stability. Although he was not able to reconcile the USSR to German rearmament, this was probably never realistic, but he was able to bring about a rapprochement with France and rebuild Germany's reputation in Europe. However, perhaps the clearest indication of his success was his ability to lead his party to three successive election victories.

Examiner says:

This introduction is clearly focused on the demands of the question. Marek now sets out a clear line of argument, which he should be able to build on in the rest of the essay. The answer already shows that it will address the crucial issue of 'how successful', suggesting that in some areas Adenauer was not completely successful, therefore achieving a balanced response. Although some vital events are mentioned the introduction does not describe them, but uses them to illustrate the direction of the argument. It is also encouraging to see that even in the introduction links between issues are made, for example between economic growth and political success.

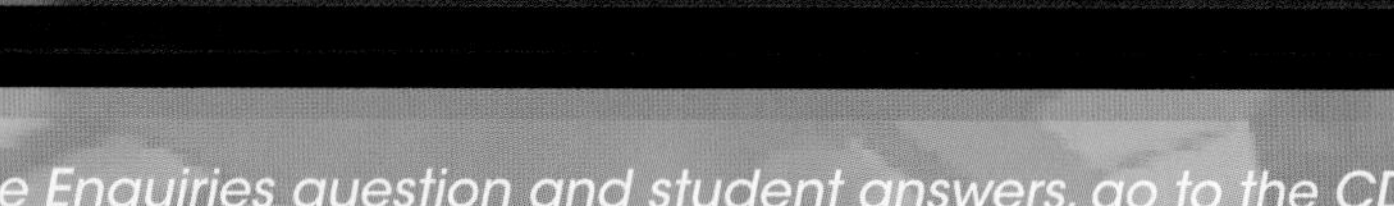
To look at the Enquiries question and student answers, go to the CD-ROM

Enquiries

In this question the issue is what led to political stability – so highlight that and deal with it directly. We're only going to consider the introduction, not the whole answer. You can find the rest of the question (part a), a model answer for part (a) and Glyn's full answer to (b) on the CD-ROM

Exam question

(b) Study all the sources.

Use your own knowledge to evaluate the interpretation that political stability in West Germany after 1949 was mainly the result of economic prosperity.

Sources

(A) An American magazine associates Adenauer's popularity with economic recovery:

Adenauer's guiding light is what he calls 'the dynamic spiritual force that outlives all politics' – Christian humanism. 'Christianity,' he says, 'is the answer to all ideologies.'

Firm in this faith, Roman Catholic Adenauer has led his conquered nation, back into the society of free nations. This is his greatest claim on the German electorate. Prosperity has been a big factor in his popularity and in the acceptance of democracy.

Eight years after the disaster of 1945, the western half of Germany is rapidly becoming the most powerful nation in Europe. US aid got the wheels of industry turning; German hard work turned revival into boom. Last week Chancellor Adenauer, touring his busy nation, watched farmers getting in what looked like the biggest harvest since World War II.

(*Time* magazine, writing just before the elections of 1953.)

(B) Statistics of economic growth. These statistics show growth rates. 1950 is the baseline at 100, so 109.6 means 9.6 per cent more food was produced in 1951 compared with 1950.

Year	All industry	Mining	Consumer goods	Food
1951	109.6	107.2	108.0	113.8
1952	114.2	112.4	110.8	121.4
1953	122.1	114.8	118.9	124.6
1954	132.4	118.6	128.0	134.2
1955	138.3	126.9	138.0	145.0
1956	144.5	132.1	144.7	150.5
1957	155.1	138.9	157.4	158.9
1958	163.1	145.4	166.9	167.3
1959	179.8	158.1	186.1	180.5
1950= 100				

(West German Ministry of Economics, 1961)

(C) This report shows the pace of economic growth and as experienced by one of West Germany's most dynamic companies, Bosch:

As a consequence of the general growth of the economy there was a rise in demand for parts for motor vehicles and engines as well as for other Bosch products. Altogether our turnover increased by nearly 25 per cent. Foreign and inland trade in household equipment made gratifying progress. The turnover of refrigerators and kitchen equipment has increased steadily and we have begun to market these products abroad.

(Company Report, 1955)

(D) A survey in the late 1960s explains stability in post-war Germany:

The vast majority of Germans were satisfied with the West German constitution in a way that was never true of the Weimar Republic. The Nazis were discredited and the Communists gained less support because of the dislike of East Germany. The army was firmly under civilian control. Lastly, the Republic was consistently prosperous and there was little unemployment in the 1950s. There was no test of democratic institutions such as there was in the Great Depression.

(Stewart Easton, *World History Since 1945*, 1968)

(E) A British journalist writes in 1952 giving some reasons for the economic growth:

The Germans have many advantages. They regard work as their national sport and not football. They do not have to pay for rearmament. On the other hand, they were literally eating out of dustbins in 1945 and 1946. The country was smashed in ruins. They have had this colossal influx of refugees to provide a labour force. You can time their amazing recovery from the currency reform of 1948. Prosperity means that they have turned away from the Nazi past.

(*Financial Times*, July 1952)

Glyn's introduction to (b):

The economic miracle was a key reason for greater stability in West Germany. Both sources B and C

offer evidence for this growth, while sources A and D link the prosperity with political stability directly. A says clearly that prosperity has been a big factor in the acceptance of democracy and D says that there was no Great Depression to test democratic institutions.

Industrial production was growing steadily as shown in B and this helped to satisfy Germans. However, the sources do mention other factors. Adenauer's leadership is stressed in A, while D points out the lack of threat from extremist parties and the army.

Examiner says:

It's good to group sources.

Examiner says:

The key points in the sources are brought out clearly without a long description – this is an introduction.

Examiner says:

There is a good use of A and D to point out other factors.

Examiner says:

This introduction gives a well-focused start to a possible discussion. The examiner would write something like 'good focus on debate' here. Though strong, let's see if this introduction could be improved. The examiner will be looking for an interpretation of sources and evidence of independent knowledge. Let's try to reassure him or her that this will be delivered.

Bibliography

Bullock, A. (1990). *Hitler: A Study in Tyranny*. London: Penguin.

Burleigh, M. (2000). *The Third Reich*. London: Macmillan.

Burleigh, M. and Wipperman, W. (1991). The Racial State: Germany, 1933–45. Cambridge: CUP.

Childers, T. 'Inflation, stabilisation and political realignment in Germany, 1924–28', in Craig, G. (1978). *Germany, 1866–1945*. Oxford: Oxford University Press.

Evans, Richard J. (2004). *The Coming of the Third Reich*. London: Penguin.

Evans, Richard J. (2006). *The Third Reich in Power*. London: Penguin.

Feuchtwanger, E.J. (1993). *From Weimar to Hitler, 1918–33*. Basingstoke: Macmillan.

Fulbrook, M. (1995). *Anatomy of a Dictatorship: Inside the GDR, 1949–89*.Oxford: Oxford University Press.

Fulbrook, M. (2000). *Interpretations of the Two Germanies, 1945–90*. Basingstoke: Macmillan.

Fulbrook, M. (2002). *History of Germany, 1918–2000: The Divided Nation*. Oxford: Blackwell.

Fulbrook, M. (2005). *The People's State: East German Society from Hitler to Honecker*. London: Yale University Press.

Hiden, J. *The Weimar Republic*. Harlow: Longman/Pearson.

Hitler, A. *Mein Kampf*, edited by D. C. Watt (1974). London: Hutchinson.

Kolb, E. (1988). *The Weimar Republic*. London: Unwin Hyman

Kershaw, I. (1998–2000). *Hitler, Hubris, Vol. 1: 1889–1936: Nemisis, vol. 2, 1936–45*. London: Allen Lane.

Kershaw, I. (1993). *The Nazi Dictatorship, Problems and Perspectives*. London: Arnold.

Koonz, C. (1987). *Mothers in Fatherland, Women and the Family and Nazi Politics*. London: Cape.

Nicholls, A. J. *The Bonn Republic: West German Democracy, 1945–90*. London: Longman.

Noakes, J. and Pridham, G. (eds) (1998). *Nazism, 1919–45, Vol.1: The Rise to Power, 1919–34*, 2nd edn). Exeter: University of Exeter Press.

Noakes, J. and Pridham, G. (eds) (1991). *Nazism, 1919–45, Vol 2: State, Economy and Society, 1933–39*. Exeter: University of Exeter Press.

Noakes, J. and Pridham, G. (eds) (1984) *Nazism 1919–45, Vol. 3: Foreign Policy, War and Racial Discrimination*. Exeter: University of Exeter Press.

Noakes, J. and Pridham, G. (eds) (1998). *Nazism , 1919–45, Vol.4: The German Home Front in World War II*. Exeter: University of Exeter Press.

O'Dochartaigh, Pól (2004). *Germany since 1945*. Basingstoke: Palgrave Macmillan.

Overy, R. (1995). *War and Economy in the Third Reich*. Oxford: Clarendon Press.

Peukert, J. (1989). *Inside Nazi Germany. Conformity, Opposition and Racism in Everyday Life*. London: Penguin.

Pinson, K. S. (1966). *Modern Germany*. New York: Macmillan.

Ross, Corey (2002). *The East German Dictatorship*. London: Arnold.

Tooze, A. (2007). *The Wages of Destruction*. London: Penguin.

Williamson, D. (2001). *Germany from Defeat to Partition, 1945-63*. London, Pearson/Longman: 2001.

Williamson, D. (2005) *Germany since 1815*. Basingstoke.

Williamson, D. (2002). *The Third Reich (third edition)*, London: Pearson/ Longman.

COLEG LLANDRILLO COLLEGE
LIBRARY RESOURCE CENTRE
CANOLFAN ADNODDAU LLYFRGELL

Glossary

Chapter 1

Armistice End to hostilities so that peace negotiations can begin.

Bolshevik Revolution In October 1917 the Russian Bolsheviks under Lenin seized power in Russia.

Coalition Government made up of members from several parties.

Compulsory state arbitration of strikes State intervention in strikes, forcing the employers and workers to agree.

Council of the League of Nations A principal organ of the League of Nations; its function was to settle international disputes.

Demilitarisation Banning of all military bases from an area.

DNVP (German National Peoples' Party) Formed in 1919, amalgamating the pre-war conservative parties.

DVP (German People's Party) Before 1918 was the National Liberal Party.

Entente Anglo-French wartime alliance against Germany.

Federation System of government whereby several states form a unity, but run their internal affairs independently.

'Fulfilment' Policy of attempting to fulfill the Treaty of Versailles in an effort to gain concessions from the Allies.

Gold standard Valuing a currency in terms of the amount of gold for which its units can be exchanged.

Habsburg Empire Austro-Hungarian Empire which collapsed in November 1918.

Heavy industry Industries in which heavy equipment is used to manufacture products or extract minerals.

Kampfbund Fighting League or Association.

Minority coalition government Coalition government without a majority.

National assembly Elected assembly that draws up a constitution.

Nationalisation Takeover of factories by the state.

Parliamentary republic Republic in which government is responsible to an elected parliament.

Plebiscite Referendum or vote by the people on a specific issue.

Proportional representation Parties are represented in parliament in proportion to the number of votes cast for them.

Putsch Attempt to seize power by force.

Red Army German Communist workers' army, named after the Russian Red Army.

Reichsrat Upper House of parliament.

Reichstag Lower House of parliament.

Reparation Commission Inter-Allied committee which worked out how much Germany should pay in reparations.

SA *Sturmabteilung* (Stormtroopers) Assault Section of the Nazi Party.

Separatists Those wanting a separate Rhineland looking to Paris as the centre of power rather than to Berlin.

Social Darwinism Application of Charles Darwin's theories of evolution and natural selection to human society.

Soviets Elected councils set up during the Bolshevik Revolution of 1917.

Spartacist League Left-wing revolutionary movement, later the KPD.

SPD (Social Democratic Party) Main working-class party in Germany.

Special interest parties Formed to campaign on specific issues.

Ufa The film studio Universal Film AG.

USPD (Independent Social Democratic Party) Party made up of former SPD members wanting more socialist reforms.

Völkisch Ideology preaching the preservation of a traditional German national and racial community.

War bonds Certificates sold by the German government during the war promising to repay buyers their money, with interest added, by a specific date.

Workers' factory councils Bodies made up of members elected by the workers to represent their interests.

Chapter 2

Article 59 Gave *Reichstag* members the right to take legal action against government members violating the constitution.

Backbenchers Members of parliament who are not members of the Cabinet and sit on the 'back benches' in the *Reichstag*.

Battle cruiser 'Pocket' or small battleship.

Cadre A core unit which can serve as a basis for mass expansion.

Charismatic leader Leader able to inspire others with devotion and enthusiasm.

Coup d'état Overthrow of a government and seizure of power illegally.

Customs union Economic union between two countries so that they can trade with each other without paying any customs duties.

Danzig Corridor Small corridor of land under Polish control to give Poland access through Germany to the port of Danzig.

Deflation Policy aimed at reducing the amount of money in circulation in order to stop prices rising.

Demilitarised Area in which military personnel and weapons are banned.

Gestapo State Secret Police.

Gold standard System of valuing a currency in terms of the amount of gold for which its units can be exchanged.

Great Coalition Consisted of the German Social Democratic Party (SPD), the Democratic Party (DDP), the Centre Party (ZTR) and the German People's Party (DVP).

Inter-Allied debts Debts owed by France and Britain to the USA.

Interest rates Rate of interest paid for the loan of money.

Investment Money invested for profit in banks or businesses.

***Land* parliaments** Parliaments of the German states (*Länder*).

Ländtag Local assembly or parliament.

Military attaché Military representative in an embassy.

Moratorium Temporary suspension of debt repayments.

November parties Parties forming the Weimar Coalition in November 1919.

Permissive attitude Tolerates behaviour and practices that go beyond normal conventions.

Reichsbanner The Social Democratic Party's paramilitary force.

Rotfront 'Red Front', the Communist Party's paramilitary force.

Stahlhelm League of Steel Helmets, a military veterans' society.

***Sturmabteilung* (Stormtroopers)** Nazi assault troops.

Tariff duties Taxes on imports.

Treaty of Versailles Signed in 1919 between Germany, the USA and the victorious Allied powers.

Weimar Republic Democratic state founded in 1919.

Chapter 3

Anschluss Annexation of Austria by Germany in March 1938.

Anti-socialist laws Laws aimed at restricting or banning the activities of socialist political parties and groups.

Asocial Category of people considered by the Nazis to be 'biologically criminal'.

Bourgeois parties Middle-class political parties of Germany.

Bureaucratic, military and big business elites The civil service, army and major industrialists and bankers.

Cadre party Party composed of a relatively small number of people trained to be the future leaders of Germany.

Civil authorities Non-military bodies that have authority over civilian affairs, such as the police, and local government.

Civil servants People employed in government ministries to carry out duties of the state.

Dual state State in which there appear to be two forms of government at work at the same time.

Ethnic Germans People of the German race who lived mainly in Poland as a result of the new frontiers drawn in 1919.

***Führer* principle** Principle that the *Führer* cannot be wrong and must be obeyed at all times.

Gauleiter Party leader in charge of a *Gau*, a regional division of the Nazi Party.

Gleichschaltung An electrical term meaning synchronisation converted to mean all aspects of life to be in line with Nazi ideology.

Intellectual workers People who work with their intellect, such as teachers, lawyers, writers, etc.

Job creation schemes Schemes to create jobs through public works programmes.

Judiciary System of courts in which judges and magistrates administer justice.

Länder Federated states independent from the central government.

***Länder* diets** Local parliaments of the federated states.

Military conscription Calling up young men to serve for two years in the army, a German tradition since the 19th century.

National Socialist Senate Influential body which would have served as the Upper House of the *Reichstag*.

Occupied and incorporated territories Territories either occupied by the German army in the war or annexed by Germany.

Old Reich Parts of Germany that lay within the frontiers of 1933.

One-party centralised Reich Form of government where only one political party can to stand for election or form the government.

Party monopoly Sole control of political, economic etc. power in a country by one party, as in a dictatorship.

Polish front Where the German and Polish armies were fighting one another during the German invasion of Poland.

Political prisoners Those imprisoned because of their political ideas.

Popular enlightenment Use of propaganda to enlighten or brainwash people into accepting Nazi ideology.

Professional diplomats Full-time officials who represented the government in its affairs with other governments.

Rival hierarchies Rival power systems, the members of which are ranked according to power.

SD (*Sicherheitsdienst*) Security service of the SS.

Unity of August 1914 Spirit uniting Germany when war broke out in 1914.

Chapter 4

Autarky Self-sufficient economic system.

Blitzkrieg Quick or 'lightning war' using bombing followed by swift attacks on opposing forces.

Congenital deformities Diseases or deformities existing from birth.

Deviants People whose behaviour does not conform to social or cultural norms.

Euthanasia Putting an end to the life of a human being who is suffering from an incurable illness.

Genetic factors Inherited factors.

Go-slows Workers with a grievance using tactics to slow down production.

Guns and butter Economy which can produce both consumer goods and arms.

Herrenvolk The ruling or racially dominant people.

Holocaust 'A sacrifice totally consumed by fire or a burnt offering'. Deliberately used to distinguish the massacre of the Jews from all other massacres and emphasise its horrendous nature.

Junkers Aristocratic landowning families of Prussia and eastern Germany.

Medieval knightly orders Organisations such as the Teutonic Knights, a military crusading order.

Mittelstand German lower middle classes: farmers, small businessmen, self-employed craftsmen and white-collar workers.

Rationalising Use of the existing resources in a rational and economic way.

Reichsbahn German national railways.

Sorbs Slavonic race related to the Czechs in south-eastern Germany and the Poles.

Total War Economy Economy where all production is dictated by the needs of war.

Untermenschen Racially inferior people.

Welfare capitalism Private businesses looking after their workers with higher wages, health care and pensions.

Work book Document containing details of a person's work place and employer.

Chapter 5

Abitur Higher school leaving exam.

Bizonia British/American merged zones.

COMECON Economic grouping of Eastern European states under the leadership of the Soviet Union.

'Democratic centralism' Marxist–Leninist principle that decisions taken at the centre should be passed down and implemented below; and that views at the grass roots should be influenced by the Communist Party and conveyed up.

Denazification Rooting out or converting former Nazis.

'False consciousness' View that, under capitalism, people were influenced by bourgeois ideology so that they did not fully understand their own class interests.

FRG Federal Republic of Germany.

GDR German Democratic Republic.

Jugendweihe Secular coming-of-age ceremony.

LPG Collective farm.

Marxist-Leninist Inspired by Marx's commitment to the overthrow of capitalism by a proletarian revolution and Lenin's 'leading role of the Party' idea.

Monopoly capitalism Marxist term for the final stage of capitalism.

Socialist intelligentsia Professional classes under Socialism.

Stasi East German secret security system.

Trizonia British/American/French merged zones.

VEB 'People's Own Factory', effectively owned and managed by the state.

Warsaw Pact Military alliance of Eastern European states under the leadership of the Soviet Union.

Chapter 6

Bundesrat Upper chamber of parliament, representing the federal states.

Bundestag Lower chamber of parliament, elected by the people in the constituencies.

'First past the post' Voting system where candidates who win the most votes are elected

Hallstein doctrine Held that the FRG should not legitimise the GDR.

Wiedergutmachung Policy of 'making good again' to survivors of Nazi brutality.

Index

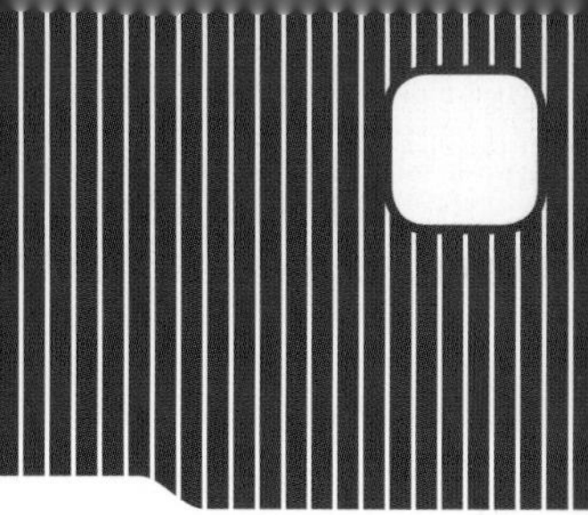

Adenauer, Konrad 147, 165, 170–1, 178–9, 181, 183, 186
- abandons GDR 145, 171–3, 183
- and Berlin Wall 162, 178, 183
- and the Nazi past 174–5
- and western alliances 145, 172, 183

agriculture 29, 39, 93, 96–7, 97, 114, 137, 147–8, 159
Anschluss (1938) 74, 115
army 19, 67, 69, 70, 71, 75

Berlin 131, 140, 141, 153, 159
Berlin Wall 147, 152, 154, 155
- Adenauer and 162, 178, 183
- building (1961) 147, 148, 153, 159, 162, 166, 173, 177

birth rate 39, 93, 109, 111
Brüning, Heinrich 44–5, 47–50, 52

CDU (Christian Democratic Union) 134, 135, 168, 171
Centre Party 21, 31, 44, 48, 51, 53, 57, 63, 64, 66
churches 63, 68, 69, 74, 84, 106
- in GDR 150–1

Cold War 138, 139, 140–1, 142–3, 153, 159, 165, 178
Communism 13, 39, 46, 138, 139–40, 140–1, 146, 147
Communists 9, 20–1, 93, 130
- *see also* KPD

concentration camps 66, 79, 82–3, 84, 107, 113, 116, 121, 129, 137
coordination *Gleichschaltung* 65–9
CSU (Christian Social Union) 135, 168, 183
currency 22, 23, 29, 38, 140, 165, 187

Dawes Plan 28, 30
deflation 45, 49, 52, 55
demilitarisation 30, 31, 41–2, 131
democracy 44, 142, 167
- FRG 165, 166–8, 177, 181, 183, 186, 187
- Weimar Republic 17–18, 40, 48, 51, 165, 167, 187

democratisation, post-war 133–6
denazification 131, 136–7, 174
Depression *see* Great Depression
DNVP (Nationalist Party) 21, 31, 41, 48, 49, 66, 70

education 67, 104–6, 108, 109, 118, 152, 157, 169
Enabling Act (1933) 62, 63–5, 72

family 109, 110–12, 121
FDP (Free Democratic Party) 136, 168, 169, 171
First World War 8–13, 19
Four Year Plan 72, 99–100, 103
Freicorps 10, 11, 12, 13, 20, 21, 22, 23
FRG (Federal Republic of Germany) 128, 141, 147, 165, 172, 174–5, 179
- constitution 165, 166–8, 183, 187
- 'economic miracle' 40, 148, 175–6, 177, 183, 186–7
- politics 166–7, 167, 167–71, 180
- social change 177–8, 183

Führer cult 39, 70, 75
Führer principle 54, 76
full employment 93–5, 113

GDR (German Democratic Republic) 128–9, 141, 143–5, 147, 155–7, 172–3, 183
- economy 137, 147–9, 159, 175
- social changes 149–53, 157

Germany
- after First World War 165
- division (1949) 138–41
- occupation of 129–43

Gestapo 79, 80, 81, 81–2, 82, 84, 113, 115, 116
Goebbels, Joseph 45, 46, 51, 52, 67, 73, 75
Göring, Hermann 11, 53, 54, 56, 64, 73, 99, 101
- and the Jews 119, 122, 123
- and SA 70, 71

Great Coalition 17, 21, 25, 44
Great Depression 93, 114, 165
- impact 42–4, 47, 48, 51, 59, 111

Heydrich, Reinhard 80, 118, 120, 122, 123
Himmler, Heinrich 70, 78–81, 82, 107, 110, 117
Hindenburg, Paul von 9, 19, 31, 40, 41, 50, 51, 56, 63, 70–1
- and Brüning 44, 48, 48–9, 50
- and Schleicher 54

Hitler, Adolf 13, 26, 39, 50, 63, 72, 129, 176
- anti-Semitism 121, 122
- assassination attempts 75, 84
- career up to 1923 19, 25–6
- consolidates power 62–78
- as *Führer* 39, 75–8
- and the Jews 39, 119–20, 121–3, 125
- Munich Putsch 25–7, 38, 55, 78
- popularity 114, 115
- portrayal of 51
- rise to power 18, 38–9, 47, 49, 51, 52–6, 59, 62, 71
- *see also* Enabling Act; *Führer* cult; Nazi Party

Hitler Youth 39, 72, 84, 105, 108, 110, 114, 115
- indoctrination 75, 105–7, 145

Holocaust 119–21, 123, 125, 175
Honecker, Erich 148, 153, 155
hyperinflation (1923) 23–4, 27

inflation 19, 95, 165, 183
- Weimar Republic 22, 23–4, 27, 28, 39, 40, 42, 48

intentionalists 119, 121, 125

Jews 11, 95, 96, 103
- anti-Semitism 39, 81, 99, 117–19, 121, 122, 125
- Hitler and 39, 119, 121–3, 125
- Holocaust 83, 119–21, 121, 125
- persecution 74, 77, 117–20, 125

Kapp Putsch (1920) 20–1, 23, 25, 27, 52

KPD (Communist Party) 12, 22, 25, 50, 51, 52, 53, 84, 93, 169
  banned in FRG 136, 170
  refounded 133, 134, 135
Kristallnacht 118–19, 125, 127

Marshall Plan 140, 165, 175, 183
Mittelstand 28, 39, 50, 95–6, 114
Munich Putsch 25–7, 38, 55, 78

NATO 131, 145, 172, 183
Nazi Party (NSDAP) 25, 26, 31, 75, 82, 114, 133, 142, 165
  Hitler's rebuilding 38–9, 45
  programme 46, 51, 55–6
  rise to power 19, 40, 44, 45–7, 51, 52, 52–3, 59
  role 1933-39 53, 72, 73–5
  see also Hitler; propaganda
New Plan 98–9, 103
Night of the Long Knives 71, 117

Papen, Franz von 44, 49, 52–4, 55, 70, 71
People's Community (*Volksgemeinschaft*) 92, 103–15
  exclusions from 103, 116–23
political parties
  in 1933 66, 69
  Soviet zone and GDR 134–5
  western zone and FRG 135–6, 166–7, 167, 167–70, 183
Potsdam Agreement (1945) 131, 137, 142, 143, 159
propaganda 67, 85–7, 89, 109
  GDR 157
  Nazi Party 39, 45, 51, 52, 75, 95, 127, 165

rearmament 39, 44, 67, 70, 77, 93, 95, 98–103, 111
refugees 129, 149, 165, 175
  from GDR 147, 148, 153, 154, 159, 166, 177

Reichskristallnacht 118–19, 125, 127
Reichstag 17, 18, 53, 55, 56, 62, 63–4
reintegration of former Nazis 174–5
reparations
  after First World War 22–3, 28, 30–1, 33, 41, 48, 93
  after Second World War 131, 137, 138, 143, 174, 175
reunification 128, 143, 159, 166
  Adenauer's rejection 145, 173
revolution 9–13, 13
Röhm, Ernst 69, 70, 71, 73, 80, 116
Rotfront 43, 45, 51
Ruhr, occupation 23, 27, 28
Ruhr uprising (1920) 20–1, 22, 23, 27

SA (*Sturmabteilung*) 25, 26, 39, 43, 45, 49, 50, 52, 69, 93
  Night of the Long Knives 71, 118
  violence 52, 57, 63, 66, 69, 82, 95, 117, 118
Schleicher, Kurt von 44, 49, 54, 55, 71
SED (Socialist Unity Party) 134, 135, 143, 150–1, 152–3, 155
Soviet Union 128, 138, 140, 141, 143, 148, 155
  Red Army 129, 130, 137
  reparations to 131, 137, 138, 142, 143, 175
  war against 75, 101–2, 120
Soviet zone 133–5, 137, 140, 165
soviets (councils) 9–10, 12, 26
Spartacist League 10, 12
SPD (Social Democratic Party) 10, 11, 17, 40, 44, 50, 51, 52, 53, 54, 84
  banned 66, 93
  FRG 168, 169–70, 171, 173, 183
  refounded 134, 135
  support for Brüning 48, 49
SS 63, 66, 79, 79–81, 82, 84
Stalin, Josef 131, 138, 142, 143
  and GDR 145, 172–3
Stalingrad 75, 165

Stasi 128, 144, 147, 155, 156, 159
Strasser, Gregor 45, 54, 71
Stresemann, Gustav 18, 25, 30–1, 41
structuralists 119, 121, 125

Thälmann, Ernst 50, 51, 82, 152
Third Reich 8, 80, 84, 89, 93–5, 128, 129
  economy 77, 93–5, 98–103
  style of government 76–8
  terror 78–84, 89, 165
  see also Hitler; Nazi Party; People's Community; propaganda
Truman Doctrine 139–40

Ulbricht, Walter 133, 143, 146–7, 148, 153, 155, 159
unemployment 22, 29, 42–4, 47, 49, 64, 69, 93–5, 98, 103
uprising of 17 June 1953 146–7, 159, 173

Versailles, Treaty of (1919) 8, 22, 23, 30, 41, 45, 48
  impact 14–17, 59

Weimar Republic 8, 32, 45, 96, 103, 116, 117
  constitution 17–18, 40, 187
  crises 19–28, 25, 27
  democracy 17–18, 40, 48, 51, 165, 167, 187
  economy 28–9, 43, 48–9
  Germans' views of 32, 57, 187
  'Golden Years' 28–9
  weakness 31, 40, 59
  see also Great Coalition; revolution; Treaty of Versailles
western zone 135–6, 165
women 32, 41, 93–4, 103, 109–12, 121, 149, 177

young people 104–8, 145, 152, 152–3, 177–8, 181
Young Plan 17, 31, 41, 44

COLEG CYMUNEDOL ABERGELE
ABERGELE COMMUNITY COLLEGE
CANOLFAN ADNODDAU DYSGU
LEARNING RESOURCE CENTRE